Balancing Copyright Law in the Digital Age

Roberto Caso • Federica Giovanella
Editors

Balancing Copyright Law in the Digital Age

Comparative Perspectives

Springer

Editors
Roberto Caso
Federica Giovanella
Facoltà di Giurisprudenza
Università di Trento
Trento
Italy

ISBN 978-3-662-52596-8 ISBN 978-3-662-44648-5 (eBook)
DOI 10.1007/978-3-662-44648-5
Springer Heidelberg New York Dordrecht London

Softcover reprint of the hardcover 1st edition 2015

Printed on acid-free paper

Springer is part of Springer Science+Business Media (www.springer.com)

Preface

This book represents the product of intensive research by experts of intellectual property law, who employ rigorous interpretative methodologies while keeping an eye on comparative law and on the effects of new technologies on law.

The idea for this book sprang from often heated debates among intellectual property scholars on the possibilities and the limits of copyright. The book draws on the research path started in a seminar held at the Faculty of Law of the University of Trento on December 6, 2013, titled "Copyright, technological evolution, and balance of rights", a path that continued during the following months. The goal of the research, concretely reached through this book, was to discuss the balancing of rights in controversies where one of the conflicting rights is copyright, in light of the revolutionary mutation that digital technologies brought with them.

Examples of these troublesome conflicts are the clash of fundamental rights, intensified by the so-called propertization of copyright; the contrast between users' access to works of authorship and the principle of exhaustion of the distribution right; the situation of conflict that exists when the protection of privacy and personal data need to be partially or totally constricted to obtain an effective enforcement of copyright; and the need for a balance between users' access to scientific literature and exclusive control of publishers.

Copyright law has been broadening its scope for decades. International treaties are often at the origin of this enlargement, which is therefore a pervasive phenomenon. This increasing wideness implies that copyright often faces other rights (frequently, fundamental rights), creating the issue of deciding what right prevails.

Decision makers need to take into account these recurring conflicts and to try to solve them. This need shows both at the lawmaking level and at the concrete case level. Sometimes the latter situation is a consequence of the former: when lawmakers do not consider the problem of balancing copyright with other rights, judges need to find a correct solution for the specific case.

Starting from the difficulties inherently connected with the task of balancing rights that respond to opposing interests, each essay analyzes techniques and arguments applied by institutional decision makers in trying to solve this dilemma.

Meanwhile, the authors also highlight the weaknesses and shadows of the analyzed approaches.

Each author applies a specific method always involving legal comparison while taking into account the European framework for copyright and related rights.

Caterina Sganga's paper, based on a deep analysis of the relations between copyright and property, springs from the interpretative *impasse* that often characterizes the conflict between copyright and other rights in European Union law. In the author's idea, this *impasse* derives from the vagueness of balancing criteria such as "proportionality" or "reasonableness". Caterina Sganga believes that the only way to overcome this problem is by assigning a specific constitutional rank to copyright. This task has become more and more complicated due to the "propertization" of copyright, critically analyzed in the work of Caterina Sganga. The paper tries to fill the emptiness of the mentioned balancing criteria, taking into account the synergies between European law and the member states' constitutional commonalities on copyright and property.

Also, *Giorgio Spedicato*'s piece concentrates on the problem of the principle of online exhaustion. The paper has its bases on the existing interpretation given by the scholars and judges and proceeds from the evidence that copyright suffers from a lack of legitimization, originating from the excessive protection provided to this right in the last years. Copyright law is often accused to be the result of lobbyism, which strengthens copyright in spite of conflicting rights of users and subsequent creators. In addition to this, in the author's view, also courts indulge the enlargement of copyright's domain. Therefore, Giorgio Spedicato stresses the role of the scholarly interpretation, in restoring the balancing that was the ontological core of copyright at its origins.

Federica Giovanella's paper, applying a law and culture methodology, concentrates on a specific subject, that is, the enforcement of copyright against Internet users suspected of illegal file sharing. In this kind of controversies, copyright inevitably collides with users' privacy and data protection. In fact, users' data need to be revealed if copyright holders want to enforce their rights directly against the users. The solutions given to this collision vary in the considered countries, namely Italy, USA, and Canada. The author hypothesizes the existence of a cultural influence on judges, who balance conflicting rights also according to the conception and the perception of copyright and data protection.

The piece by *Valentina Moscon* focuses on a highly topical issue: the phenomenon of Open Access to scientific literature. Under a "law and technology" as well as a comparative perspective, the paper highlights how the advent of digital technologies fosters collaborative logic that, with old tools such as contracts, creates new forms of sharing within—and not in contrast with—copyright laws. Valentina Moscon analyzes the current obstacles to a broader diffusion of Open Access, which she identifies with the lack of coherent regulation. Therefore, the author hopes for a deeper and better intervention by lawmakers, able to balance copyright with the demand for open access to knowledge.

Our gratitude goes to the Faculty of Law of the University of Trento and to its staff, which promoted and sponsored the conference from which this book sprouted. We greatly thank the authors for the enthusiasm and commitment shown in the research and the realization of their essays.

Trento, Italy

Roberto Caso
Federica Giovanella

Authors' Short Biographies

Prof. Roberto Caso is associate professor of Private Comparative Law and codirector of the Law and Technology Research Group at the University of Trento (Italy)—Faculty of Law. He teaches Private Law, Comparative Intellectual Property Law, and ICT Law. Roberto Caso is author and editor of many books and articles on Intellectual Property, Privacy and Data Protection, and Contract Law. He is member of the International Association for the Advancement of Teaching and Research in Intellectual Property (ATRIP).

Federica Giovanella is postdoc fellow and member of the LawTech Research Group at the Faculty of Law of the University of Trento. She holds a Ph.D. in Private Comparative Law from the same University. She has been a visiting scholar at the "Max Planck Institute for Innovation and Competition" in Munich and the "Centre for Intellectual Property Policy" of McGill Law School in Montreal. Her research interests concentrate on copyright, privacy and data protection, as well as liability issues arising from new technologies.

Valentina Moscon holds a Ph.D. in Private Comparative Law on Copyright Law and Digital Rights Management. She is currently fellow of the LawTech Research Group (University of Trento—Faculty of Law) and postdoc researcher on "Intellectual Property and knowledge transfer in the University" at the same institution. She was a scholarship holder at the "Max Planck Institute for Innovation and Competition" from May 2013 to March 2014. She had previously been a visiting scholar at the "Institute for Information Law" in Amsterdam and at the "Institute of European and Comparative Law" of Oxford. She teaches Copyright Law in Music and Contract Law and is the author of several publications in the fields of private law and comparative private law.

Caterina Sganga is assistant professor of law at the Central European University (Budapest). She holds a Ph.D. in Private Comparative Law from Scuola Superiore Sant'Anna, Pisa; an LL.M. from Yale Law School; and an LL.B. and J.D. from University of Pisa. Her research focuses on comparative copyright law and the interplay between intellectual property and fundamental rights.

Giorgio Spedicato is research fellow and adjunct lecturer in Intellectual Property Law at the University of Bologna. He holds a degree cum laude in Law from the University of Bari, an LL.M. and a Ph.D. in Information Technology Law from the University of Bologna, as well as a Certificate in International Copyright Law from the University of Amsterdam. He has been a visiting research scholar in Intellectual Property at the "Benjamin N. Cardozo School of Law" in New York and at the "Max Planck Institute for Innovation and Competition" in Munich.

Contents

EU Copyright Law Between Property and Fundamental Rights: A Proposal to Connect the Dots

Caterina Sganga

Contents

Abstract Although scholars and stakeholders have long analyzed and tried to limit the clashes between copyright and fundamental rights caused by the recent developments of EU copyright law, none of their proposed solutions has been proven successful. This chapter is based on the assumption that the cause of this impasse lies in the systematic chaos generated by the incompatibility of EU and national copyright models.

Since its onset, EU copyright law has substantially departed from Member States' common traditions, while Article 17.2 of the European Charter of Fundamental Rights (ECFR) completed the paradigm shift by formalizing the definition of copyright in proprietary terms. Due to the vagueness of CJEU's "fair balance" test and the different approaches of the ECFR and national constitutions to the functions, limits, and hierarchical rank of property rights, this classification has broadened the divide between EU and national case laws and caused several interpretive short circuits before national courts.

The chapter argues that the only way out from the stalemate is a systematic reordering of this otherwise fragmented multilevel framework. To this end, it starts with a description of the main symptoms of the EU paradigm shift (§ 2) and

---

C. Sganga (✉)
Central European University, Budapest, Hungary
e-mail: sgangac@ceu.hu

R. Caso, F. Giovanella (eds.), *Balancing Copyright Law in the Digital Age*,
DOI 10.1007/978-3-662-44648-5_1

compares the effects of copyright propertization before the CJEU and in selected Member States (§ 3). Then it proposes an integrated interpretation of CJEU's precedents in light of the common constitutional traditions (§ 4) and concludes by providing examples of how the new interpretative framework may help to restore the lost balance on more solid and stable systematic bases (§ 5).

1 The Need to Go Back to the System

In the last two decades, the headlong rush of copyright law towards the achievement of high levels of protection has neglected, if not created, the risk of conflict between authors' prerogatives and users' fundamental rights. To restore the balance that once characterized the discipline, scholars and stakeholders have advocated for legal reforms,[1] proposed to take advantage of the flexibility of the current legislative framework,[2] or supported the creation of model private agreements as tools to leverage, rather than oppose, natural market tendencies.[3] So far, none of these solutions have been successfully worked out. There is an inner and somewhat overlooked reason why all the approaches thus suggested are, and most probably will be, destined to fail. In fact, the ultimate cause of the current *impasse* lies in the systematic chaos generated by the interplay between EU and national legal sources. EU copyright law has substantially departed from Member States' common core, abandoned the paths traced by the civil and common law traditions, and embraced rationales that are far removed from the inspirations of both models.[4] This silent revolution has generated several interpretative short circuits in the practice of national courts, such as the disapplication of exceptions in light of their potential negative impact on the commercial exploitation of the work.[5] The already critical imbalance between exclusive rights and free uses, which are traditionally provided to allow the enjoyment of users' fundamental rights *vis-à-vis* copyright enforcement, has thus significantly worsened. At the same time, the Court of Justice of the European Union (CJEU) has not been able to draw up any clear criteria to be used by national courts when pursuing the "fair balance" mentioned in several EU Directives, given the much greater emphasis placed on broadening the scope of

[1] For a comprehensive overview, see Van Eechoud et al. (2004). See also IVIR (2007).

[2] See, e.g., Hugenholtz and Senftleben (2011).

[3] Especially in the fields of cross-border licensing, collective management, and ISPs' liability. For an interesting analysis of the positions of different stakeholders in the European Union, see Mazziotti (2013).

[4] See *infra*, § 2.

[5] See *infra*, note 84.

the *acquis communautaire* than on providing rules of thumb to systematize the subject.[6] It is not surprising that, when facing such a chaos, the fragmented and atomistic *modus operandi* of copyright scholarship and case law is not of any help in untying the interpretative knots. To complete the picture, Article 17 of the European Charter of Fundamental Rights (ECFR), dedicated to property rights, has formalized the qualification of copyright in proprietary terms by stating, rather cryptically, in its second paragraph that "intellectual property shall be protected."[7] The definition stands in clear contrast with the historical aversion of the civil law tradition towards an extension of property rights to cover intangible goods and with the absence of intellectual property from most of the Member States' constitutions,[8] and it is thus destined to create much misunderstanding in its national implementation. But the problems arising from the clash between the EU and Member States' sources do not end here. The ECFR does not define any hierarchy among rights and liberties protected, while national constitutions have traditionally ranked fundamental rights, either fully or at least up to a certain extent, according to specific value-laden options.[9] For the common constitutional traditions of Member States, property is a right internally limited by its functionalization to social goals, while for the ECFR it is a fundamental liberty that can be subject to limitation dictated by public interests.[10] In those national jurisdictions where constitutional property rules apply also to intellectual property, the propertization of copyright has been used to uphold the legislative limitation of author's rights in light of their social function.[11] On the contrary, the effects of Article 17 on CJEU's case law have been either limited or dangerously contradictory, while the "fair balance" looks at copyright and fundamental rights as equally ranked rights.[12]

With such a chaotic and scattered background, every possible attempt to solve the conflict between copyright and fundamental rights is condemned to produce ephemeral or no results and to be frustrated by further interpretative short circuits. In fact, no balance can be coherently pursued and no legal certainty can be achieved until the elements composing this multilevel framework are properly conceptualized and understood and their interactions resystematized. In this context, as much as the propertization of EU copyright law constitutes the final threat posed by the

---

[6] As emphasized by Griffiths (2013), p. 77. See also, more generally Van Eechoud (2012), p. 1; Derclaye (2010), p. 247.

[7] On the cryptic nature of Article 17 ECFR, see Geiger (2009), p. 115.

[8] See *infra*, note 21.

[9] On the relationship between the ECFR and national constitutions and, more generally, on the impact of the Charter on the protection of fundamental rights in Europe in light of CJEU's case law, see the overview provided by Advocate General Kokott in Kokott and Sobotta (2010). On convergences and divergences in the multilevel protection of fundamental rights see Besselink (2012), p. 63.

[10] See *infra*, § 4.

[11] See *infra*, § 3.

[12] Ibid.

systematic chaos, it may equally play a fundamental role in building the framework necessary to emerge from the *impasse*.

Starting with the main symptoms of the paradigm shift of EU copyright in the words of legislator and courts (§ 2), this article attempts to trace a possible path for this new systematic reconstruction. A brief diachronic comparison of the effects of propertization in the EU and selected Member States (§ 3) provides the elements necessary to connect the dots and merge the lessons coming from the common constitutional traditions of Member States with the indications formulated by the CJEU (§ 4). The paper concludes with some practical examples of how the new framework may help in reinterpreting EU copyright law in order to restore the lost balance on solid and stable systematic bases (§ 5).

2 The "Propertization" of EU Copyright Law

The use of property rhetoric to support the quest for expansion of the scope and term of protection of copyright is not a new phenomenon. In eighteenth century England, the Stationers' Company, a corporation enjoying full control over printing activities, defines copyright as "undoubted property" to lobby for reclaiming the privileges lost due to the nonrenewal of the Printing Act.[13] After the enactment of the Statute of Anne, which reduces the duration of printing monopolies, a comparable argument is used to advocate for the existence of an absolute and perpetual common law copyright, independent of the rights created by law.[14] In the same span of years, publishers from Paris fight to strengthen their position by claiming the existence of a *propriété literaire*, defined as perpetual natural right,[15] while a few decades later, after the Revolution, authors' rights are statutorily qualified in terms of property rights, which represent the highest expression of the new freedom acquired with the defeat of the *Ancient Regime*.[16] Several American colonies use analogous definitions until the advent of the federal Constitution and the first federal Copyright Act, which opt for a neutral, utilitarian approach.[17] Here also, exactly as it happened in England after the Statute of Anne, local publishers push

[13] The definition was used in the "Bill for the Encouragement of Learning and for Securing the Property of Copies of Books to the rightful Owners thereof." The text is reported by Rose (1993), pp. 36 ff.

[14] *Millar v. Kinkaid*, 4 Burr. 2303, 98 Eng. Rep. 210 (1751), *Tonson v. Collins*, I Black W. 301, 321, (1760), and the most cited *Donaldson v. Becket*, 4 Burr. 2408, 98 Eng. Rep. 251 (H.L. 1774).

[15] Particularly in the *Mémoire de d'Héricourt*. See Edelman (2004), pp. 239 ff.

[16] The same proprietary metaphor appears in the definition of "public domain" used by Le Chapelier in the report on the 1791 decree. See Moyse (1998), p. 1 and his ample bibliographical references.

[17] U.S. Constitution, art. I, section 8, cl. 8.

for an expansion of the scope and term of protection by arguing for the existence of a common law copyright, clearly worded in proprietary terms.[18]

Although the historical process of formation of copyright and *droit d'auteur* shows in both cases the presence of strong property rhetoric, the paths followed by the two models diverge at a very early stage. The most direct explanation of the phenomenon—less political and more technical—lies in the opposite semantic implications of the word "property" in civil and common legal systems.[19] In the Anglo-Saxon tradition, the lexeme is a synonym of ownership or asset and does not represent an autonomous, characterizing legal category. Hence, the qualification of a right in terms of "property" does not carry systematic consequences, nor does it have an impact on its regulation.[20] The characteristics of intellectual property rights descend, in fact, only from their monopolistic nature and the utilitarian rationales underlying their protection. On the contrary, the continental paradigm is heavily influenced by the Pandectist tradition, which limits the subject matter of property to tangible goods, and links the definition of a right in proprietary terms to the application of specific rules concerning the creation, circulation, and protection of the entitlement.[21] According to these dogmas, intellectual property is not a form of property, nor can it ever be. France constitutes an exception, where property is a concept characterized by weak classificatory power.[22] Its scarce cogency explains why the personalist nuance of the *propriété literaire* could predominate and distance author's rights from the property model delineated by the *Code Napoleon* and why the consequences of such a development share very little with the effects of the recent copyright propertization.[23]

French literary property mirrors the sacred link between author and work, where the work represents the materialization of author's personality.[24] This aspect is of such key importance to the development of the model as to have influenced the way that exclusive rights and exceptions are conceptualized. Personality rights, unlike monopolies, are not supposed to be tightly controlled in their exercise, while their superior hierarchical status limits the number of cases where flexible clauses are needed to balance them with other conflicting rights. Consequently, exclusive

[18] *Wheaton v. Peters*, 33 U.S. (8 Pet.) 590 (1834). For a more detailed comment see Joyce (2005), p. 325.

[19] The literature is immense. An essential comparative overview is provided by Gambaro (2011), p. 205. For a broader discussion, see Mattei (2000), pp. 13 ff.

[20] Mostly due to the "property as a relationship" approach. See Gambaro (2011), pp. 220 ff.

[21] For a historical reconstruction, see Schrage (1996), pp. 35 ff.; more broadly, on the objective scope of civil law property, see, in the same book, Mincke (1996), pp. 655 ff.

[22] This is one—and maybe the most important—reason why the French *droit d'auteur* is considered as a bridge between the civil and common law traditions of copyright. On this line, Ginsburg (1990), p. 991; see also Kerever (1989), pp. 4 ff. The historical roots of French exceptionalism are analyzed by Halperin (2008).

[23] As shown by the development of moral rights. See Desbois (1978), pp. 388 ff.; *contra* Lucas (1998), pp. 350 ff.

[24] On the particular relevance of the "sacred bond," see Willem Grosheide (1994), p. 207.

author's rights are shaped in broad and flexible terms, while exceptions and limitations are exhaustively determined by law.[25] Dissimilarly, the Anglo-Saxon model has a strong utilitarian inspiration, where the incentive offered to authors is justified by the social need to create a marketplace for ideas and to stimulate the creation and diffusion of knowledge. Since copyright is a monopoly granted for public goals and not an idiosyncratic natural right, exclusive rights are listed in a close and exhaustive manner, while exceptions are worded as flexible clauses, so as to allow courts the possibility to implement the law according to its underlying goals.[26]

EU copyright law departs from both models. Its pronounced market rationales are rooted in the original lack of competence of the Community in the field, and the consequent need to ground its intervention on the necessity to remove obstacles to the internal market.[27] Born as a sterile creature, EU copyright is unable to embed the philosophical inspirations that have characterized the continental and Anglo-Saxon traditions since their onset.

The shift is already visible even in the earliest consultative documents. The goals of harmonization, according to the first Green Papers and subsequent follow-ups, are to strengthen the internal market and to stimulate competitiveness and investments.[28] Meanwhile, the necessity to balance market needs with the promotion of access and participation to cultural life is confined to mere declamatory statements or introduced in the context of goals of production and commercialization of cultural goods and services.[29] Similar words can be found in the first Directives, which repeatedly mention the need to protect investments,[30] to stimulate the

---

[25] Strowel (1993), pp. 144–147. For a comparative analysis of the two approaches see Senftleben (2004), pp. 22 ff.; and Guibault (2002), pp. 17 ff.

[26] Similar conclusions can be found in Geller (1994), pp. 170 ff.; Strowel (1993), pp. 250 ff.; Ginsburg (1990), pp. 133 ff.

[27] See, among others, Keeling (2003), pp. 28 ff. The conflict between intellectual property and fundamental freedoms are particularly evident in the early CJEU's case law, e.g. in *Deutsche Grammophon v. Metro*, C-78/70, ECR 487 (1971), *Coditel v. Ciné Vog Films*, C-62/79, ECR 881 (1980), *Warner Bros and Metronome Video v. Christiansend*, C-158/86, ECR 2605 (1988), *EMI Electrola v. Patricia Im-und Export*, C-341/87, ECR 79 (1989).

[28] As in the *Green Paper on copyright and the challenge of technology – Problems in copyright calling for immediate action*, COM (88) 72 final, 17 June 1988, 3; *Follow-up to the Green Paper – Working programme of the Commission in the field of copyright and neighbouring rights*, COM (90) 584 final, 17 January 1991, 2–3; *Green Paper on Copyright and Related Rights in the Information Society*, COM (95) 382 final, 25 July 1995, 10. For further comments, see Van Eechoud et al. (2004), pp. 5 ff.; see also Mazziotti (2008), pp. 46 ff.

[29] *Green Paper on Copyright and the Challenge of Technology*, *supra* note 28, 5; *Follow-up*, *supra* note 28, 4; *Green Paper on Copyright and Related Rights*, *supra* note 28, 10–12.

[30] Directive 91/250/EEC of 14 May 1991 on the legal protection of computer programs, OJ L-122, 17 May 1991, 42–46 [hereinafter Software 1 Directive], Recital 2; Directive 92/100/EEC of 19 November 1992 on rental right and lending right and on certain rights related to copyright in the field of intellectual property, OJ L-346, 27 November 1992, 61–66, [hereinafter Rental Right Directive], Recital 7; Directive 93/83/EEC of 27 September 1993 on the coordination of certain rules concerning copyright and rights related to copyright applicable to satellite broadcasting and

industrial development,[31] and to remove obstacles to the internal market.[32] Directive 2001/29/EC (InfoSoc) completes the departure from the continental model with two further steps: firstly, the explicit introduction of a utilitarian rationale in its recitals[33] and, secondly, for the first time, the definition of copyright in proprietary terms inspired not by jusnaturalism but by its utilitarian function of promoting and protecting creativity.[34] No correspondent change, however, can be witnessed in the approach to limitations and exceptions. On the contrary, Recital 32 specifies that the list provided by Article 5 should be deemed exhaustive, following the good old continental paradigm. At the same time, Recital 31 rejects the adoption of a pure common law utilitarian rationale and negates the possibility to introduce flexible balancing clauses, by stating that national legislators shall intervene on exceptions only if a lack of harmonization may have an impact on the internal market. Similar arguments are advanced in the Directives enacted after 2001.[35]

The paradigm shift is inspired by the aim of granting to copyright a "high level of protection,"[36] which the EU legislator seems to consider desirable in any case and representing an end in itself. This assumption has led several scholars to affirm the adoption of a new "property logic," according to which author's rights are so idiosyncratic that they need not to be justified in light of any further aim.[37] The use of "logic," instead of "dogmatic definition," is understandably grounded on the almost complete absence of an explicit proprietary qualification of copyright in EU

cable retransmission OJ L-248, 6 October 1993, 15–21, [hereinafter Satellite Directive], Recital 5; Directive 96/9/EC of the European Parliament and of the Council of 11 March 1996 on the legal protection of databases, OJ L-077, 7 March 1996, 20–28, [hereinafter Database Directive], Recital 7.

[31] Software 1 Directive, Recital 3; Rental Right Directive, Recital 6; Satellite Directive, Recital 9; Directive 93/98/EEC of 29 October 1993 harmonizing the term of protection of copyright and certain related rights, OJ L-290, 24 November 1993, 9–13, [hereinafter Copyright Term Directive], Recital 10; Database Directive, Recital 3.

[32] Software 1 Directive, Recitals 4–5; Rental Right Directive, Recitals 1–3; Satellite Directive, Recitals 2, 21; Copyright Term Directive, Recitals 2, 9, 11, 17, 25; Database Directive, Recital 3.

[33] Directive 2001/29/EC of the European Parliament and of the Council of 22 May 2001 on the harmonisation of certain aspects of copyright and related rights in the information society, OJ L-167, 22 June 2001, 10–19 [hereinafter InfoSoc Directive], Recitals 2, 10 and 11.

[34] Id. Recital 9.

[35] See, e.g., Directive 2001/84/EC of the European Parliament and of the Council of 27 September 2001 on the resale right for the benefit of the author of an original work of art, OJ L-272, 13 October 2001, 32–36, Recitals 10, 11, 13, 14; Directive 2004/48/EC of the European Parliament and of the Council of 29 April 2004 on the enforcement of intellectual property rights, OJ L-157, 30 April 2004, 16–25, Recitals 1, 3, 8, 9, 10; Directive 2011/77/EU of the European Parliament and of the Council of 27 September 2011 on the term of protection of copyright and certain related rights, OJ L-265, 27 September 2011, 1–6, Recital 21. Even in the recent Directive 2012/28/EU of the European Parliament and of the Council of 25 October 2012 on certain permitted uses of orphan works, OJ L-299, 27 October 2012, 5–12, which has different targets, similar rationales are recalled in Recital 4.

[36] InfoSoc Directive, Recital 4.

[37] As emphasized by Peukert (2011), p. 67.

legislative and judicial texts, at least until the advent of the Charter of Nice and the ECFR.

Despite being new, Article 17 of the ECFR does not represent a revolutionary norm. The ECtHR, following the EU Commission, already had the opportunity to apply to intellectual property Article 1 of the first Additional Protocol to the European Convention of Human Rights (ECHR), although without providing any significant systematic explanations.[38] Yet the dry language of the text and the many divergent official translations have raised substantial interpretative questions. The English version of the ECFR states that intellectual property "shall be protected," suggesting an interpretation of Article 17.2 as a constitutional declamation of a maximalist approach to copyright protection. On the contrary, the plain use of the verb "to be" in, e.g., German, Italian, and French (*est*, *wird*, *è*) seems to indicate the mere reception of the existing judicial practice, justified by the inclusion of intellectual property under the competences of the Union after the Treaty of Lisbon. The permanence of a balance between copyright and fundamental rights in EU law may support the second, less alarming interpretation.[39] This does not mean, however, that Article 17 represents a merely descriptive provision without substantial effects. To see this, suffice it to mention the impact of its introduction on CJEU's case law.

In an increasing number of decisions, the Court refers to Article 17 to define copyright as a property—and thus fundamental right—and to operate a "fair balance" between equally ranked rights. Since the ECFR and the ECHR do not set any internal hierarchy, while the majority of national constitutions downgrade the hierarchical rank of property in light of its social function, this trend has naturally magnified the divide between EU and State sources. In addition, although the CJEU has already specified that Article 17.2 does not ensure absolute and unlimited protection to copyright, the vagueness of the balancing criteria has already led the Court to tautologically assert the existence of the balance on the mere ground that the law claims to have taken into account all the interests at stake.[40] At the same time, the weak prescriptive nature of the "fair balance" makes national courts unable to understand and apply the test, marginalizing their role in the process. The consequent judicial inertia leaves unsolved the potential conflict between EU and national constitutional provisions and, with this, the question of the impact of Article 17 ECFR on the discretion left to Member States in adapting EU copyright law to the principles and values inspiring their legal systems.

The divide separating EU and Member States' copyright models becomes more evident still when juxtaposing the effects of copyright propertization in recent

---

[38] The most relevant decisions are *Dima v. Romania*, App. No. 58472/00 (2005); *Melnychuk v. Ukraine*, (2006) 42 *EHRR* 42; *Anheuser-Busch Inc. v. Portugal* (2005), 44 EHHR 42. See Helfer (2008), p. 1.

[39] Geiger (2009), p. 121.

[40] Id. at p. 77.

CJEU's decisions with those of the equation of copyright and constitutional property in past national experiences.

3 The Different Effects of Propertization: EU vs. Member States

With a few limited exceptions, the civil law tradition excludes the possibility of extending the subject matter of property to cover intangible goods and, thus, intellectual property.[41] At the same time, due to the high degree of specificity and technicality of the subject, courts have generally found it impractical to use property rules to fill gaps in its regulation, thus making its dogmatic categorization in proprietary terms practically useless. Dissimilarly, scholars and a number of national constitutional courts have opened up the category of constitutional property to include an ample range of economic rights, interests, and expectations, including also intellectual property.[42]

Since 1971, the German *Bundesverfassungsgericht* has applied Article 14 GG to uphold the legitimacy of legislative interventions limiting authors' exclusive rights when required by public interest.[43] In the most paradigmatic case, *Schoolbook*,[44] the Court rejected plaintiffs' claim of expropriation, grounded on a provision that allowed the reprint of excerpts from literary, music, and artistic works in anthologies destined to didactic, educational, or religious purposes,[45] stating that the author's freedom to dispose of his economic rights is not absolute, due to the "special nature and character of this (...) right."[46] On the contrary, "in defining the content of copyright according to Article 14 GG, [the legislator] should provide rules adequate to assure an exploitation of the work which is coherent with the nature and social relevance of copyright."[47] These rules usually take the form of exceptions and limitations and guarantee an adequate balance of copyright with private interests of higher hierarchical rank such as, in this case, the interest for young generations to have access to the most relevant literary and artistic works.[48]

---

[41] See *supra* notes 21 and 22.

[42] For further comments and doctrinal references to the divide between statutory and constitutional property in civil law, with particular regard to intellectual property, see Dreier (2013), p. 94.

[43] See, e.g., 18 BVerfGE 85 (1964); 31 BVerfGE 29 (1971); 31 BVerfGE 270 (1971); 31 BVerfGE 275 (1971); 49 BVerfGE 382 (1978); 79 BVerfGE 1 (1988); 79 BVerfGE 29 (1988); 81 BVerfGE 12 (1989); 81 BVerfGE 208 (1990). For a more detailed analysis, see Braegelmann (2009–2010), p. 99.

[44] *Schoolbook case*, 31 BVerfGE 229 (1971).

[45] § 46, *Urheberrechtsgesetz*, BGBl I (1965).

[46] *Schoolbook*, *supra* note 44, at 241.

[47] Ibid.

[48] Id. at 247–248.

A similar reference to the social function of property in order to justify the otherwise unauthorized use of a protected work appears in the *Broadcast Lending* case,[49] where the *Bundesverfassungsgericht* affirms the legitimacy of a rule that allows the nonprofit reproduction of works for schools that have already acquired a license for single uses. Analogously, the *Church Music* case legitimates the unauthorized performance of music pieces in nonprofit events in light of the "social character of intellectual property," although the Court requires the attribution of fair compensation in order to respect the principle of equitable balance among opposite interests.[50] In the following decades, several other decisions affirmed the validity of this interpretation, using it also to support the interpretative expansion of the boundaries of existing exceptions, like in the recent and famous *Germania 3* case.[51]

German case law is the clearest and most detailed example of the impact of social function on the constitutional propertization of copyright. Other countries, such as France, show similar interpretative trends in several doctrinal contributions, although their courts are relatively silent on the issue.[52] At the opposite side of the spectrum, countries like Italy witness the radical exclusion of the application of constitutional property guarantees on intellectual property rules, in line with the doctrinal aversion against the dogmatic definition of patents, trademarks, and copyright in proprietary terms.[53] As early as in 1978, the Italian Constitutional Court declared the unconstitutionality of the nonpatentability of pharmaceutical products but specified that the reference to constitutional property should be rejected because "the particular characteristics of intangible goods (...) suggests the inopportunity to ascribe them to the property model described by Article 42.1 Cost."[54] More than a quarter of century later, the Court dismissed on procedural grounds a claim of unconstitutionality of the reduction of the term of protection granted to pharmaceutical patents, thus avoiding the decision of whether or not the act amounted to an illegitimate expropriation of property rights.[55] Except for a

[49] 31 BVerfGE 248 (1971).

[50] 49 BVerfGE 382 (1978).

[51] BVerfGE, June 29, 2000, 2001 GRUR 149. For further analysis, see Geller (2009–2010), pp. 907 ff.

[52] See, e.g., Buydens and Dusollier (2008) (especially the contributions of C. Caron (p. 240), and M. Vivant (p. 290), and their broad bibliographical references). However, the *Conseil Constitutionnel* has very recently upheld Act no. 2012-287, which allows the digitalization and reissuing of no longer exploited copyrighted books, on the ground of the fact that the right to property can be limited for reasons of public interests. Cons. Const., décision no 2013-370 QPC, 28 février 2014, JORF du 2 mars 2014, p. 4120.

[53] As clearly shown by Corte Cost., 4 July 1996, n. 236, in *Giur. Cost.*, 1996, 2135. See Moscarini (2006), pp. 161 ff.

[54] "Although the assimilation is possible up to a certain extent, e.g. in case of expropriation of patents under Articles 60 ff. of the R.D. n. 1127/1939" (author's translation). Corte Cost., 20 March 1978, n. 20, in *Giur. Cost*, 1978, 446.

[55] Corte Cost., 21 June 2005, n. 345, in *Giur. Cost.*, 2005, 327.

decision on trademarks,[56] where Article 42.2 Cost. was applied to state that the ownership and enjoyment of intangible goods should be regulated in light of their social functions, and one on copyright,[57] all the other precedents ascribe intellectual property rights to freedom of economic activity and protection of competition.[58]

However, also in those countries where courts and scholars accept the qualification of authors' exclusive rights in terms of constitutional property when the issue at stake concerns the legitimacy of State interventions on copyright law, such a reconstruction is seldom used in cases of conflicts between copyright and fundamental rights in private relationships. Once again, the reason for the divergence may be identified in the traditional judicial deference towards statutory law and the rigidity of exceptions, as shown by the conspicuous number of precedents on the clash between copyright and freedom of expression.[59] In any case, regardless of whether copyright propertization appears only in rulings addressing the constitutionality of copyright statutes, the assumption that its final consequence is the social functionalization and internal limitation of authors' rights, rather than their progressive expansion, remains perfectly valid.

The evolution of CJEU's case law leads, instead, to substantially different results.

In *Laserdisken*,[60] the Court applied for the first time Article 1 of the First Additional Protocol of the ECHR to argue that the protection of copyright as property right represents a case of justified limitation of the freedom to impart and receive information allowed by Article 10 ECHR, which was deemed to be violated by the exclusion of international exhaustion by the InfoSoc Directive. However, no explanation is provided as to the criteria applied for the balance, although the proportionality of the intervention is taken for granted in light of the need to protect copyright.

A completely different approach is adopted in *Promusicae*,[61] in an area—the interplay between copyright enforcement and privacy rights—where the *acquis communitaire* was at that time still underdeveloped. Requested to decide whether EU law obliges Member States to introduce an obligation for Internet Service Providers (ISPs) to communicate users' personal data in the context of civil proceedings, the Court finds that the "fair balance" and other balancing criteria mentioned in the legislative texts, interpreted in light of Articles 17 and 57 of the Charter of Nice, call for a negative answer. These general rules "leave to Member

---

[56] Corte Cost., 3 March 1986, n. 42, in *Giur. Cost.*, 1986, 330.

[57] Corte Cost., 23 March 1995, n. 108, in *AIDA*, 1995, 297.

[58] See Moscarini (2006), pp. 162 ff.

[59] See Hugenholtz (2001), pp. 343 ff. But see Geiger (2006), pp. 375, 394–396, reporting a series of decisions from the Netherlands, Germany and Austria where freedom of expression prevails over copyright and trademark. See also Strowel and Tulkens (2005), pp. 287 ff.

[60] *Laserdisken ApS v. Kulturministeriet*, Case C-479/04, [2006] ECDR 30.

[61] *Productores de Música de España (*Promusicae*) v Telefónica de España SAU*, Case C-275/06, [2008] ECR I-271.

States the necessary discretion to define transposition measures which may be adapted to the various situations possible,"[62] in order for them to fulfill their obligation to "take care to rely on an interpretation of the directives which allows a fair balance to be struck between the various fundamental rights protected by the Community legal order."[63] Moreover, "when implementing the measures transposing those directives, the authorities and courts of the Member States must (...) also make sure that they do not rely on an interpretation of them which would be in conflict with those fundamental rights or with the other general principles of Community law, such as the principle of proportionality."[64] In this case, the conflict would arise if the Court had opted for a broader interpretation of the communication duties to be imposed on ISPs.

Promusicae may have been read as an imperative call for national courts to apply constitutional clauses horizontally when required to protect fundamental rights *vis-à-vis* copyright enforcement. Instead, the decision ended up representing only the starting point of a path where the concept of "fair balance" has been—maybe voluntarily—left empty, making the balancing criteria useless at a national level but at the same time allowing the CJEU to use them flexibly, according to its contingent policy goals.[65]

This attitude appears crystal clear when comparing *Promusicae* with three similar cases: on one side, *Scarlet Extended*[66] and *Netlog*[67] (2011), concerning the possibility of imposing on ISPs the duty to implement general monitoring systems to check and block the exchange of infringing materials, and, on the other side, *Bonnier Audio*[68] (2012), which looks at the compatibility with the right to privacy of a new Swedish law granting right holders, also in the context of civil proceedings, the right to obtain users' personal data from ISPs in order to identify and prosecute infringers.

Both in *Scarlet Extended* and in *Netlog*, the CJEU specifies that although Article 17.2 ECFR protects intellectual property rights, "there is [...] nothing whatsoever in the wording of that provision or in the Court's case-law to suggest that that right is inviolable and must for that reason be absolutely protected."[69] Recalling *Promusicae*, the Court reaffirms that "national authorities and courts must strike a fair balance between the protection of copyright and the protection of the

---

[62] Id. at para 67.

[63] Id. at para 70.

[64] Id. at para 68.

[65] See the critiques moved by Drassinower (2009), p. 991.

[66] *Scarlet Extended SA v Société belge des auteurs, compositeurs et éditeurs SCRL (SABAM)*, Case C-70/10, 24 November 2011.

[67] *Belgische vereniging van Auteurs, Componisten en Uitgevers CVBA (SABAM) v. Netlog NV*, Case C-360/10, 16 February 2012.

[68] *Bonnier Audio AB and Others v Perfect Communication Sweden AB*, Case C-461/10, 19 April 2012.

[69] *Netlog*, para 41; *Scarlet Extended*, para 43.

fundamental rights of individuals who are affected by such measures."[70] The need to protect copyright does not justify the imposition of a general monitoring obligation that would impair, on one side, ISPs' freedom of economic initiative due to its costs and, on the other side, users' right to impart and receive information due to its inability to distinguish between legal and illegal contents.[71] A few months later, *Bonnier Audio* reaches opposite results. According to *Promusicae*, an interpretation of EU copyright law in line with fundamental rights protection excludes the existence of an obligation for Member States to implement communication duties *vis-à-vis* ISPs. States, however, are free to provide otherwise, and thus Sweden is deemed to have correctly exercised its discretion when letting copyright enforcement prevail over users' privacy in the context of civil proceedings.[72]

Nothing in the text of the decisions helps to provide an understanding of why and how the same "fair balance" between privacy and copyright could produce such different outputs in so short a time frame. The vagueness of the balancing criteria seems to reduce CJEU's intervention to mere cosmetic statements, which hardly set a clear direction to resolve conflicts between copyright and fundamental rights.[73] Such blurriness would not hurt if the Court played a neutral role in the creation and development of EU copyright law. But this has long not been the case.

As a matter of fact, the CJEU has repeatedly tried to broaden the scope of EU harmonization and to introduce new limits to State discretion. An example of this attitude can be found in the recent *Eva-Maria Painer* case,[74] where the Court admits that the InfoSoc Directive leaves Member States free to adapt the public security exception to their own needs,[75] but at the same time it circumscribes the scope of the exception with several well-known, but again vague, criteria. Principles and rules, such as proportionality and the three-step test, are listed without providing any further explanation on their specific application in the case at hand.[76] Parallel to this, the goals of the Directive are reduced to the mere assurance of a high level of copyright protection,[77] while the "fair balance" is analyzed only briefly.[78] No reference whatsoever is made to Article 17 ECFR and its possible implications for the balancing exercise.[79]

---

[70] *Netlog*, para 43; *Scarlet Extended*, para 45.

[71] *Netlog*, paras 46–50; *Scarlet Extended*, paras 48–52.

[72] *Bonnier Audio*, paras 55–57.

[73] The mere "cosmetic" nature of the CJEU's constitutionalization of copyright law is also emphasized by Griffiths (2013), p. 78.

[74] *Eva-Maria Painer v. Standard VerlagsGmbH et al.*, Case C-145/10, 1 December 2011.

[75] Id. at paras 101–103.

[76] Id. at paras 105–110.

[77] Id. at para 107.

[78] Id. at para 135.

[79] See recently, e.g., *Nintendo Co. Ltd and Others v PC Box Srl and 9Net Srl*, Case C-355/12, 23 January 2014, and *UPC Telekabel Wien GmbH v Constantin Film Verleih GmbH and Wega Filmproduktionsgesellschaft GmbH*, Case C-314/12, 27 March 2014.

One might be tempted to argue that the impact of the ECFR on the CJEU has been only slightly more than nonexistent. However, precedents such as *Luksan*[80] depict a completely different scenario.

The *casus belli* here is the decision of the Austrian legislator to grant to producers, rather than to directors, the exploitation rights over cinematographic works. The Court not only finds Austrian law incompatible with the European framework[81] but also uses Article 17.1 ECFR to define the legislative act as a deprivation of property rights legitimately acquired under EU law.[82] Although a proper argumentation in support of the statement is missing, the link between Article 17.1 and 2 is clearly spelled out[83] and creates for the first time a connection between copyright and the ECtHR's case law on property rights. The same property logic emerges in the judicial construction of the mandatory nature of the right to receive a fair compensation in case of private copy exception, which goes beyond what is provided by the InfoSoc Directive, and stands in clear contrast with the extreme favor for private ordering characterizing the field of exceptions and limitations.

The Strasbourg Court's fragmented reading of Article 1 of the First Protocol of the ECHR, coupled with the high technicality of copyright law, makes it hard to predict the consequence of this *revirement*. However, whatever the evolution of CJEU's case law might be, the interpretation adopted in *Luksan* represents a sort of final and last call to take copyright propertization seriously. The need to revise the approach to the problem becomes particularly pressing when faced with the questionable results already caused by the encounter of the new EU paradigm shift with the relatively rigid background of Member States' laws and judicial practices. Vivid examples of these distortions are the use of the three-step test as an additional filter to the application of exceptions,[84] often leading to their practical disapplication, or the rigid reluctance to apply constitutional clauses horizontally and to extend exceptions by analogy when required to satisfy similar balancing needs.[85]

Before the European harmonization, the continental model of authors' rights and its traditional deference towards statutory law have hindered the ability of judges to play an active role in balancing copyright with other conflicting interests.[86] Still, the

[80] *Martin Luksan v. Petrus van der Let*, Case C-277/10, 9 February 2012.

[81] Id. at para 67.

[82] Id. at paras 69–70.

[83] Id. at para 68.

[84] A comparative overview of national cases is provided by Hugenholtz and Senftleben (2011), pp. 18 ff., and by Griffiths (2009), p. 489.

[85] The decision of the Tribunal of Rome in the *Peppermint* case and the final decisive intervention of the national authority for privacy protection constitute some of the most paradigmatic examples of the phenomenon. Ord. Trib. Roma sez. IX civ. 9 February 2007 and 14 July 2007, in *Diritto dell'Internet*, n. 5/2007, 465, with comments of R. Caso and G. Scorza. The case is analyzed in depth in this book by F. Giovanella, who proposes the adoption of an analytical framework based on national cultural influences to understand and implement the balance between copyright enforcement and the right to privacy.

[86] See Hugenholtz (2001), p. 346. See also Strowel and Tulkens (2005), p. 287.

application of constitutional property clauses to copyright has represented an occasion to emphasize the social function of author's rights and the need to pursue an effective balance. Today, the interaction of national path dependence with the vagueness of the concept of "fair balance" and the controversial indications offered by EU Directives have reinforced the passive attitude of the judiciary and made it more inflexible than ever before.[87] At the same time, the uncertainties surrounding the relation of the new EU constitutional property model with Member States' common constitutional traditions have relegated the social function doctrine to the corner.[88] As a result, the clause has never been used in the context of national implementations of EU copyright law, nor has the CJEU ever referred to it when applying Article 17 to cases related to copyright balance.

The inconsistencies generated by the unclear interplay between multilevel sources make it impossible to regulate the conflicts between copyright and fundamental rights in a manner compatible with the backgrounds characterizing all the systems involved. Short circuits and interpretative *impasses* like those affecting EU copyright law can be metaphorically compared to the consequences of not completely understood, and thus mishandled, chemical reactions. In such cases, the most rational way out is to separate and analyze the single components of the process and then to reconnect them in a new, internally coherent interpretative framework.

4 A Proposal to Connect the Dots

With the introduction of the concept of social function, several modern Constitutions have significantly intervened on the hierarchical rank of property, engendering a qualitative mutation in the nature of its limitations, which have become an integral part of the structure of the right.[89] The effects of the innovation have been the same regardless of whether national Constitutions downgraded property to a mere economic right, as in the case of Italy,[90] or defined it in terms of fundamental right, as in the case of Germany, where the link between property and the goals of the new *Sozialstaat* is summarized by the powerful statement *Eigentum verpflichtet* (property obliges).[91] The concept of social function also emerges in judicial

[87] As in Hugenholtz and Senftleben (2011), p. 10.

[88] See *infra*, note 108.

[89] For an analysis of the role played by social function in national constitutions, see Van Banning (2001), pp. 148 ff.

[90] See, among all, Salvi (1994), pp. 9 ff.; Gambaro (1995), pp. 40 ff.; explicitly on the hierarchical downgrade of property rights Natoli (1976), pp. 34 ff.

[91] See Alexander (2003), p. 733; see also Kommers and Miller (2012), pp. 630 ff.

decisions in countries like France, where the Constitution is silent.[92] Decades of precedents have contributed to the development of a complex doctrine, which emphasizes, above all, the variable implications of the clause according to the social relevance of the good(s) owned, or the connection between property and the duty of civil solidarity.[93] As a result, proprietors' idiosyncratic interests are smeared, while property moves away from the category of inviolable rights and the top of the pyramid of rights protected.[94]

Although social function represents one of the most characterizing traits of continental property, the clause does not appear in any of the EU texts, where it is generally substituted by the notion of general/public interest.[95] "General interest" is also the lexeme used in Article 1 of the First Additional Protocol of the ECHR, the content of which is only minimally specified by the ECtHR, due to the Court's high deference towards national socioeconomic and distributive policies.[96] Only those acts that "take the legislature's decision outside the margin of appreciation"[97] are considered inappropriate and disproportionate, while the admissibility of the limitation is assessed on the ground of the existence of a legitimate goal and of the reasonableness and proportionality of the balance between intervention and goals pursued. The evaluation of the Court is centered either on the social function of property, i.e. on the reasons underlying the limitation, or, more often, on the economic loss suffered by the right holder.[98] Due to this tendency, the property depicted by the ECtHR is predominantly a bundle of economic utilities[99]; the missing specification of the interplay between powers, limits, and social obligations

---

[92] As clearly stated by the French Conseil Constitutionnel in two historical decisions. Cons. const. 25 July 1989, 89-256 D.C., 53, and Cons. const. 8 January 1991, RIPIA n. 163-1991, 326. See Libchaber (2006), pp. 659 ff.

[93] Recently spelled out by the Italian Constitutional Court, when interpreting Art. 42 Cost. in light of the ECtHR's case law on property rights. Corte Cost., 24 October 2007, n. 348–349, available at www.cortecostituzionale.it.

[94] Van Banning (2001), p. 149.

[95] Nevertheless, scholars draw a parallelism between general interest and social function. See, e.g., Calliess (2007), p. 456.

[96] The Court's clearest affirmation of the deference can be found in *Handyside v. United Kingdom*, 1 EHRR 737 (1976): "*The second paragraph of Article 1 sets the Contracting States as the sole judges of the necessity of an interference.*" Similarly, e.g. *Draon v. France*, 42 EHHR 40 (2006), and *Scordino v. Italy*, 45 EHHR 7 (2007).

[97] *Sporrong and Lonnroth v Sweden* 5 EHRR 35 (1983), 69.

[98] For an overview of the ECtHR's case law in the field of property, among all, see Helfer (2008), pp. 7–11. More generally, see Shutte (2004); Çoban (2004), pp. 124 ff.; Harris et al. (2009), pp. 655 ff.

[99] See Allen (2006), pp. 123 ff., analyzing the emphasis put on economic losses in the ECtHR's balancing test. However, the nature of the interest underlying property protection plays an interesting role. The deference towards commercial property, for example, is much less strong than the one shown when the right to habitation comes into play. Compare, *e.g.*, the approach adopted in *Gasus dosier- und fördertechnik GmbH v. The Netherlands*, (1995) 20 EHRR 403 with *Venditelli v. Italy*, (1995) 19 EHRR 464. For a more detailed analysis, see Shutte (2004), pp. 46 ff.

makes Article 1 of the First Protocol a mere guarantee against State interferences, which, as a consequence, says little or nothing about the hierarchical rank of property and its balance with other conflicting rights.

CJEU's decisions, although limited in number, offer more detailed arguments. The first definition of property as fundamental right subject to limitations in light of public interest can be found in *Hauer v. Land Rheinland-Pfalz.*[100] The case represents also the first connection of the Luxembourg Court's case law with the ECtHR's precedents, with the difference that the CJEU explicitly refers to social function as the lowest common denominator of Member States' common constitutional traditions and as the founding element of any legislative interventions on property rights.[101] Five years before, in *Nold,*[102] the Court was even clearer in stating that "if rights of ownership are protected by the constitutional laws of all the Member States [. . .] the rights thereby guaranteed, far from constituting unfettered prerogatives, must be viewed in the light of the social function of the property and activities protected thereunder."[103] *Nold* recognizes that social function belongs to the common core of Member States' property law and draws internal limits to the structure of the right, allowing EU interventions on national property rights when required by public interest.[104] On the basis of this principle, which was further developed in *Van der Bergh Foods Ltd. v. Commission,*[105] the CJEU has repeatedly found EU interference on national laws justified by the need to pursue socially relevant goals such as the protection of fundamental rights[106] and, to a much greater extent, the correct functioning of the internal market.[107] The more frequent use of market arguments may be causally connected with the original competences of the Union and the late appearance of fundamental rights in the Court's case law.

Several scholars have argued that the advent of the ECFR and its direct reference to the ECHR represent two decisive steps towards the creation of a new EU constitutional property model, which would diverge drastically from the

[100] *Hauer v. Land Rheinland-Pfalz*, Case C-44/79, [1979] ECR 3727.

[101] Id. at paras 20 and 32.

[102] *Nold v. Commission*, Case C-4/73, [1974] ECR 491.

[103] Id. at para 14.

[104] Ibid.

[105] *Van den Bergh Foods Ltd. v. Commission*, Case T-65/98R [2004] ECR II-4653.

[106] See., *e.g.*, *Alliance for Natural Health et al. v. Secretary of State for Health and National Assembly for Wales*, Cases C-154/04 and C-155/04 (2005), ECR I-6451, which states the admissibility of the restriction to protect public health.

[107] As in, *e.g.*, *Regione autonoma Friuli-Venezia Giulia e Agenzia regionale per lo sviluppo rurale (ERSA) v. Ministero delle Politiche Agricole e Forestal*i, Case C-347/03 (2005), ECR I-3785; *Commission v. Germany*, Case C-113/82, 19 April 1983; *Zuckerfabrik v. Hauptzollamt Aachen et al.*, Cases C-23 to 36/06 (2008), OJ C-158, 2; *Unitymark Ltd, North Sea Fishermen's Organisation v. Department for Environment, Food and Rural Affairs*, Case C-535/03 (2006), ECR I-2689.

personalist-solidarist inspiration of many national constitutions.[108] The absence of an internal hierarchy among fundamental rights, the dilution of social function in the vague concept of general (or public) interest, the qualification of property in terms of fundamental liberty, and the focus on guarantees and minimum economic content of the right might indeed support this fear. Still, the fact that the ECFR eschews a hierarchy and defines property as a fundamental liberty does not necessarily imply the abandonment of the social function clause, as shown by the German Constitution.[109] Similarly, the concept of social function is not completely unknown to European courts, although it has never been properly articulated in their arguments. Last, but not least, Article 6 of the Lisbon Treaty defines common constitutional traditions as general principles of EU law, thus allowing them to play a relevant role in aligning the development of EU constitutional property with the milestones reached by decades of national judicial contributions.[110]

Past national experiences illustrate well how reading copyright propertization through the lens of social function may help in attributing to authors' exclusive rights an indicative hierarchical rank and orienting their balance with conflicting public and private interests. Today, Article 17 ECFR clearly requests national legal systems to overcome the reluctance against this dogmatic categorization and broaden the reach of their constitutional property clauses to cover also intellectual property. At the same time, the indications coming from the EU may also contribute to the "renaissance" of social function. The interpretation of the clause as rule directed only at legislators has historically slowed down, if not blocked, its horizontal application, thus making it impossible for property to share with contracts and torts the same path of "constitutionalization."[111] The situation may—and most probably should—now change in light of the CJEU's recommendations. In *Promusicae*, as well as in its general case law on fundamental rights protection, the Court has clearly stated that not only legislators but also courts are in charge of implementing EU law in a manner that is not conflicting with fundamental rights or other general principles of Community law, such as the principle of proportionality.[112] This implies also the need for a horizontal application of constitutional clauses if required to guarantee the respect of fundamental rights in the context of private relations, and there is no reason to believe that property clauses would constitute an exception. If this were the case, the social function of constitutional property could play a fundamental role in guiding courts when they are requested to rule on conflicts between copyright and fundamental rights. Moreover, in light of

[108] Rodotà (2005), p. 159, argues that EU law brings the property "constitutional clock" back of a whole century.

[109] Graziadei (2011), p. 194.

[110] The implications of the EU multilevel constitutionalism have been so broadly analyzed by scholars that it is impossible to provide a full account of the wide array of literature on the subject. Suffice it to mention, for a comprehensive overview of the doctrinal and judicial debate on the interplay between the ECHR and national constitutions, Lenaerts (2012), p. 375.

[111] On which, see *infra*, note 133.

[112] *Promusicae*, *supra* note 61, para 68.

Article 6 of the Treaty of Lisbon, the clause may help to attribute an indicative hierarchical status to author's exclusive rights *vis-à-vis* conflicting right and thus to fill up, on stronger dogmatic bases, the empty spot left by the CJEU in the definition of the meaning of "fair balance," with undoubtedly positive effects for legal certainty and the coherent development of EU harmonization.

The effects of this new systematic reconstruction are potentially numerous and range from a new interpretation of exceptions, limitations, and the three-step test to the correction of the most evident distortions of digital copyright contracts. The development of more sophisticated national judicial approaches may not only avoid interpretative short circuits at a State level but also contribute, with a bottom-up approach, to resolving the inconsistencies affecting CJEU's case law.

5 Potential Effects of the New Systematic Reconstruction

One of the most important roles that social function can perform is to assist judges in developing adequate criteria to follow *Football Association Premier League*,[113] which states that the restrictive interpretation of exceptions should in no way hamper their effectiveness and the fulfillment of their purposes.[114] Once the exception is read as a limit imposed on copyright in light of its functionalization to social goals[115] and once its legal function is clearly spelled out, *Football Association* may support, on a more solid and systematic basis, the extension by analogy of the rule to cases not explicitly provided by law but still sharing the purpose of protecting the same fundamental right. Such an approach would contribute to the creation of even clearer points of reference for the application of the "fair balance" and proportionality test, thus helping to achieve higher legal certainty in a field where inconsistencies are a matter of routine.

It has already been noted that the horizontal application of constitutional clauses on exceptions might be precluded by Article 5.5 InfoSoc and its three-step test, which is deemed to exclude the judicial creation or expansion of free unauthorized uses.[116] The test, in fact, subordinates the implementation of exceptions to specific cases that do not conflict with the normal exploitation of the work and do not unreasonably prejudice the legitimate interests of the right holder. The language of the Directive, which uses the vague phrase "shall be applied," does not shed light on the subjective scope of the provision.[117] This uncertainty is mirrored in the bipolar

---

[113] *Football Association Premier League Ltd and Others v QC Leisure and Others*, Case C-403/08, and *Karen Murphy v Media Protection Services Ltd*, Case C-429/08, (2012) EWHC 108.

[114] Id. at paras 163–164. The same argument is used in *Eva-Maria Painer*, *supra* note 74, para 133.

[115] On the same line, see Geiger (2013), pp. 157 ff., who also gives account of the doctrinal contributions on the theory of social function of intellectual property (p. 156, note 9).

[116] Senftleben (2004), p. 118.

[117] InfoSoc Directive, Article 5(5).

approach of Member States, which either interpret Article 5.5 as a rule directed at legislators, and avoid implementing it in their laws, or read it as a rule addressed to judges, thus embedding it in their copyright statutes.[118] Irrespective of the option chosen, a number of national courts have used the three-step test to exclude the application of legally granted exceptions on the basis of their negative impact on the commercial exploitation of the work.[119] Although CJEU's decisions such as *Infopaq II*[120] may suggest an interpretation of Article 5.5 as a mere criterion to scrutinize the legitimacy of the legislative introduction of new limitations, the Court has not taken a definite position on the issue yet, leaving the door open to contrary interpretations.

To read the three-step test as an additional *ex post* filter undoubtedly frustrates the goal of legal certainty that the continental model has always pursued by means of closed and exhaustive lists of exceptions.[121] At the same time, their judicial disapplication can hardly be reconciled with those of CJEU's precedents that assume that the fair balance between copyright and fundamental rights has been realized by the broad and flexible catalog of free uses provided by Article 5 InfoSoc and its national implementations.[122] Although Member States are free to implement the provision according to their national needs, the CJEU still requires an implementation of EU law that is coherent with the goal of protecting fundamental rights (*Promusicae* et seq.) and an interpretation of exceptions that does not hinder the practical fulfillment of their function (*Premier League*). These precedents should logically prevent mere market arguments from supporting the disapplication of exceptions when such rules are used within the borders of their legitimate function, and their implementation is needed to guarantee the enjoyment of users' fundamental rights.

The social function of property may also inspire a more balanced interpretation of the first and third prongs of the three-step test. If the main social function of exceptions is to act as a safeguard to fundamental rights *vis-à-vis* copyright enforcement, the term "special cases" should be read by legislators as including every free use necessary to guarantee their protection. Similarly, the legitimacy of authors' interests should be evaluated on the basis of their proprietary nature and thus by a concept of property protected in light and within the limits of its social function.[123] This suggests the acceptability of those exceptions that regulate the borders of exclusive rights in accordance with their purposes and that can be used to prevent their *de facto* abuse. If the three-step test is meant to be directed also at judges, then the social function doctrine indicates again the necessity for courts to

---

[118] On the various national approaches to the test, see Griffiths (2009), pp. 495 ff.

[119] *Supra* note 84.

[120] *Infopaq International A/S v Danske Dagblades Forening*, Case C-302/10, 17 January 2012.

[121] Geiger et al. (2010), p. 119. But see *contra* Cohen Jehoram (2005), p. 359; and Lucas (2010), p. 277, who see the three-step test as a tool to prevent possible abuses of exceptions.

[122] Geiger et al. (2010), p. 120.

[123] See *supra* note 115.

read its first and third prongs in view of the goal of fair balance and horizontal protection of fundamental rights. This implies not only the impossibility of basing on mere economic grounds the disapplication of exceptions required to safeguard the enjoyment of a fundamental right but also the need to extend them by analogy to specific similar cases, even if not contemplated by law, when the purpose of protecting the same fundamental right is at stake.

The new systematic approach to copyright propertization may also contribute to solving the distortions caused by the compression or nullification of users' prerogatives in EULA standardized clauses. With the exception of Directive 2011/83/EC, which introduces information duties on TMPs,[124] the only EU text addressing the issue of copyright contracts is the InfoSoc Directive, which leaves contractual parties free to determine the applicability of exceptions "to ensure fair compensation for the rightholders insofar as permitted by national law."[125] The remission of the copyright balance to contractual determination, which signs a clear departure from the model of imperative exceptions adopted by Directive 96/6/EC on database protection[126] and Directive 2009/24/EC on software protection,[127] is not destined to change soon, notwithstanding the intense round of consultations recently launched by the Commission on the matter.[128] Here, where the conflict between copyright and fundamental rights arises in the context of a private agreement, the interpretative nodes to be solved are whether and to what extent parties can agree on the restriction of legitimate uses and whether or not the negative effects of such a restriction on users' fundamental rights may impact on the validity of the contract, clause excluding the applicability of the exception(s). While the answer is straightforward for that minority of legal systems that declares exceptions mandatory,[129] the issue becomes more problematic when the legislator is silent on the issue.

National courts and scholars agree on the fact that exceptions do not confer subjective rights and thus deny their imperative nature.[130] Dogmatically speaking, the theory is hard to confute. No subjective right exists if, as in the case of exceptions, the biunivocal link between subject and object is missing. While the exclusive right on a specific work arises at the moment of its creation, and

[124] Directive 2011/83/EU of the European Parliament and of the Council of 25 October 2011 on consumer rights, OJ L 304-64, 22 November 2011, Article 5(1)(h) and Article 6(1)(r).

[125] InfoSoc Directive, Recital 45.

[126] Database Directive, Article 15.

[127] Directive 2009/24/EC of the European Parliament and of the Council of 23 April 2009 on the legal protection of computer programs, OJ L 111/16, 5 May 2009, Article 5 (2)–(3), and Article 6.

[128] As for the case of the Public Consultation on the Review of the EU Copyright Rules, launched by the Commission in December 2013. The questionnaire is available at http://ec.europa.eu/internal_market/consultations/2013/copyright-rules/docs/consultation-document_en.pdf (last access September 12, 2014).

[129] Like Belgium, Ireland and Portugal. See Guibault (2008), pp. 537 ff.

[130] For a comparative overview, see Baulch et al. (1999). Before the introduction of the InfoSoc Directive, however, a number of national courts ruled in favor of the imperative nature of exceptions. See Guibault (2002), pp. 91 ff.

immediately generates the necessary connection between holder and object of the right, exceptions are generically attributed to an indefinite potential user and on any indefinite potential works. As a consequence, no corresponding obligation arises for the author until the interest materializes in a specific user and in a specific context.

The dogmatic nature of exceptions is closer, instead, to the category of "objective rights," elaborated in Germany at the beginning of the twentieth century on the basis of the *Reflexwirkung* theory and subsequently developed in different forms throughout Europe.[131] An objective right is the reflex of the introduction of legal provisions that mainly pursue public goals, while the right holder is the subject who becomes, in a specific time and circumstance, the target of a protection justified by the safeguard or fostering of the public interest. The term "objective right" is used in clear contrast with the concept of subjective right, which is recognized and protected as a result of the positive legislative evaluation of a specific private, idiosyncratic interest. The main distinction between objective and subjective rights lies in the creation, in the latter case, of a correspondent duty on everyone or on a definite subject, with clear consequences in terms of judicial remedies available.[132] In the case of exceptions, the general interest to achieve a balance between copyright and fundamental rights becomes an objective right and finds application in favor of a specific subject every time the protection of his or her fundamental right(s) is subordinated to the possibility of exercising the exception itself.

In lack of significant case law in the field, the only precedents available to orient the analysis are those concerning the horizontal effect of fundamental rights on contractual relations. Although not all the Member States have experienced similar degrees of judicial development, in the last decade the path of "constitutionalization" of contract law has been followed by an increasing number of countries. Common criteria used in the scrutiny of the agreement are the proportionality of the contractual restriction imposed on the exercise of fundamental rights and the gravity of the prejudice as compared with the goals pursued by the contract, where proportionality plays the most important role.[133] Seeming as if courts would had wanted to draw a parallelism between legal and contractual interventions, these elements show an impressive similarity to the criteria used for assessing the legitimacy of legislative limitations of property rights or, more generally, fundamental rights.

If translated into the area of digital copyright contracts, these judicial doctrines may support the denial of effectiveness of an EULA clause that restricts users' prerogatives attributed by law, when such a restriction is neither proportionate nor necessary to pursue the goal underlying the license contract, which is to authorize otherwise illegitimate uses. In fact, no authorization is needed for acts included in the scope of exceptions, nor can their limitation be deemed essential to the

[131] The *Reflexwirkung* theory originates from Jellinek (1919), pp. 70 ff.

[132] As in Gervais (1961), pp. 246–247.

[133] For an overview of the most relevant judicial and scholarly interventions, see Mak (2008), pp. 45 ff. See also, more generally, Cherednychenko (2007) and Grundmann (2008).

protection of authors' rights, if they are integral to laws that aim to protect the moral and material interests of the author.[134] This does not exclude, however, the need for a case-by-case judicial analysis, which may alter the balance in favor of authors' rights—they being also fundamental rights—if the circumstances so require.

The qualification of exceptions in terms of objective rights makes it hard to justify an *ex officio* judicial intervention on a freely stipulated agreement and has already hindered the effective application of consumer protection tools on EULA clauses compressing free uses.[135] Yet when the application of the exception is necessary for the enjoyment of a user's fundamental right, and the gravity of the prejudice caused by its restriction is not proportionate to the goals pursued by the contract and to the (social) function of copyright law, a judicial enforcement of such terms may result in an indirect violation of the fundamental right, the protection of which underlies the statutory limitation. As a consequence, although the objective right conferred by the exception may not constitute the ground for an independent cause of action, the actual impairment of a user's fundamental right may surely be used as a defense against the licensor's claims. This would allow the "fair balance" between conflicting interests to operate also when their regulation is remitted to private ordering, thus bridging the gap between copyright law and copyright contracts created by the InfoSoc Directive and progressively broadened by the CJEU. Social function, once again, is fundamental to a specification of the content of the balancing test—in this case, the proportionality of the contractual restriction—and to the orientation of its application.

Conclusions

With a more thorough reconstruction of its content and implications in light of Member States' legal framework, the paradigm shift and propertization caused by EU law and the ECFR may turn from a problematic mine zone to a stimulating opportunity to rethink and reframe EU copyright law. A new, systematic approach to the subject, based on a deconstructed analysis of the implications that copyright propertization should have if correctly embedded in Member States' legal systems, may lead to several positive results. First, it may assist national legal formants in solving the most controversial interpretative short circuits generated by the clash between multilevel legal sources. Second, it may ensure more legal certainty in the formulation and application of the criteria to be used when pursuing the "fair balance" between copyright and fundamental rights, at the same time achieving a greater coherence with the values underlying the legal systems involved. Third, it may help national courts to abandon the traditional passive and deferential attitude towards statutory law and gain a more prominent role in the process of developing

(continued)

[134] Guibault (2002), p. 269.

[135] Id. at p. 272.

EU copyright law. A more solid set of State case laws may create a positive bottom-up pressure on EU courts to take more seriously into consideration the relevance of national legal traditions and to avoid the inconsistencies generated by a poorly directed harmonization. If the EU and national dots are reorganized and connected in a more ordered and structured fashion, property may finally cease to constitute a dangerous rhetoric tool and start instead to perform the role of a new, effective, and long-waited systematic framework.

References

Alexander G (2003) Property as a fundamental constitutional right? The German example. Cornell Law Rev 88:733

Allen T (2006) Property and the Human Rights Act of 1998. Hart, Oxford

Baulch L, Green M, Wyburn M (eds) (1999) ALAI study days – the boundaries of copyright: its proper limitations and exceptions. Australian Copyright Council, Redfern

Besselink LFM (2012) General report. In: Laffranque J (ed) The protection of fundamental rights post-Lisbon: the interaction between the Charter of Fundamental Rights of the European Union, the European Convention on Human Rights and national constitutions. Tartu University Press, Tallin, p 63

Braegelmann T (2009–2010) Copyright Law in and under the Constitution – the constitutional scope and limits to Copyright Law in the United States in comparison with the scope and limits imposed by constitutional and European Law on Copyright Law in Germany. Cardozo Arts Entertain Law J 27:99

Buydens M, Dusollier S (eds) (2008) L'intérêt général et l'accès à l'information en propriété intellectuelle. Bruylant, Bruxelles

Calliess E (2007) The fundamental right to property. In: Ehlers D (ed) European fundamental rights and freedoms. De Gruyter, Berlin, p 456

Cherednychenko OO (2007) Fundamental rights, contract law and the protection of the weaker party. Sellier, Munich

Çoban AR (2004) Protection of property rights within the European Convention on human rights. Ashgate, Aldershot

Cohen Jehoram H (2005) Restrictions on copyright and their abuse. Eur Intellect Prop Rev 27:359

Derclaye E (2010) Infopaq International A/S v Danske Dagblades Forening: wonderful or worrisome? Eur Intellect Prop Rev 53:247

Desbois H (1978) Le droit d'auteur en France, 2nd edn, mise a jour 1973. Dalloz, Paris

Drassinower A (2009) From distribution to dialogue: remarks on the concept of balance in copyright law. J Corporation Law 34:991

Dreier T (2013) How much 'Property' is there in intellectual property? The German civil law perspective. In: Howe H, Griffiths J (eds) Concepts of property in intellectual property law. Cambridge University Press, Cambridge, p 94

Edelman B (2004) Le sacre de l'auteur. Dalloz, Paris

Gambaro A (1995) Il diritto di proprietà. Giuffrè, Milano

Gambaro A (2011) Property rights in comparative perspective: why property is so ancient and durable. Tulane Eur Civil Law Forum 26

Geiger C (2006) Constitutionalising intellectual property law. The influence of fundamental rights on intellectual property in Europe. Int Rev Intellect Prop Competition Law 37:375

Geiger C (2009) Intellectual property shall be protected!? – Article 17(2) of the Charter of Fundamental Rights of the European Union: a mysterious provision with an unclear scope. Eur Intellect Prop Rev 31

Geiger C (2013) The social function of intellectual property rights, or how ethics can influence the shape and use of IP law. In: Dinwoodie GB (ed) Intellectual property law: methods and perspectives. Edward Elgar, Cheltenham, pp 153–176

Geiger C, Griffiths J, Hilty RM, Suthersanen U (2010) Declaration on a balanced interpretation of the three-step test in copyright law. J Intellect Prop Inf Technol E-Commerce Law 1:119

Geller PE (1994) Must copyright be forever caught between marketplace and authorship norms? In: Sherman B, Strowel A (eds) Of authors and origins. Essays on copyright law. Oxford University Press, Oxford, p. 170

Geller PE (2009–2010) A German approach to fair use. Test cases for TRIPS criteria for copyright limitations. J Copyright Soc U S A 57

Gervais A (1961) Quelques réflexions à propos de la distinction des "droits" et des "intérêts. Mélanges en l'honneur de Paul Roubier. Dalloz, Paris, p 246

Ginsburg J (1990) A tale of two copyrights: literary property in revolutionary France and America. Tulane Law Rev 64

Graziadei M (2011) Disciplina internazionale e circolazione dei modelli proprietari. L'incidenza del diritto internazionale sul diritto civile. Napoli

Griffiths J (2009) The 'Three-Step Test' in European copyright law – problems and solutions. Intellect Prop Q 4:428–457

Griffiths J (2013) Constitutionalising or harmonising? The Court of Justice, the right to property and European copyright law. Eur Law Rev 38: 65

Grundmann S (2008) Constitutional values and European contract law. Wolters Kluwer, Alphen an den Rijn

Guibault L (2002) Copyright limitations and contracts: an analysis of the contractual overridability of limitations on copyright. Kluwer Law International, The Hague

Guibault L (2008) Relationship between copyright and contract law. In: van Derclaye E (ed) Research handbook on the future of EU copyright law. Edward Elgar, Cheltenham, p 537

Halperin JL (2008) Histoire du Droit des Biens. Dalloz, Paris

Harris DJ et al (2009) O'Boyle & Warbrick: law of the European convention on human rights. Oxford University Press, Oxford

Helfer L (2008) The new innovation frontier? Intellectual property & the European Court of human rights. Harv Int Law J 49:1

Hugenholtz PB (2001) Copyright and freedom of expression in Europe. In: Dreyfuss TC et al (ed) Expanding the boundaries of intellectual property: innovation policy for the knowledge society. Oxford University Press, Oxford, p. 3443

Hugenholtz PB, Senftleben M (14 November 2011) Fair use in Europe: in search of flexibilities. http://ssrn.com/abstract=1959554. Last access 12 Sept 2014

IVIR (2007) Study on the implementation and effect in Member States' laws of directive 2001/29, Final Report (February 2007). http://www.ivir.nl/publications/guibault/Infosoc_report_2007.pdf. Last access 12 Sept 2014

Jellinek G (1919) System der subjektiven offentlichen Rechten. Mohr, Tubingen

Joyce C (2005) A curious chapter in the history of judicature: Wheaton v. Peters and the rest of the story (of copyright in the New Republic). Houston Law Rev 42:325

Keeling DT (2003) Intellectual property rights in EU law: free movement and competition law. Oxford University Press, Oxford

Kerever A (1989) Révolution Française et droit d'auteur. Revue Internationale du droit d'auteur 141

Kokott J, Sobotta C (2010) The charter of fundamental rights of the European Union after Lisbon. EUI Working Paper AEL 2010/6. http://cadmus.eui.eu/bitstream/handle/1814/15208/AEL_WP_2010_06.pdf?sequence=3. Last access 12 Sept 2014

Kommers DP, Miller RA (2012) The constitutional jurisprudence of the Federal Republic of Germany. Duke University Press, Durham

Lenaerts K (2012) Exploring the limits of the EU charter of fundamental rights. Eur Constitutional Law Rev 8:375

Libchaber R (2006) La propriété, droit fondamental. In: Cabrillac R et al (eds) Libertés et droits fondamentaux, 12th edn. PUF, Paris, p 659
Lucas A (1998) Droit d'auteur et numérique. Litec, Paris
Lucas A (2010) For a reasonable interpretation of the three-step test. Eur Intellect Prop Rev 6:277
Mak C (2008) Fundamental rights in European private law. Kluwer Law International, Alphen aan den Rijn
Mattei U (2000) Basic principles of property law. A comparative legal and economic introduction. Praeger, Westport
Mazziotti G (2008) EU digital copyright and the end-user. Springer, Berlin
Mazziotti G (2013) Copyright in the EU digital single market. Reports of the CEPS Digital Forum, June 2013. http://ssrn.com/abstract=2307855. Last access 12 Sept 2014
Mincke W (1996) Objects of property rights. In: Van Maanen GE, Van Der Walt A (eds) Property law on the threshold of the 21st century. Maklu, Antwerpen-Apeldoorn, pp 655 ff
Moscarini A (2006) Proprietà privata e tradizioni costituzionali comuni. Giuffrè, Milano
Moyse PE (1998) La nature du droit d'auteur: droit de propriété ou monopole? McGill Law J 43:1
Natoli U (1976) La proprietà. Appunti dalle lezioni. Giuffrè, Milano
Peukert A (2011) Intellectual property as an end in itself. Eur Intellect Prop Rev 67:68
Rodotà S (2005) Il progetto della Carta europea e l'art. 42 Cost. In: Comporti M (ed) La proprietà nella Carta Europea dei diritti fondamentali. Milano, p 159
Rose M (1993) Authors and owners. The invention of copyright. Harvard University Press, Cambridge
Salvi C (1994) Il contenuto del diritto di proprietà, in Commentario del codice civile diretto da P. Schlesinger. Giuffrè, Milano
Schrage EJH (1996) Jus in re corporali perfecte disponendi: property from Bartolus to the New Dutch Civil Code of 1992. In: Van Maanen GE, Van Der Walt A (eds) Property law on the threshold of the 21st century. Antwerpen-Apeldoorn, p. 35
Senftleben M (2004) Copyright, limitations, and the three-step-test. Kluwer Law International, The Hague
Shutte CB (2004) The European fundamental right of property. Kluwer, Deventer
Strowel A (1993) Droit d'auteur et copyright. Divergences et convergences. Bruylant, Brussels
Strowel A, Tulkens F (2005) Freedom of expression and copyright under civil law: of balance, adaptation, and access. In: Griffiths J, Suthersanen U (eds) Copyright and free speech: comparative and international analyses. Oxford University Press, Oxford, p. 287
Van Banning TRG (2001) The human right to property. Intersentia, Antwerpen
Van Eechoud M (2012) Along the road to uniformity – diverse readings of the court of justice judgments on copyright work. J Intellect Prop Inf Technol E-Commerce Law 3:1
Van Eechoud M et al (2004) Harmonizing European copyright law. The challenges of better lawmaking. Kluwer Law International, Alphen aan den Rijn
Willem Grosheide F (1994) Paradigms in copyright law. In: Sherman B, Strowel A (eds) Of authors and origins. Essays on copyright law. Clarendon, Oxford, p 207

Online Exhaustion and the Boundaries of Interpretation

Giorgio Spedicato

Contents

Abstract It is a common perception that copyright has been struck by a serious crisis of legitimacy. This crisis can be traced to a variety of causes, but the main one would seem to lie in the (over)protectionist drift by which copyright legislation has been affected, and which has led to a radical shift in the balance of interests that has been achieved over time. However, the balancing of interests is not an activity exclusively entrusted to lawmakers, for it also involves judges and legal scholars. This essay explores the ability of the three "legal formants" to ensure that the EU copyright regulatory framework stays fit for purpose in the digital environment by referring to the widely debated question whether the digital marketplace is an appropriate context into which to expand the principle of exhaustion of the

G. Spedicato (✉)
Department of Legal Studies, University of Bologna, Bologna, Italy
e-mail: giorgio.spedicato@unibo.it

R. Caso, F. Giovanella (eds.), *Balancing Copyright Law in the Digital Age*,
DOI 10.1007/978-3-662-44648-5_2

distribution right. In the first place, a few considerations on the interests protected by the principle of exhaustion are proposed, arguing that there is no reason why this principle should become any less necessary in the online distribution. In the second place, it is considered the way lawmakers and judges have addressed the question of whether and under what conditions a principle of online exhaustion can be recognized. In the third place, it is discussed how some solutions based on a nonformalistic and nontextualist interpretation of the norms can make it possible to overcome the objections that have so far prevented the principle of online exhaustion from being recognized for digital works other than computer programs.

1 Technological Evolution, Balancing of Interests, and the Three Drivers of Legal Innovation

According to an account that seems to afford an accurate picture of the situation,[1] the phenomenon of rampant copyright infringement on the Internet—a practice that poses a serious threat to the full development of digital markets[2]—can be explained at least in part by pointing to the crisis of legitimacy that has struck copyright, in particular,[3] and intellectual property, in general.[4]

---

[1] Cf. Peukert (2012), pp. 163 ff.

[2] However, the empirical evidence of the negative impact of Internet piracy on sales of legal products is less straightforward than what the copyright industry generally claims: see for example, in this regard, the study "*Digital Music Consumption on the Internet: Evidence from Clickstream Data*," authored by L. Aguiar and B. Martens and published in 2013 by the European Commission Joint Research Centre (the study is available at ftp://ftp.jrc.es/pub/EURdoc/JRC79605.pdf), where, based on a data set provided by Nielsen NetView (Nielsen company's Internet audience measurement service), the authors conclude that "[t]aken at face value, our findings indicate that digital music piracy does not displace legal music purchases in digital format." The International Federation of the Phonographic Industry (IFPI), on the other hand, has labeled this study as "flawed and misleading," observing that "[t]he findings seem disconnected from commercial reality, are based on a limited view of the market and are contradicted by a large volume of alternative third party research that confirms the negative impact of piracy on the legitimate music business" (the IFPI response is available online at http://www.ifpi.org/content/library/IFPI-response-JRC-study_March2013.pdf). Among the vast literature about the impact of Internet piracy on the markets for copyright goods, see Liebowitz (2005), pp. 439 ff., suggesting that given our current state of knowledge, we should conclude that file sharing hurts copyright owners and is one of the main causes responsible for most of the recent decline in sales; Zentner (2006), pp. 63 ff., arguing that peer-to-peer usage reduces the probability of buying music by an average of 30 %; Peitz and Waelbroeck (2006), pp. 449 ff., concluding that the effects of end-user copying on a particular industry depend on the particular features of that industry.

[3] On the bad image of copyright, see Ginsburg (2002), pp. 61 ff.; and Gendreau (2006), pp. 209 ff.

[4] Cf., for example, Geiger (2008), p. 103. For a different approach, based on cognitive science, see Goodenough and Decker (2009), pp. 345 ff.

Indeed, copyright is increasingly being perceived by users as a legal scheme far removed from common sense,[5] a device aimed not at guaranteeing a "fair balance of rights and interests between the different categories of rightholders, as well as between the different categories of rightholders and users," as the idea is ecumenically stated in Recital 31 of Directive 2001/29 (InfoSoc Directive),[6] but rather at making sure that some right holders (i.e., the copyright industry) can reap monopolistic profits on the backs of other right holders (i.e., authors),[7] as well as against the interests of users.[8]

This crisis of legitimacy can probably be traced to a variety of causes, but the main one would seem to lie in the (over)protectionist drift by which copyright legislation has been affected,[9] and which has led to a radical shift in the balance of interests that has been achieved over time.[10] The roots of this protectionism go back a long way, but the phenomenon picked up speed only in the latter half of the 1990s, when lawmakers found themselves having to adapt the copyright system to the challenges brought about by the digital revolution,[11] a process that, for the most part, has resulted in a progressive extension of the scope[12] and term[13] of copyright

[5] Patry (2012), p. 56, has significantly defined copyright laws as "a faith-based enterprise, passed according to theological claims and slogans that are contrary to both common sense and independent economic studies." See also Litman (2006), p. 29, who has observed that "a number of the rules that copyright lawyers take for granted are so very counterintuitive that people commonly refuse to believe that they could possibly be the rules."

[6] Directive 2001/29/EC of the European Parliament and of the Council of 22 May 2001 on the harmonisation of certain aspects of copyright and related rights in the information society, in *OJ*, no. L 167, 22 June 2001, 10 ff. On the language of the directive, see Hilty and Nérisson (2012), p. 76, noting that "the quest for balance appears only rhetorical since international law only moves towards more protection granted to those able to block access to works."

[7] See Feldman and Nadler (2006), pp. 587 f. An example of the underlying economic mechanism in the music industry is provided by Fisher III (2004), pp. 54 ff.

[8] On the copyright wars between right holders and consumers, see Patry (2009), pp. 1 ff.

[9] Some scholars however have criticized the use of the term overprotection (as well as the opposite term underprotection) as it is based on the questionable assumption that it is possible to identify an optimal level of intellectual property protection: see, in this sense, Ricolfi (2006), pp. 305 ff.; and Efroni (2010), p. 410.

[10] See Hilty and Nérisson (2012), pp. 2 ff. For a more thorough analysis of the topic see Spedicato (2013), pp. 115 ff.

[11] Cf., in this regard, WIPO (2002).

[12] See, by way of example, the protection granted to nonoriginal databases under Article 7 of Directive 96/9/EC on the legal protection of databases and the expansion of the scope of the rights of reproduction and communication to the public under Articles 2 and 3 of the cited InfoSoc Directive.

[13] See Council Directive 93/98/EEC of 29 October 1993 harmonizing the term of protection of copyright and certain related rights, in *OJ*, No. L 290, 24 November 1993, 9 ff., which has been repealed and replaced by Directive 2006/116/EC of the European Parliament and of the Council of 12 December 2006, in *OJ*, No. L 372, 27 December 2006, 12 ff., and finally amended by Directive 2011/77/EU of the European Parliament and of the Council of 27 September 2011, in *OJ*, No. L 265, 11 October 2011, 1 ff. See also the Copyright Term Extension Act (CTEA) of 1998, Pub. L. 105–298, which has extended copyright terms in the United States.

protection,[14] with an accompanying restriction of the exceptions and limitations to the exercise of exclusive rights. In this sense, the crisis of legitimacy affecting copyright can be said to reflect the larger credibility gap for the political class, often accused of being more receptive to the lobbying of the copyright holders than to the claims advanced by society.[15]

It is worth recalling, even so, that the balancing of interests in copyright legislation is not an activity exclusively entrusted to lawmakers, for in different ways and to different degrees it also involves other subjects. Indeed, no less important, particularly but not only in common law countries, is the role of the judges, who are tasked with shaping into concrete relations the abstract designs by which the lawmakers have sought to balance the different interests at stake. The balancing of interests done by the judges can, in this sense, be regarded as second-order balancing (or metabalancing, as it has been described by legal theorists),[16] since it works on the basis of the balancing the lawmakers have designed, and of course this latter design cannot be ignored without violating the democratic principle and, no less importantly, the principles of legality and legal certainty.[17] The need for judges to respect these basic principles, however, may promote a natural tendency toward interpretive formalism and, more broadly, toward judicial deference.[18] This is particularly true when major technological shifts are involved,[19] and as much as these attitudes may be understandable, the risk is that they may undermine the ability of judges to find the best balancing of the interests at stake.[20]

---

[14] On this expansionist trend, see Netanel (2007), pp. 3 ff. and the essays in Dreyfus et al. (2001).

[15] See, for example, Hugenholtz (2000), p. 501, pointing out the "unprecedented lobbying, the bloodshed, the vilification, the media propaganda, the constant hounding of EC and government officials" during the legislative process for the adoption of Directive 2001/29/EC. With reference to the U.S. legislation, see J. Litman (2006), pp. 144 f., observing that, in the Digital Millennium Copyright Act, "[t]here is no overarching vision of the public interest [. . .]. Instead, what we have is what a variety of different private parties were able to extract from each other in the course of an incredibly complicated four-year multiparty negotiation. Unsurprisingly, they paid for that with a lot of rent-seeking at the expense of new upstart industries and the public at large." See also Merges (2000), pp. 2236 f.; and Landes and Posner (2003), pp. 220 ff., on industry's successful lobbying campaign for the extension of the copyright term.

[16] See, in this sense, Pino (2010), pp. 202 ff.

[17] Cf. G. Pino (2010), p. 203.

[18] See *Eldred v. Ashcroft*, 537 U.S. 186 (2003), where the US Supreme Court stated that any extension of the terms of copyright protection is compliant with the requirement of the "limited time" set forth by Article I, Section 8, Clause 8 of the United States Constitution, as long as the extension itself is limited instead of perpetual. In his dissenting opinion, Justice Stevens observed that, by adopting such a formalistic approach to the constitutional provision, "the Court has stated that Congress' actions under the Copyright/Patent Clause are, for all intents and purposes, judicially unreviewable." On the consequences of the *Eldred* decision, see Samuelson (2003), pp. 547 ff.

[19] As the US Supreme Court put it in *Sony Corp. of America v. Universal City Studios, Inc.*, 464 U.S. 417 (1984), "sound policy, as well as history, supports our consistent deference to Congress when major technological innovations alter the market for copyrighted materials."

[20] Cf., also in this regard, Lucas (2010), pp. 310 f.

A useful contribution, in light of this background, can thus come from the interpretations put forward by legal scholars, who can exert an indirect influence on the law in force by persuading judges[21] that the lawmakers' balancing of the interests ought to be reconsidered in response to the new socioeconomic and technological context.[22]

It is worth considering in some depth the ability of the three "legal formants"[23] to "ensur[e] that the EU copyright regulatory framework stays fit for purpose in the digital environment."[24] But since the discussion can easily branch out in too many directions, it will be best to focus on one specific issue that, as has been rightly pointed out, "is integral to the balance between authors and the public that lies at the heart of [...] copyright law."[25] To this end, I will restrict my view to the widely debated question whether the digital marketplace[26] is an appropriate context into which to expand the principle of exhaustion of the distribution right—i.e., the principle under which, once a copy of a protected work has been legally purchased, the copyright holders will be limited in their ability to control any further distribution of that copy.

I will thus start out with a few considerations on the interests protected by the principle of exhaustion, arguing that there is no reason why this principle should become any less necessary in the online distribution of intangible copies. I will then consider the way lawmakers and judges have addressed the question of whether (and, if so, under what conditions) a principle of online exhaustion can be recognized.[27] And, finally, I will discuss how some solutions based on a nonformalistic and nontextualist interpretation of the norms can make it possible to overcome the objections that have so far prevented the principle of online exhaustion from being recognized for digital works other than computer programs.[28]

For the sake of brevity, I will confine my analysis to the EU legal framework, so as to then be able to expand that analysis in future works.

---

[21] See Sacco (1991), p. 349, observing that scholars "has no other power than the one that comes from his capacity to persuade."

[22] A few examples are Geiger et al. (2008), pp. 707 ff.; and Bently et al. (2013).

[23] I use here the well-known definition by Sacco (1991), p. 343.

[24] Cf. European Commission, *Public Consultation on the review of the EU copyright rules*, available at http://ec.europa.eu/internal_market/consultations/2013/copyright-rules/docs/consultation-document_en.pdf, 2.

[25] Serra (2013), p. 1785.

[26] Hereinafter, I will use the expression "digital markets" to refer to online markets of copyright works that are not put into circulation as tangible objects (*i.e.* intangible copies).

[27] I use here the expression "online exhaustion" rather than "digital exhaustion," as the latter may also refer to the distribution of tangible objects (e.g. DVD) in which copies in digital format are fixed.

[28] See also Targosz (2010), p. 340, who has pointed out that in order to solve the issue of online exhaustion, "literal interpretation will not be of much help."

2 The Interests Protected by the Principle of Exhaustion and Their Persistence in Digital Markets

Since the landmark decision of the Court of Justice of the European Union in the *Deutsche Grammophon* case,[29] the judicial and legislative recognition[30] of the principle of exhaustion has been a basic element on which to ensure that the protection of intellectual property rights is consistent with the free movement of goods[31] in such a way as to avoid an unjustified and artificial partitioning of the common market, an outcome that would be repugnant to the essential purpose of the EU Treaty.[32]

As much as the Community origin of the principle of exhaustion is closely related to the regulation of the internal market and to the general interest in ensuring its competitive functioning,[33] the principle is often regarded as a device aimed at achieving a balance among essentially individual interests: on one hand, the copyright holder's interest in controlling the number of copies of the work brought to market and, on the other, the purchaser's interest in retaining the ability to resell any individual copy he may own.[34]

There are important outcomes that follow once right holders are legally prevented from controlling the further circulation of the copies put on the market by the right holders themselves or indirectly with their consent,[35] and among these consequences are those that affect the interest of consumers in having access to

[29] CJEC, 8 June 1971, case C-78/70, *Deutsche Grammophon v Metro SB*, in *OJ*, No. C 65, 29 June 1971, 14. On this case see Cohen Jehoram (1973), pp. 345 ff.; and Olivier (1971–1972), pp. 516 ff.

[30] The principle of Community exhaustion is now expressly stated in Article 5(c) of Directive 96/9/EC on the legal protection of databases, Article 1(4) of Directive 92/100/EEC on rental right and lending right, Article 4 of Directive 2009/24/EC on the legal protection of computer programs, Article 4(2) of Directive 29/2001/EC on copyright in the information society, as well as Article 7 of Directive 2008/95/EC on the harmonisation of trade mark law and Article 16 of Council Regulation 2100/94 on Community plant variety rights.

[31] As pointed out by Sarti (1996), pp. 72 ff., the principle of exhaustion has its historical roots in the need to protect the freedom and certainty of trade. It is worth noting that this objective is fully consistent with the very first objective for the European Community to harmonize the copyright laws of its Member States, which was not to improve copyright protection as such but to remove the legislative barriers that could have a negative impact on trade in the Community: see, in this sense, Cohen Jehoram (1994), p. 821.

[32] Cf. CJEC, 8 June 1971, *cit.*, para. 12.

[33] On the historic origins of the principle of exhaustion in the EU, see Westkamp (2007a), pp. 291 ff.; and Schovsbo (2012), pp. 174 ff.

[34] Cf. Cohen Jehoram (1996), p. 280, who, referring to the explanation of the exhaustion principle provided by the patriarch of intellectual property law, Josef Kohler, observes that "he regarded this rule as a necessary demarcation line between two colliding properties: the intellectual property right of the producer and the common proprietary right the of the owner of a copy of a product he has bought." In this sense, see also Bertani (2011), p. 348.

[35] On the character of the manifestation of the will through which the exhaustion takes place, see Sarti (1996), pp. 82 ff.

protected works under favorable economic conditions, as well as stably over time.[36] The first point here is that, throughout the time that the work is still being distributed by the right holder, the secondary markets will generally make lower prices available, thus making the work accessible to consumers with less purchasing power.[37] The second point is that (unlike trademark and, to some extent, patent protection) copyright protection does not lapse just because the protected work is no longer being distributed by the right holder, and so in the interim period, in a situation where the work is no longer being distributed but has not yet passed into the public domain, the secondary markets may facilitate access to the work by those who are interested in it.[38]

However, in order to protect copyright holders from an excessive curtailment of their rights,[39] the principle of exhaustion has traditionally been subjected to specific conditions and limitations: on one hand, the principle is deemed to be applicable only when a tangible copy[40] of the work has had a transfer of ownership[41] by the right holder or with his consent[42]; on the other hand, exhaustion only affects the right to distribute the single copy put on the market[43] and only applies within the EU market.[44]

---

[36] For a more thorough analysis of the market effects of the principle of exhaustion, see Reese (2003), pp. 583 ff.

[37] Cf. Perzanowski and Schultz (2010), p. 894.

[38] Cf. Reese (2003), p. 595.

[39] But it is worth considering that the principle of exhaustion has positive effects on the right holders' economic interests as well. See, in this sense, Katz (2011), observing that consumers "may be more willing to purchase an item if they know they can later resell it in a secondary market." In the same sense, see Glusman (1995), p. 716.

[40] Cf. § 3 below.

[41] Cf. CJEU, 17 April 2008, case C-456/06, *Peek & Cloppenburg*, para. 36, commented by Von Lewinski (2009), pp. 175 ff.

[42] In other words, it is necessary for the right holder to bring a copy of the work to market or to otherwise authorize third parties to do that, a circumstance that, one might add, clearly evinces the right holder's legally protected interest in controlling the number of copies available on the market and in setting their price. See Sarti (1996), p. 17.

[43] And in this way, the law preserves the copyright holder's interest in economically exploiting the work in other ways. Cf. CJEC, 28 April 1998, case C-200/96, *Metronome Musik v Music Point Hokamp*, in *OJ*, No. C 209, 4 July 1998, 5, where the Court of Justice has stated that the introduction of an exclusive rental right, which is not subject to the principle of exhaustion, is fully compatible with Community law.

[44] As a consequence of a clear political choice made by the EU legislator, international exhaustion is expressly excluded in the EU: cf. CJEU, 12 September 2006, case C-479/04, *Laserdisken*, in *OJ*, No. C 281, 18 November 2006, 10, where the European Court of Justice has deemed legitimate Article 4(2) of the InfoSoc Directive, although it preclude a Member State from acknowledging a principle of international exhaustion in its domestic legislation. The opposite approach has been taken in the U.S.: see, in this regard, *Kirtsaeng V. John Wiley & Sons, Inc.*, 133 S. CT. 1351 (2013), stating that the principle of exhaustion is not subjected to geographic limitations: on the Kirtsaeng case, see Rub (2013), pp. 41 ff.

One can easily appreciate, however, that the conditions and limitations just described saddle digital markets with problems not amenable to easy solutions, in that

(*i*) the copies of the work put out in the marketplace are not embodied into tangible objects[45];

(*ii*) the agreements for the use of intangible copies are typically qualified by right holders as *licenses* rather than *sales*,[46] from which it should follow that ownership of those copies does not transfer to the user;

(*iii*) even if we set aside the question of the proper legal characterization for an act through which the right holder put an intangible copy on the market over the Internet—that is, whether this should be characterized as an act of distribution or as one of making available to the public[47]—any transfer of the work the lawful purchaser may make to a third party will require that purchaser to perform one or more acts of reproduction of the work, and those acts do not fall within the scope of the principle of exhaustion; and

(*iv*) the geographic limits imposed on the principle of exhaustion cannot easily be enforced on the Web, which by definition is a *worldwide* network.[48]

Aside from the problems just outlined, the very opportunity of extending the principle of exhaustion to the online distribution of intangible copies has been called into question.[49] One of the reasons for this objection is that, whereas the first purchaser's resale of a *tangible* copy deprives that person of any ability to use that copy, quite the opposite is the case with the resale of *intangible* copies: here, it would be difficult, without adopting technological protection measures,[50] to prevent resellers from keeping and using a copy of a work after they have resold it. On the other hand, it has been argued, while markets for tangible copies are based on goods that deteriorate over time, online markets for intangible copies are based on copies of perfect quality that never deteriorate.[51] The two aforementioned factors, it

---

[45] But cf. Spedicato (2011), where, referring to the well-known distinction between *corpus mysticum* and *corpus mechanicum*, I have defined a computer file as a *corpus quasi-mechanicum*. Indeed, although a file is not a tangible object (i.e., a *corpus mechanicum* in the strict sense), it cannot be denied that it has a physical dimension (and thus it cannot be qualified simply as *corpus mysticum*).

[46] The critical aspects of such a commercial practice are highlighted, ex multis, by Winston (2006), p. 133, who has observed that without "thoughtful extension of the principles of intellectual property into the domain of licenses, the balance between the rights of the intellectual property owner and the public interest in intellectual property shifts away from the public interest."

[47] On this issue, see, for example, Ricolfi (2002), pp. 48 ff.

[48] But for some early critical thoughts on the Internet as a borderless network, see Goldsmith and Wu (2006), pp. 13 ff. On this topic, see also Boschiero (2007), pp. 58 ff.

[49] For a first survey, see Targosz (2010), pp. 343 ff.

[50] Cf. U.S. Copyright Office, *DMCA Section 104 Report*, August 2001, xix, available at http://www.copyright.gov/reports/studies/dmca/sec-104-report-vol-1.pdf.

[51] Cf. European Commission, *Public Consultation on the review of the EU copyright rules*, *cit.*, 13. For a different perspective, based on the possibility to implement an aging file system technology that progressively degrades the digital copy after each duplication, see Hess (2013), pp. 2007 ff.

is believed, would unreasonably undermine the economic interests of copyright holders[52] and would conflict with the specific subject matter of copyright protection, which, as has been rightly pointed out by the EU Court of Justice, protects the right of copyright holders to receive an "appropriate" remuneration for each use of the protected work, that is, a remuneration reasonable "in relation to the actual or potential number of persons who enjoy or wish to enjoy" the work.[53]

Ultimately, according to those who object to online exhaustion, the likely benefits from any expansion of the principle would not outweigh the likely increase in harm.[54]

Even though this position may proceed from true premises, it only takes into account the individual interests involved in the principle of exhaustion, neglecting to consider that, as was previously pointed out, this principle plays a fundamental role, in combination with competition rules, in maintaining the competitive structure of the European single market.[55] Much progress has been made in this last respect by moving closer toward integration among national markets within the EU, but certainly there is still much to be done in the context of digital markets, at least according to the European Commission, which has recently expressed its concern about the fact that, while the Internet is borderless, online markets in the EU are still fragmented by multiple barriers.[56]

It bears pointing out in this regard that many sectors of the online markets for digital goods show a high degree of concentration, which is likely to distort

[52] Cf. U.S. Copyright Office, *op. loc. cit.*, according to which "digital transmissions can adversely effect the market for the original to a much greater degree than transfers of physical copies." In the same sense, see also Kupferschmid (1998), p. 848.

[53] In this sense, see CJEU, 4 October 2011, joined cases C-403/08 and C-429/08, *FAPL*, paras. 108–109, commented by Smith and Silver (2011), pp. 399 ff.; Clifton (2011), pp. 38 ff.; Riziotis (2013), pp. 72 ff. The same point is also made in the opinion of Advocate General Bot delivered on 24 April 2012 in the case C-128/11, *UsedSoft*, para. 81, and in the opinion of Advocate Generale Jääskinen delivered on 12 December 2012 in the joined cases C-201/11 P, C-204/11 P and C-205/11, *UEFA v Commission*, para. 43.

[54] U.S. Copyright Office, *op. loc. cit.* In the same vein, see also Wiebe (2009), p. 117.

[55] Cf. Drexl (2012), p. 4, who emphasizes that "the close link between the exhaustion principle and EU competition law characterized European law from the very beginning." On the convergence between the principle of exhaustion and competition rules, see also Rognstad (2008), pp. 427 ff.

[56] See, in this regard, European Commission, *Communication from the Commission to the European Parliament, the Council, the European Economic and Social Committee and the Committee of the Regions – A Single Market for Intellectual Property Rights. Boosting creativity and innovation to provide economic growth, high quality jobs and first class products and services in Europe*, COM(2011) 287 final, Brussels, 24 May 2011, 9. On the market distortions caused by differences in VAT rates within the EU, and especially differences between the VAT rates applied to physical and digital variants of what is rightly acknowledged to be "essentially the same product," as in the case of hard copy and electronic books, see European Parliament, *Simplifying and Modernising VAT in the Digital Single Market*, Brussels, September 2012, available at http://www.europarl.europa.eu/studies.

competition and lead to the charging of supracompetitive prices.[57] As Advocate General Kokott has pointed out in the *FAPL* case, "it forms part of the logic of the internal market that price differences between different Member States should be offset by trade."[58] From such a perspective, the principle of exhaustion can serve as a fundamental tool in putting downward pressure on the prices of copyrighted works,[59] in such a way as to forestall *ex ante* those market distortions that antitrust measures are designed to drive back only *ex post*.

For the reasons outlined above, we ought to at least recognize that, subject to certain conditions, there is still merit for the principle of online exhaustion to be carefully considered.

3 The International Legislator's (Purported) Clarity in Rejecting Online Exhaustion

Despite clearly being one of the most trade-related aspects of intellectual property rights,[60] the principle of exhaustion has not been specifically addressed in the TRIPS agreement. That is because the negotiating parties could not find a common perspective on such a fundamental topic,[61] especially as concerns the question whether the principle should apply internationally. It is for this reason that Article 6 TRIPS charts a strictly neutral course on this question, by providing the basic freedom of each contracting party to establish its own exhaustion regime, so long as there is no violation of Article 3 (on national treatment) and Article 4 (on the most-favored-nation treatment).

In light of the same need to bridge the gap among different national approaches to the exhaustion rule, the contracting parties are recognized as having a similar

---

[57] It is precisely out of those concerns that the European Commission and the US Department of Justice have recently brought parallel proceedings against Apple and five international publishers on charges of colluding to limit retail price competition for e-books. For the EU case, see *Summary of Commission Decision of 12 December 2012 relating to a proceeding under Article 101 of the Treaty on the Functioning of the European Union and Article 53 of the EEA Agreement*, case COMP/39.847—E-BOOKS, in *OJ*, No. C 73, 13 March 2013, p. 17 ff. For a comment on the case, see Daly (2013), pp. 350 ff.; and Linklater (2012), pp. 20 ff.

[58] See the opinion of Advocate General Kokott delivered on 3 February 2011 in the joint cases C-403/08 and C-429/08, *FAPL*, para. 192.

[59] Cf. Perzanowski and Schultz (2010), p. 894. On the relationship between the principle of exhaustion and price competition, see specifically Ghidini (2006), p. 40; and Mattioli (2010), pp. 246 ff.

[60] See, in this sense, Cohen Jehoram (1996), p. 292.

[61] See Bercovitz (2008), p. 145, who critically points out that "it is difficult to admit that an international agreement whose purpose is to eliminate the obstacles that may arise from the protection of intellectual property rights for international trade does not establish an international exhaustion principle." On the history and interpretation of Article 6 TRIPS, see Correa (2007), pp. 78 ff.; and Gervais (1998), pp. 60 ff.

freedom under Article 6(2) of the WIPO Copyright Treaty of 1996 (WCT),[62] under which nothing in the treaty may be construed in such a way as to affect the freedom to determine "the conditions, if any, under which the exhaustion of the distribution right applies after the first sale or other transfer of ownership of the original or a copy of the work with the authorization of the author."[63] It is worth noting that neither the exhaustion rule contained in Article 6(2) nor the very definition of the distribution right contained in Article 6(1) excludes their applicability to digital copies. However, the agreed statement concerning Article 6 WCT, which is an essential instrument for interpreting the provisions of the Treaty, make it clear that "the expressions "copies" and "original and copies," being subject to the right of distribution [. . .], refer exclusively to fixed copies that can be put into circulation as tangible objects."[64]

In this way, the international legislator for the first time appears to take a clear position[65] in the multifaceted debate on which right the online distribution of intangible copies of a work should be made to fall under:[66] this form of distribution, the WCT unambiguously states, is protected under the right to make the work available to the public, which would foreclose (at least on a *prima facie* basis) any possibility of expanding the principle of exhaustion to intangible copies distributed on online markets.[67]

The principle finally set forth in the WCT seems to have deeply influenced the approach of the Community legislator on the question of online exhaustion. And indeed the analysis of EU copyright legislation shows that the very year the WCT was approved marks a turning point in the way this question has been treated.

---

[62] Whose wording has been "the result of lengthy debates on numerous text versions intending to be sufficiently neutral and flexible, so as to meet the concerns of all delegations," as pointed out by Reinbothe and von Lewinski (2002), p. 83.

[63] On the exhaustion rule, as set forth in the WCT, see also Goldstein (2001), pp. 255 f.

[64] As explained by Reinbothe and von Lewinski (2002), p. 87, "such clarification was deemed necessary, not least because the application of the distribution right under the Copyright Treaty to digital transmissions had been discussed at some length, and was eventually dismissed, by the Committee of Experts."

[65] However, as explained in WIPO (2003), p. 203, "the agreed statement only indicates the minimum level of protection. The minimum obligation consists in extending the right of distribution to the making available of tangible copies. It follows from the nature of minimum obligations that there is no obstacle under the WCT to extend the application of a right beyond the scope and level prescribed therein. This means that it is possible to extend the right of distribution to distribution through reproduction through transmission, and to apply this broader right of distribution in accordance with the 'umbrella solution'."

[66] On this debate, see Ficsor (2002), pp. 145 ff.

[67] Cf. Ficsor (1995), pp. 138 f., as quoted in Ficsor (2002), p. 209, where it is pointed out that digital distribution, due to the fact that it is not distribution after reproduction but distribution through reproduction, is not subject to any exhaustion.

To see this, we can start out from Directive 91/250/EEC (Software Directive),[68] noting that—even though the 1988 Green Paper on copyright and the challenge of technology had specified some caveats[69] and the CJEU had already singled out cases in which the principle of exhaustion did not apply to the exploitation of a work in an intangible form[70]—no such concerns are reflected in the directive, where the Community legislator did not yet take care to distinguish tangible copies of computer programs from intangible ones in stating how the principle of exhaustion was to apply. This can probably be explained by looking at the specific structure of the software market in the early 1990s. Indeed, while the commercial exploitation of protected products such as cinematographic works[71] and sound recordings was seen to depend importantly on the ability to protect those objects in an *intangible* form, the software market in the pre-Internet era was still fundamentally based on the sale of *tangible* items. In other words, when the Software Directive was adopted in 1991, the time of software *as a service* was yet to come.[72]

For this reason, Article 4(1)(c) of the directive provides a very broad definition of distribution,[73] a definition in which, as was just mentioned, no distinction is made between tangible and intangible copies; and without further specification, the same article states that "the first sale in the Community of a copy of a program by the right holder or with his consent shall exhaust the distribution right." As some scholars have pointed out, absent any indication to the contrary in the Software Directive, the exhaustion rule set forth in Article 4(1)(c) is broad enough to apply to intangible copies distributed online.[74]

The same approach is adopted in Directive 92/100/EEC (Rental and Lending Rights Directive).[75] The landscape begins to change, however, with the 1995 Green

---

[68] Council Directive 91/250/EEC of 14 May 1991 on the legal protection of computer programs, in *OJ*, No. L 122, 17 May 1991, 42 ff. This directive has been codified by Directive 2009/24/EC of the European Parliament and of the Council of 23 april 2009 on the legal protection of computer programs, in *OJ*, No. L 111, 5 May 2009, 16 ff.

[69] Cf. European Commission, *Green Paper on Copyright and the Challenge of Technology – Copyright Issues Requiring Immediate Action*, COM (88) 172 final, Brussels, 7 June 1988, 150.

[70] Cf. CJEC, 18 March 1980, case C-62/79, *Coditel v Ciné Vog Films*, in *ECR*, 1980, 881 ff., commented by Harris (1980), pp. 163 ff., and CJEC, 13 July 1989, case C-395/87, *Tournier*, in *OJ*, No. C 207, 12 August 1989, 10, commented by Françon (1990), pp. 50 ff.

[71] Cf. CJEC, 17 May 1988, case 158/86, *Warner Brothers and Others v Christiansen*, in *OJ*, No. C 159, 18 June 1988, p. 4, para. 14, where the Court observed that "the market for the hiring-out of video-cassettes reaches a wider public than the market for their sale and, at present, offers great potential as a source of revenue for makers of films."

[72] On the definition of "software as a service," see Regnell et al. (2011), p. 71.

[73] Which generically includes "any form of distribution to the public, including the rental, of the original computer program or of copies thereof."

[74] As long as the person who resells the first copy does not continue to use any copy left with him, as it has been correctly pointed out by Walter and von Lewinski (2010), p. 136.

[75] Cf. Article 1(4) of the Council Directive 92/100/EEC of 19 November 1992 on rental right and lending right and on certain rights related to copyright in the field of intellectual property, in *OJ*, No. L 346, 27 November 1992, 61 ff.

Paper on copyright and related rights in the Information Society,[76] in which the European Commission appears to take a broader view on the issue of the digital dissemination of works and on the exhaustion of the relative right. This was a time, in the mid-1990s, when the Internet was beginning to shape up as a network carrying huge potential for commerce, and the Commission accordingly felt it necessary to distinguish the sale of goods from the supply of services, including online services, in treating the question of how the principle of exhaustion was to apply, observing in that regard that

> [w]hether a distribution right is capable of being exhausted by an exploiting act of the rightholder [. . .] depends upon the form in which the protected work or related matter is exploited. If it is incorporated in a material form it is subject to the rules on free movement of goods and, in consequence, to the principle of Community exhaustion. [. . .] On the other hand, if the work or related matter is not incorporated in a material form but is used in the provision of services, the situation is entirely different. [. . .] In fact, given that the provision of services can in principle be repeated an unlimited number of times, the exhaustion rule cannot apply.

One year after the release of the Green Paper of 1995, the policy direction the Commission set out in that document can be seen to be reflected in Directive 96/9/EC (Database Directive),[77] which is quite unlike the Software Directive of 1991 in its treatment of online exhaustion. Even without specifying that the right of distribution only applies to tangible copies of a database, thus leaving open the question of which exclusive right online distribution should be made to fall under,[78] Recital 33 of the Database Directive explicitly states that "the question of exhaustion of the right of distribution does not arise in the case of on-line databases, which come within the field of provision of services," and this "also applies with regard to a material copy of such a database made by the user of such a service with the consent of the rightholder."[79]

The EU legislator seems here quite straightforward in framing the rule that the principle of exhaustion does not apply to digital copies distributed online. However, the language of Recital 33 is less clear than would appear at first sight. For example, on a literal interpretation of the second sentence of Recital 33, users who have legitimately downloaded a permanent copy of the database on their hard drive

---

[76] Cf. European Commission, *Green Paper on Copyright and Related Rights in the Information Society*, COM(95) 382 final, Brussels, 19 July 1995, 56 ff.

[77] Directive 96/9/EC of the European Parliament and of the Council of 11 March 1996 on the legal protection of databases, in *OJ*, No. L 77, 27 March 1996, 20 ff.

[78] Cf. Walter and von Lewinski (2010), pp. 721 f., pointing out, however, that the wording of Recital 31 seems to suggest a preference of EU legislator for classifying online transmission as a kind of distribution.

[79] Cf. European Commission, *Commission Communication – "Follow-up to the Green Paper on copyright and related rights in the information society,"* COM(96) 568 final, Brussels, 20 November 1996, p. 19, where the Commission pointed out that in the course of the debate on the challenges posed by new technologies for copyright and related rights, a "large number of interested parties took the view that any legislative initiative should spell out explicitly that the right applicable to the provision of online services may not be subject to exhaustion."

cannot resell the hard drive without first deleting the database from it[80]—but one could seriously doubt that it was really the legislator's intent to arrive at such a conclusion. In more general terms, if on one hand there is no doubt that the principle of exhaustion does not apply to the provision of services, on the other hand there is no bright-line rule on which basis to unambiguously state what is covered by the definition of online databases and so what the circumstances are under which a database ought to be qualified as a service. More to the point, it is not clear whether the provision of services ought to include those cases in which the right holder allows purchasers of a database to download a copy on their hard drive so as to enable them to consult the database offline.

A similar ambiguity can also be found in the InfoSoc Directive of 2001. Indeed, on one hand, this directive seems clearer than the Database Directive in providing that the right of distribution only applies to copies of the work incorporated in a tangible item,[81] but, on the other hand, Recital 29—apart from offhandedly confirming that "the question of exhaustion does not arise in the case of services and on-line services in particular"—is set up in a way almost identical to Recital 33 of the Database Directive, with the consequence that we are left with the same interpretive doubts just pointed out with respect to the latter directive. And, as we will see, despite the apparent clarity of the relevant norms, the very same doubts have been raised by the CJEU in the *UsedSoft* case.

4 The More Reflective Attitude of the Court of Justice

As much as there may have been only a handful of occasions so far in which European judges have been asked to rule on the validity of the principle of online exhaustion, their position, as expressed in the case law, seems to be more nuanced than the legislator's apparent stark rejection. Indeed, although some German courts initially expressed doubts in regard to that question,[82] the landscape seems to be changed after the landmark decision the CJEU rendered in 2012 in the *UsedSoft* case,[83] finding that the authorized downloading from the Internet of a copy of a computer program can actually give rise to the exhaustion of the right of distribution of that copy within the EU.[84]

---

[80] See, on this specific example, Walter and von Lewinski (2010), p. 723.

[81] Cf. Recital 28 of the InfoSoc Directive.

[82] For a survey of the relevant German cases, see Cook (2010), pp. 363 f. On the legal debate in Germany see Overdijk et al. (2011), pp. 36 f.

[83] CJEU, 3 July 2012, case C-128/11, *UsedSoft GmbH v Oracle International Corp*. On the *UsedSoft* decision, see, ex multis, Hilty et al. (2013), pp. 263 ff.; Jani (2012), pp. 21 ff.; and Senftleben (2012), pp. 2924 ff.

[84] In the same vein, see also Sarti (1996), pp. 93 f.

The Court's reasoning is based on a rigorous interpretation of Article 4(2) of Directive 2009/24/EC (which codifies the Software Directive of 1991), under which, as we saw earlier, "the first sale in the Community of a copy of a program by the right holder or with his consent shall exhaust the distribution right within the Community of that copy," regardless of whether the copy is tangible or intangible.

The CJEU has laid out the rationale behind its decision by offering both a consequentialist argument and an economic one. In the former respect, the Court argued that without a broad interpretation of the term *sale*,[85] the effectiveness of the principle of exhaustion would be undermined, since right holders could contract around the rule by merely designating the contract a *license* rather than a *sale*.[86] In the latter respect, the Court argued that the sale of a copy incorporated in material objects is fully analogous, from an economic perspective, to the sale of a copy downloaded from the Internet, since transmission of a copy over the Internet is functionally equivalent to the supply of a material object.[87]

The CJEU does not fail to notice that the moment the principle of exhaustion is extended to intangible copies, the act of making such copies available over the Internet must necessarily be qualified as an act of "distribution" within the meaning of Article 3(1) of the InfoSoc Directive and not as an act of "making available to the public," this in deliberate contrast to the position taken by the European Commission.[88] Even so, we saw earlier that the exclusive rights provided under the Software Directive recognize the right holder as having not only a reproduction and a modification right but also an all-embracing exploitation right inclusive of "any form of distribution to the public," and this inclusion led the CJEU to include the online distribution of a work within the definition of *distribution* set forth in Article 4(1)(c) of the Software Directive of 2009, with the obvious and inevitable consequences that follow as concerns the applicability of the exhaustion rule under that directive.[89]

---

[85] Which, according to the CJEU, necessarily encompasses every agreement by which a person, in return for payment, transfers to another person the ownership in a (tangible or intangible) object that belongs to him. Under this perspective, the downloading of a copy of a computer program from the right holder's website and the conclusion of a license agreement for that copy that grants the user, in return for payment of a lump sum, the right to use that copy for an unlimited time have to be interpreted as "an indivisible whole," whose effect is to transfer the ownership of that copy to the user: i.e. a "sale" of the copy of the computer program in accordance with Article 4(2) of Directive 2009/24/EU.

[86] In the same vein as the CJEU's reasoning, see Sarti (1996), p. 342. For a comparative perspective on the contractual overridability of the exhaustion rule, see Longdin and Lim (2013), pp. 541 ff.

[87] In this vein, see also Tjong Tjin Tai (2003), pp. 207 ff.; Bertani (2000), p. 415.

[88] Cf. para. 50 of the *UsedSoft* decision.

[89] Cf. the AG's opinion in the *UsedSoft* case, para. 56, where it is pointed out that "under Directive 2009/24, the distinction between sale and rental is the 'summa divisio' on which both the application or otherwise of the exhaustion rule and the scope of that rule depend."

In this regard, however, the CJEU takes care to point out that its decision is grounded in the nature of the Software Directive as a *lex specialis* relative to the InfoSoc Directive.[90] At the same time, however, the Court does not explicitly say that the principle of exhaustion does not apply to the online distribution of works subject to the InfoSoc Directive. Quite the contrary, the language used by the Court to say that the InfoSoc Directive excludes online exhaustion for the works within its scope is at best dubitative.[91] So the proposition that in the *UsedSoft* decision there is to be found an implied *obiter dictum* barring the principle of exhaustion in connection with works other than computer programs should at least be closely scrutinized.

That view is borne out by the doubts raised in the opinion delivered by Advocate General Bot. Indeed, as the Advocate General argues, Recitals 28 and 29 of the InfoSoc Directive are neither clear nor unambiguous in excluding that the principle of exhaustion can apply to online transmission,[92] a view that runs contrary to a widely accepted interpretation of those two recitals that are commonly taken as evidence that the principle of exhaustion by contrast applies only to forms of distribution mediated by a tangible object.

Unfortunately, the CJEU does not specifically address on the merits the Commission's argument that EU law does not provide for exhaustion of the distribution right where services are concerned, and in particular the Court fails to clarify whether the act of enabling users to download a work from the Internet, in such a way as to grant them a right to use their copy in perpetuity, should properly be characterized as a provision of services or as a sale of goods. Indeed, the Court, with specific regard to computer programs, confines itself to finding that

[90] C.f. Article 1(2) of Directive 2001/29, which states that such directive "shall leave intact and shall in no way affect existing Community provisions relating to [...] the legal protection of computer programs." The lex specialis nature of the Software Directive has been reaffirmed by the Court of Justice in the Nintendo case: cf. CJEU, 23 January 2014, case C-355/12, Nintendo, para. 23, commented by Minero (2014), pp. 335 ff.

[91] Cf. CJEU, 3 July 2012, *cit.*, para. 60, where the Court observes that "*even supposing* [emphasis mine] that Article 4(2) of Directive 2001/29 [...] indicated that, for the works covered by that directive, the exhaustion of the distribution right concerned only tangible objects that would not be capable of affecting the interpretation of Article 4(2) of Directive 2009/24."

[92] Cf. the AG's opinion in the *UsedSoft* case, para. 75 f., where it is observed that "a converse reading of the first sentence of Recital 28 in the preamble to that directive, which provides that '[c] opyright protection under this Directive includes the exclusive right to control distribution of the work incorporated in a tangible article,' implies that that right also includes other forms of distribution. Indeed, the second sentence of that recital, relating to exhaustion, does not limit exhaustion to one particular form of distribution.

Recital 29 in the preamble to Directive 2001/29 is not without ambiguity either. While it appears to draw a distinction between the sale of goods, to which the exhaustion rule would apply, and the provision of services, to which that rule would be inapplicable, the fact remains that online services, as defined by EU law, include the sale of goods online. Thus, for example, by the standard of the wording of that recital, the exhaustion rule should not apply to an online purchase of a CD-ROM in which the copy of the computer program is incorporated. To my mind, however, the distinction as to whether the sale takes place remotely or otherwise is irrelevant for the purposes of applying that rule."

> to limit the application [. . .] of the principle of the exhaustion of the distribution right under Article 4(2) of Directive 2009/24 solely to copies of computer programs that are sold on a material medium would allow the copyright holder to control the resale of copies downloaded from the Internet and to demand further remuneration on the occasion of each new sale, even though the first sale of the copy had already enabled the right holder to obtain an appropriate remuneration. Such a restriction of the resale of copies of computer programs downloaded from the internet would go beyond what is necessary to safeguard the specific subject-matter of the intellectual property concerned.

It is not clear whether that reasoning of the court can also be made to apply to works other than computer programs. Indeed, while the aforementioned nature of the Software Directive as a *lex specialis* would suggest a negative answer, it must also be mentioned, on the other hand, that the principle of proportionality set forth in Article 52(1) of the Charter of Fundamental Rights of the EU—a principle implicitly invoked by the CJEU—should apply in an analogous way to all works of authorship, from which it follows that those norms that restrict the resale of a user's legitimately purchased copies should be subjected to a test of validity based on the same interpretive criteria.

Somehow, though, the CJEU appears to have deliberately left open an interpretative window on the question whether the principle of online exhaustion can be extended to works and other materials protected under the InfoSoc Directive.[93] This window, however, has promptly been closed by the Regional Court of Bielefeld in a case decided in March 2013 concerning the online distribution of e-books and audiobooks.[94] Indeed, the German court, seizing precisely on the *lex specialis* nature of the Software Directive, found that the principles set out by the CJEU in the *UsedSoft* case cannot be applied to digital contents governed under the InfoSoc Directive.

The Court of Bielefeld stated, in this regard, that a contract under which a copyright holder grants users the right to use an intangible copy of a work for personal use—including by downloading a copy from the Internet—and in which a clause is contained that expressly prohibits resale of the copy or its transfer to third parties may not be interpreted as granting users a right comparable to that granted to owners of a material good.[95] More than that, the German court, ignoring the concerns expressed in this regard by the Advocate General and the CJEU in the *UsedSoft* case, is unambiguous in holding that the act by which a copyright holder grants users a perpetual right to use copies downloaded from the Internet amounts to an act of making the work available to the public pursuant to Article 3 of the

[93] Cf., in the same vein, Hilty et al. (2013), p. 284, observing that "a broader applicability of the ECJ decision does not seem to be a priori precluded."

[94] Landgericht Bielefeld, 5 March 2013, case No. 4 O 191/11. For a brief comment, see Linklater (2013), pp. 685 f. The decision of the Regional Court of Bielefeld has been upheld by the Court of Appeal of Hamm, 15 May 2014, case No. 22 U 60/13, in GRUR, 2014, pp. 853 ff.

[95] But see Fairfield (2007), p. 411, who is trenchant in stating that "[a]n owner of virtual property owns the same rights that the owner of a book does."

InfoSoc Directive and so that, even in light of Recitals 28 and 29 of the same directive, the principle of exhaustion does not apply.[96] Even while recognizing that the principle of exhaustion has been deemed by some German legal scholars to be applicable to online distribution,[97] the Court of Bielefeld clearly gives greater weight in this case to a textual interpretation of legislative sources,[98] arguing that *ubi lex voluit dixit*: if the legislator had actually wanted to generally extend the principle of exhaustion to acts of online distribution, such an extension would have been expressly stated in the InfoSoc Directive. And since no such express recognition can be found in that directive, any analogical interpretation of the principle of exhaustion is thereby ruled out.[99]

The Court of Bielefeld further specifies that, even if we recognized a general principle of online exhaustion, its applicability would in any event be paralyzed by the impossibility of transferring files to third parties without violating the exclusive right of reproduction. This problem had been solved by the CJEU in its finding that a secondary purchaser of a copy of a computer program is a "lawful acquirer" of that copy within the meaning of Article 5(1) of the Software Directive of 2009 and so that the secondary purchaser is allowed to reproduce the work without the right holder's consent where the act of reproduction is necessary for the use of the computer program in accordance with its intended purpose. No comparable rule, however, can be found in the InfoSoc Directive,[100] with the consequence that the principle of online exhaustion would in any event be precluded on a practical level even if it were to be recognized on a theoretical one.

On a deeper analysis, the discrepancy between the CJEU and the Court of Bielefeld can be explained by pointing not only to the different laws applicable in the two cases and the different outcomes such application brings about but also to the different approaches the two courts took to the principle of exhaustion. While the CJEU, in line with its well-established case law, lays emphasis on the importance of this principle as a tool with which to protect the general interest in avoiding the partitioning of the market,[101] the German court takes a more individualistic

[96] Cf. Landgericht Bielefeld, 5 March 2013, *cit.*, 20.

[97] Cf. Landgericht Bielefeld, 5 March 2013, *cit.*, 19, where the judges explicitly refer to Hoeren and Försterling (2012), pp. 642 ff.; and Hartmann (2012), pp. 980 ff.

[98] The same approach has been adopted by the U.S. District Court for the Southern District of New York in the *ReDigi* case [*Capitol Records, LLC v. ReDigi Inc.*, 934 F. Supp. 2D 640 (S.D.N.Y. 2013)], concerning the resale of "used" digital music files originally purchased from the iTunes store, where the judge, in rejecting the expansion of the first sale doctrine to cover digital files, has observed that "[w]hile technological change may have rendered Section 109 (a) unsatisfactory [. . .], it has not rendered it ambiguous" and "amendment of the Copyright Act in line with ReDigi's proposal is a legislative prerogative that courts are unauthorized and ill suited to attempt." On the *ReDigi* case, see Capobianco (2013), pp. 391 ff. For a comparison between the *UsedSoft* and the *ReDigi* rulings, see Moon (2013), pp. 193 ff.

[99] Cf. Landgericht Bielefeld, 5 March 2013, *cit.*, 17.

[100] But see § 5.3 below.

[101] Cf. par. 62 of the *Usedsoft* decision.

perspective through an analysis narrowly focused on the conflicting interests of the copyright holder and the purchaser of a digital copy of the work,[102] arguing (quite apodictically) that while the right holder's economic interest can only be satisfied by preventing the work from finding its way in the highly elusive secondary digital markets, the purchaser's interest is satisfied merely by enabling him to use a digital good at a lower price than the one at which the corresponding material good is available. This appears to be, however, a rather superficial application of the proportionality test set forth in Article 52(1) CFR. Indeed, in order to properly assess whether the principles of necessity and proportionality "in the narrow sense"[103] are a valid and sufficient basis on which to restrict purchasers to the right to transfer their copies, the German court should have followed the CJEU[104] in taking due account that different technological solutions can, and in the future increasingly will,[105] guarantee for right holders that if a legitimate purchaser should redistribute a digital copy, the originally purchased copy will be automatically deleted, thus reinstating a proper balance between the different interests at stake.

5 A Three-Step Argument for Recognizing the Online Exhaustion Principle

As was noted earlier, the claim that the InfoSoc Directive rules out the possibility of recognizing a general principle of online exhaustion is based on a reading of Articles 3 and 4 of the same directive, especially in light of Recitals 28 and 29. In short, and summing up the argument so far made:

(*i*) online distribution always entails the supply of a service (not the sale of a good), an activity in regard to which Recital 29 states that the question of exhaustion simply "does not arise"; and

(*ii*) online distribution must always be construed, not as an act of distribution but as one of making the work available to the public under Article 3 of the directive, and under paragraph 2 of the same article, the latter activity expressly excludes exhaustion of the right.

---

[102] Cf. Landgericht Bielefeld, 5 March 2013, *cit.*, 12.

[103] On the different subprinciples that constitute the proportionality principle, namely legitimate ends, suitability, necessity, and proportionality in the narrow sense, see Klatt and Meiste (2012), p. 8.

[104] Cf. CJEU, 3 July 2012, *cit.*, para. 79.

[105] In this respect, it is worth noting that the corporations that own and manage the two largest digital marketplace in the world (i.e., Amazon and iTunes) have already filed patent application for technologies allowing the forwarding and deletion of digital contents: see the US Patent Application No. 20130060616 filed by Apple, Inc., for an invention titled "Managing access to digital content items" and the US Patent No. 8364595 assigned to Amazon Technologies, Inc., for an invention titled "Secondary market for digital objects." On the above-mentioned patents, see Streitfield (2013).

On top of these two critical questions, as we have seen, there comes another that has been worked out in two contrary ways by the CJEU and the Regional Court of Bielefeld, namely:

(*iii*) online distribution in any event entails the need to reproduce the work through a series of acts that never exhaust the copyright holder's right.

Each of the three critical issues just listed will now be taken up in turn in an attempt to show how a nonformalist and nontextualist approach to the InfoSoc Directive makes it possible to overcome at least some of the obstacles that come in the way of our recognizing a general principle of online exhaustion.

5.1 First Step: Distinguishing Between Services "as Services" and Services "as Goods"

The principle under Recital 29 of the InfoSoc Directive—stating that the question of exhaustion does not arise in connection with services, and online services in particular—is fully established in EU law, at least since the landmark decision that the CJEU rendered in the *Coditel I* case.[106] It is therefore crucial to understand whether online distribution of a copyrighted work should be characterized as the supply of a service or as the sale of a good[107]—a question that the CJEU did not clarify in the *UsedSoft* case.[108]

As Advocate General Bot has rightly observed,[109] Recital 29 is far from clear in that regard, since it offers no general definition of the two concepts, choosing to instead illustrate their meaning by example, namely by characterizing as "services by nature" the rental and lending of original and copies of a work and as an "item of goods" a CD-ROM, "where the intellectual property is incorporated in a material medium."[110] It would thus appear that under EU law, the goods/services dichotomy corresponds to the tangible/intangible objects dichotomy already pointed out in the *Coditel I* case. But that such correspondence does not accurately describe the application of the principle of exhaustion can be appreciated in Recital 29 itself, considering that under this recital, the principle does not cover also *material* copies

[106] Cf. CJEC, 18 March 1980, *cit.*

[107] On the gradual overlap between these two categories and the resulting problem of their characterization, see Santini (1979), pp. 415 ff.

[108] It is worth recalling, in a comparative perspective, that unlike European Union, "application of the first sale doctrine to digital works in the United States does not focus on the distinction between goods and services" and "[s]ometimes the different analytical framework can lead to different results," as it happens, for example, in the case of a lawful copy of an online digital transmission burned onto a CD, which would fall under the first sale doctrine in the U.S. (but not in the EU): see, in this regard, Peters (2010), p. 331.

[109] Cf. para. 76 of the AG's opinion in the *UsedSoft* case.

[110] Cf. also Schovsbo (2012), p. 180, observing that the sharp distinction between online and off-line transactions can arguably be criticized for placing too much weight on formalities.

of a work made by a user of a service with the consent of the right holder.[111] Furthermore, in stating that the question of exhaustion does not arise in connection with "online services," Recital 29 fails to provide for that term a definition suitable for this specific context, considering as well that the definition of "online services" one should want to look to here, in view of the *ratione materiae*—the definition offered in Recital 18 of Directive 2000/31/EC[112]—includes the activity of "selling goods on-line" within the scope of "services" and so is much too broad to be usefully brought to bear on the problem of exhaustion.[113]

The arguments just outlined bring out the substantial fallacy where the criterion for applying the principle of exhaustion is sought by uncritically superimposing the dichotomy between tangible and intangible objects on top of the dichotomy between good and services. To this end, as has been rightly underscored in the legal literature,[114] we have to attempt a "coherent theory of when to treat online offerings of copyrighted works as "services" and when to still treat them as "goods," in spite of their intangible and immaterial nature."

There is no space here to enter into such a theory in any depth, but one thing can definitely be pointed out: it cannot but proceed from an acknowledgment of the economic rationale according to which the principle of exhaustion will eventually be excluded where the supply of services is concerned. As the Court of Justice has commented in the *Coditel I* case, the economic assumption at the basis of the principle is that the right holder "receives his remuneration upon the sale of the protected product" (so-called criterion of marketing). What calls for scrutiny is the

[111] Note, too, that the U.S. Copyright Office, *op. loc. cit.*, goes in the opposite direction in its finding that "a lawfully made tangible copy of a digitally downloaded work, such as a work downloaded to a floppy disk, Zip™ disk, or CD-RW, is clearly subject to section 109," which regulates the application of the first-sale doctrine. However, when it comes to services in the strict sense—what in this contribution I am calling "services as services"—it is certainly correct that the principle of exhaustion does not apply. That is because we lack here the essential element of the principle of exhaustion, namely, the right holder's intention to bring a copy of the work to market: without that intention, it is pointless to determine whether or not a copy made with the right holder's consent is material. Consider, for example, digital rental: although the digital renter has the copyright owner's consent to make a copy of the work and that copy is not transitory, there seems to be no question that the user (the digital renter) may not resell that copy.

[112] Directive 2000/31/EC of the European Parliament and of the Council of 8 June 2000 on certain legal aspects of information society services, in particular electronic commerce, in the Internal Market, in *OJ*, No. L 178, 17 July 2000, 1 ff.

[113] Indeed, even though under the E-Commerce Directive the online sale of goods (and so of tangible items) embodying original works of authorship is treated as a supply of services, it clearly amounts to an act of distribution under Article 4 of the InfoSoc Directive, with the consequence that those items become subject to the principle of exhaustion: in this sense, see also Wiebe (2009), p. 115. If online services were understood as defined by Recital 18 of the E-Commerce Directive, we would therefore have to even exclude that the principle of exhaustion applies to online sales of tangible copies of a work, thus implicitly introducing a distinction between "real" and "virtual" transactions, a distinction that has no basis in any single provision of the InfoSoc Directive or in the directive as a whole.

[114] Dreier (2013), p. 139.

correctness of the Court's conclusion that "if there is no material medium the criterion of marketing cannot be used to determine the extent of the exclusivity of the right."[115]

It is worth noting that in the *Coditel I* decision, exhaustion is expressly excluded for "performing rights," or what the Court describes as "copyrights where there is no material medium." What does not seem entirely convincing in the Court's reconstruction is exactly the equivalence between "performing rights" and "copyrights where there is no material medium," as well as the consequent implicit claim that there can be no sale of a protected product absent a material medium. Indeed, the validity of the Court's conclusion appears to be conditional on the contingent fact that, at the time of the *Coditel I* judgment, the only commercially viable solution for selling a copy of a work was by fixing that copy in a material medium. But, as is known, the scenario has radically changed with the development of the Internet as a medium for distributing digital copies. It would seem, therefore, that the concept of "performing rights"—where the right holder's remuneration is indeed not based on an act of sale in such a way as to make it impossible to apply the "criterion of marketing"—should properly be understood under the heading of "non-copy related rights"[116] rather than under that of rights "where there is no material medium," considering that a work no longer needs to be fixed in a material medium since the beginning in order for it to be exploited by exercising copy-related rights, and likewise, as the *UsedSoft* case clearly shows, even a copy not fixed in a material medium can be the object of a sale.[117]

Therefore, taking the CJEU's reasoning to a higher level of abstraction, and adjusting to the Internet era the nonexhaustion principle stated in *Coditel I*, it would be more accurate to conclude that the principle of exhaustion does not apply where no copy is sold,[118] since it is only in that circumstance that "the criterion of marketing cannot be used to determine the extent of the exclusivity of the right."

---

[115] Cf. CJEC, 18 March 1980, *cit.*, 894.

[116] The distinction between "copy-related rights" and "non-copy-related rights" is clearly made in WIPO (2003), p. 228, fn. 226, where it is pointed out that "[c]opy-related rights (such as the right of distribution, the right of rental or the right of public lending (where recognized)) cover acts by means of which copies are made available to the public; typically for 'deferred' use, since the act of making available and the perception (studying, watching, listening to) of the signs, images and sounds in which a work is expressed or a sound recording (that is, the actual 'use') by the members of the public differ in time. Noncopy-related rights(such as the right of public performance, the right of broadcasting, the right of communication to the public by wire), on the other hand, cover acts through which works or objects of related rights are made available for direct – that is not 'deferred' – use (perceiving, studying, watching, listening to) by the members of the public."

[117] See, in this sense, also Wiebe (2009).

[118] Not surprisingly, drawing a distinction between different forms of exploitation, the Court of Justice has pointed out in the *Warner Brothers* decision that copyright works "may be the subject of commercial exploitation, whether by the way of public performance or of the reproduction and marketing of the recordings made by them." The Court therefore seems to suggest a distinction that is based not on a dichotomy between material and immaterial media but on a dichotomy between copy-related and noncopy-related rights.

In fact, in all cases where a copy is sold by the right holder or with his consent, he receives a remuneration consistent with the specific subject matter of intellectual property protection,[119] regardless of whether the copy is fixed in a material medium,[120] and thus the economic criterion for applying the exhaustion rule (i.e., the "criterion of marketing") is fully satisfied.[121]

So the dichotomy we should match to the one between goods and services in applying the principle of exhaustion is not that between tangible and intangible objects, as Recital 29 of the InfoSoc Directive would suggest, but rather that between selling a work and making it available (through an act other than a sale) or, on a more general level, that between forms of exploitation that entail a transfer of ownership of a copy of the work and forms that do not.[122] Indeed, as was just observed, the copyright holder's legally protected interest in obtaining an appropriate remuneration for the use of a copy is satisfied the moment that copy is sold, and so there is no reasonable basis on which the he should be able to further profit from subsequent transfers of ownership—provided, of course, that these subsequent transfers do not increase "the actual or potential number of persons who enjoy"[123] the work.

The interpretive problem thus shifts to a different issue. The problem will be how to determine that there has actually been a transfer of ownership of a copy from the right holder to a user and, in particular, that a sale has taken place. Here it seems to me that there is no compelling reason why the definition of a sale offered in *UsedSoft* ought to apply exclusively to software and cannot be generalized to other copyright-protected works.[124] Now, it bears recalling here the CJEU's view that the applicability of the principle of exhaustion must be considered on a broad interpretation of the term *sale*

---

[119] See § 2 above.

[120] This can easily be appreciated by considering that when a digital copy of a book is sold to a user, that user is asked to make just one payment in exchange for the download, regardless of how many times that copy will be used, but when the same copy is digitally rented to that user, the service requires a new payment with each new use of that copy (for a fraction of the price, that would be charged for purchasing a copy). For a clear example of such economic mechanism, see the functioning and the pricing strategy of the Amazon's Kindle Textbook Rental Service, available at http://www.amazon.com/gp/feature.html?docId=1000702481.

[121] Recital 28 of the InfoSoc Directive would seem to confirm such approach when, after pointing out that "copyright protection [...] includes the exclusive right to control distribution of the work incorporated in a tangible article," it states in more general terms that the first sale of the original of a work or copies thereof—and not the first sale of a tangible copy—by the right holder or with his consent exhausts the right to control resale of that object in the Community.

[122] The need to overtake unnecessary differences in the legal treatment of tangible and intangible versions of essentially the same good is also clear in the project of reform of the VAT system in the EU, in the context of which has been pointed out that "equal treatment of physical and digital version of like products should be priority number one": cf. European Parliament, *op. cit.*, 9.

[123] See CJEU, 4 October 2011, *cit.*, para 109.

[124] Indeed, although the CJEU defines a sale by express reference to software, for that is the object of the dispute before the Court, it is a *different* definition that the Court relies on in arguing the Software Directive to be a *lex specialis* relative to the InfoSoc Directive: the Court proceeds not from the definition of *sale* but from that of *distribution* contained in those same directives.

> as encompassing all forms of product marketing characterized by the grant of a right to use a copy of a [work], for an unlimited period, in return for payment of a fee designed to enable the copyright holder to obtain a remuneration corresponding to the economic value of the copy of the work of which he is the proprietor.

In this way, the CJEU points out that, regardless of the legal terms the parties use in a contract,[125] the contract will be deemed a sale (not a license) if through it *i*) the right holder receives a remuneration corresponding to the economic value of the copy of the work and (*ii*) the user is granted a right to freely use the copy for an unlimited (or, I would add, for a substantially unlimited)[126] time.[127]

So, from the standpoint of the way the contract frames the rights acquired by the parties, what distinguishes the sale of a good from the supply of a service is the user's ability under the contract to enjoy a copy of the work without time limits and without the right holder's further intervention or, otherwise stated, without encroaching on the user's autonomy as to when and how he may use the copy.[128]

---

[125] Cf. Sarti (1996), p. 404, rightly pointing out that the question whether exclusive rights can be extended and whether the principle of exhaustion applies does not turn on the *nomen iuris* given to the activities the right holder is interested in prohibiting but rather depends on the effects these activities have on the availability of the work. In the same vein, see also Musso (2008), pp. 370 f. An example will make this clearer: according to the Amazon's Kindle Store Terms of Use (available at https://www.amazon.com/gp/help/customer/display.html/ref=hp_left_v4_sib?ie=UTF8&nodeId=201014950), "Kindle Content," namely any digital content obtained through the Kindle Store, such as books, newspapers, magazines, and journals, "is licensed, not sold"; however, users have to click on an icon labeled "buy now" in order to download a copy of the work and, upon payment of a fixed price, obtain a nonexclusive right to view, use, and display the Kindle Content in an unlimited number of times. In the light of the above, it could be seriously questioned whether the agreement between Amazon and the user is a license or a sale. The courts, especially in the United States, have tended to lay greater emphasis on the intention of the parties even in deciding how the transaction between them is to be defined: see *MAI Sys. Corp. v. Peak Computer, Inc.*, 991 F.2d 511 (9th Cir. 1993) and *Triad Sys. Corp. v. Se. Express Co.*, 64 F.3d 1330 (9th Cir. 1995) and the more recent *Vernor v. Autodesk, Inc.*, 555 F. Supp. 2d 1164 (W.D. Wash. 2008), commented by Kamenetz (2011), pp. 155 ff. In this last case, the district court developed a three-step test under which "a software user is a licensee rather than an owner of a copy where the copyright owner (1) specifies that the user is granted a license; (2) significantly restricts the user's ability to transfer the software; and (3) imposes notable use restrictions." The test was subsequently applied in *MDY Indus., LLC v. Blizzard Entertainment, Inc.*, 629 F.3d 928 (9th Cir. 2010), where it yielded the same result.

[126] One should consider as "substantially unlimited," for example, *i*) a time exceeding the copyright term or (*ii*) a time that, having regard to the nature of the work and to its degree of technical (or commercial) obsolescence, is effectively equivalent, under an economic perspective, to an unlimited time (e.g., 30 years for a computer program).

[127] In the same sense, see also Court of Milan, 3 June 2002, in *AIDA*, 2002, 838 ff. For a clear example of the "perpetual possession approach" in the context of the U.S. legal system, see Carver (2010), pp. 1920 ff.

[128] Cf. Wiebe (2009), who rightly pointed out that transfer of ownership implies "rendering control by the seller and taking control by the acquirer," so that "not the transport medium is important but the end result which is the permanent control of the user over a copy."

This view finds support as well in the opinion that Advocate General Kokott delivered in the *FAPL* case, where the difference is rightly pointed out between services that "differ from goods in that they cannot be re-used per se" and services that "do not differ significantly from goods" insofar as they can be "downloaded from the Internet [and] can easily be passed on in electronic form." Whereas services in the first class (i.e., services properly enjoyed "as services") "cannot be passed on as such," such that "there is actually no scope for an "exhaustion" of the right to the service," services in the second class (i.e., those enjoyed "as goods") should be treated as tangible goods. In other words, one can hardly disagree here with the Advocate General's view that, under the basic principles on the free movement of goods enshrined in the EU Treaty, it would be arbitrary to apply to "services as goods" a set of rules different from those that govern tangible goods,[129] since that would wind up restricting the freedoms guaranteed by the principle itself to a degree not justified by the need to protect the specific subject matter of intellectual property rights.[130]

The approach suggested here—on which the goods/services dichotomy is best rendered through the dichotomy between forms of according as they do or do not entail a transfer of ownership of a copy of the work, regardless of whether that copy is tangible or intangible—brings with it, too, an additional benefit, in that on this basis the principle of exhaustion, as framed in the Software, Database, and InfoSoc Directives, can be reduced to unity by doing away with what appears to be an untenable distinction between different types of copyright works.[131] And, after all, when the CJEU in the *Donner* decision found that "the protection of the right of distribution cannot [. . .] be deemed to give rise to a disproportionate or artificial partitioning of the markets"[132] unless necessary to protect the specific subject matter of copyright, it also pointed out that this holds not only for the distribution of tangible goods but also for the delivery of services enjoyed "as goods," as is the case with "the sale of computer software, musical works, e-books or films via the

[129] Cf. para. 185 of the AG's opinion in the *FAPL* case.

[130] It is worth quoting *in extenso* the conclusion reached by the AG Bot in his opinion delivered in the *UsedSoft* case, para. 83: "the rightholder has received appropriate remuneration where he has been paid in return for the grant of a right to use a copy of a computer program. Allowing him to control the resale of that copy and, in that event, to demand further remuneration, on the pretext that the copy was fixed on a data carrier by the customer after having been downloaded from the internet, instead of being incorporated by the rightholder in a medium which was put on sale, would have the effect not of protecting the specific subject-matter of the copyright but of extending the monopoly on the exploitation of that right."

[131] This can be appreciated by considering as well that the principle of exhaustion can do a much better job at balancing interests in goods other than software products, which are much more liable to become technologically obsolete, and so where the need to guarantee that they will be widely available on the market over the long-to-medium term is less crucial than is the case with, say, audiovisual or literary works.

[132] Cf. CJEU, 21 June 2012, case C-5/11, *Donner*, para. 35, commented by Lauterbach (2013), pp. 13 ff.

Internet," since the "restrictions on the fundamental freedoms must, as a rule, be justified by reference to the same principles."[133]

5.2 *Second Step: Challenging the Conventional Wisdom on the Nonexhaustion Rule Set Forth in Article 3 (3) of the InfoSoc Directive*

A second critical point in regard to the question of recognizing a general principle of online exhaustion lies in the circumstance previously considered that, after the adoption of the WIPO Copyright Treaty,[134] the online distribution of intangible copies of a work is mostly deemed to be an act of making the work available to the public and so is subject to the nonexhaustion rule set forth in Article (3)3 of the InfoSoc Directive. I will not be trying to poke holes in this legal construction.[135] Nevertheless, I will be trying to show that the Court of Justice, despite the unambiguous rendering of Article 3(3) of the InfoSoc Directive, has at least implicitly recognized as well that the right of making a work available to the public is subject to a limited form of exhaustion of the right itself.[136]

Indeed, it is now an established principle of Community case law that the right of communication (including the right of making works available) to the public can be deemed to have been infringed only on condition that an unauthorized third party has made the work available to a "new" public, that is, to a range of potential users broader than the group to which the original act of communication of the work was directed,[137] assuming as well that the second act of communication to the public was carried out using the same techniques as the first.[138]

---

[133] Cf. para. 175 and 183 of the AG's opinion in the *FAPL* case. See also Ricolfi (2004), p. 384.

[134] See § 3 above.

[135] But I do have many reservations in that regard if, in light of the foregoing remarks, we grant that the exclusive distribution right is best construed as a right of exploitation based on transferring ownership of a permanent copy of the work. See also, in this sense, CJEU, 3 July 2012, *cit.*, para. 52, where the Court observes that "the existence of a transfer of ownership changes an 'act of communication to the public' provided for in Article 3 of [the InfoSoc Directive] into an act of distribution referred to in Article 4 of the directive [. . .]."

[136] In this vein, see also BGH, 7 November 1980, case I ZR 24/79, *Kabelfernsehen in Abschattungsgebieten*, in *GRUR*, 1980, pp. 413 ff., concerning the exhaustion of cable rights.

[137] Cf. CJEU, 7 December 2006, case C-306/05, *SGAE*, in *ECR*, 2006, p. I-11543 ff., para. 40, commented by Bateman (2007), pp. 22 ff.

[138] Cf. CJEU, 7 March 2013, case C-607/11, *ITV Broadcasting and Others*, para. 26 and 39, in *OJ*, No. C 123, 27 April 2013, 6, commented by Baggs and Hansson (2013), pp. 363 ff.

This principle—which the CJEU developed in *EGEDA*[139] and *SGAE*[140] by interpreting Article 11*bis*(1)(ii) of the Berne Convention in light of the explanatory guide published by the WIPO in 1978[141]—is based on the premise that "the decisive factor for determining whether a communication is "to the public" lies in the extent of the circle of potential recipients of the communication and [emphasis mine, on] *its economic significance for the author*."[142] Indeed, when a copyright holder carries out or authorizes the first communication to a given public, any further acts of communication directed at the same public (and using the same techniques) do not amount to an independent economic exploitation of the work[143] and so do not require the right holder's authorization.

That principle has just recently been upheld by the CJEU in the *Svensson* case,[144] involving an action against third parties who were linking to protected contents published online without the right holder's authorization. Although the Court in this case held that providing clickable links to protected works must be characterized as an act of communication to the public within the meaning of Article 3(1) of the InfoSoc Directive,[145] it also acknowledged that where such an act concerns "the same works as those covered by the initial communication and [is] made [...] by the same technical means [it] does not lead to the works in question being communicated to a new public,"[146] so long as the users enabled to access the works through the links provided by the unauthorized third party could access those works independently[147] by logging directly onto the website on which the same content had initially been communicated. Indeed, in this case, such users

> must be deemed to be potential recipients of the initial communication and, therefore, as being part of the public taken into account by the copyright holders when they authorised the initial communication. Therefore, since there is no new public, the authorisation of the copyright holders is not required for a communication to the public such as that in the main proceedings.

Now, it seems to me that, as much as Article 3(3) of the InfoSoc Directive may appear unambiguous, the CJEU doctrine of the "new public" requirement makes it possible to advance the theory that a limited principle of exhaustion can also be

---

[139] Cf. ECJ, 3 February 2000, case C-293/98, *EGEDA*, in *ECR*, 2000, I-651 ff., commented by Edelman (2001), pp. 1094 ff.

[140] Cf. CJEU, 7 December 2006, *cit.*, para. 40 f.

[141] Cf. WIPO (1978), pp. 66 ff.

[142] See the opinion of Advocate General Sharpston delivered on 13 July 2006 in the case C-306/05, *SGAE*, para. 54.

[143] See the opinion of Advocate General La Pergola delivered on 9 September 1999 in the case C-293/98, *EGEDA*, para. 24.

[144] Cf. CJEU, 13 February 2014, case C-466/12, *Svensson and Others*. For some early thoughts on this case, see Targosz (2014).

[145] Cf. para. 20 of the *Svensson* decision.

[146] Cf. paras. 24-25 of the *Svensson* decision.

[147] Cf. para. 27 of the *Svensson* decision.

applied to the right to communicate a work to the public. That is because the two rules appear to rest on the same underlying economic rationale. Indeed, as was noted earlier, the background economic assumption forming the basis of the principle of exhaustion is that a right holder who sells a copy of a work receives a remuneration consistent with the specific subject matter of intellectual property protection. Therefore, enabling a right holder to control the further circulation of that copy would go beyond the scope of the exclusive rights (and in particular beyond the scope of the right to distribute the work). Similarly, when a right holder communicates or authorizes a third party to communicate a work to a quantitatively and qualitatively determined (or determinable) public, then he receives (or has the chance to receive) a remuneration that can be deemed "appropriate" under the normative standard the CJEU introduced in its *FAPL* decision. Therefore, allowing a right holder to control further acts of communication to the same potential recipients would go beyond the scope of the exclusive rights (and, in particular, beyond the scope of the right to communicate the work or make it available to the public).

Ultimately, if we compare the economic rationale behind the exhaustion principle with that behind the "new public" requirement,[148] we can extract a further general principle under which the right holder's exclusive rights are deemed to have been exhausted when (and to the extent that) the acts the right holder carried out in exploiting the work have already yielded a reasonable remuneration, that is, one proportionate to the actual or potential number of persons who enjoy the work.

If the solution just offered should prove acceptable, we will have to conclude that when a right holder transfers the right to use a digital copy to a user in return for a remuneration corresponding to the economic value of the copy, the act by which said transfer is made (as by enabling the user to download the copy from the right holder's own website) exhausts the right to control any further distribution of that copy, so long as the transfer is made for an unlimited time—and the rule should hold independently of whether the initial act of exploitation is deemed an act of distribution or one of communicating the work to the public.[149]

---

[148] In reality, the "new public" requirement is understood by the CJEU as the element absent which an act can no longer be qualified as one of communication to the public (cf. para. 24 of the *Svensson* decision). But it seems to me, in light of the way the right of communication to the public is defined, that an act of communication need not be directed at a new public in order to count as an act of communication, even though it is no longer afforded any exclusivity, for the relative right has been exhausted.

[149] Indeed, even on this latter construction, consider someone who resells a digital copy he has purchased (thereafter deleting the resold copy so as not to multiply the number of persons who can enjoy the work): if the resale is carried out using the same technical means (i.e., the Internet), then this person can be said to have communicated the work to the public in such a way as not to interfere with the copyright holder's exclusive rights, for it is not to a "new public" that the work has been communicated but to the same public as that of the original communication. The purchaser's resale will be all the more legitimate if carried out without making the digital copy available to the public, as by privately negotiating the terms of the transaction and sending the

5.3 *Third Step: Distinguishing Acts of Reproduction According to Their Intended Purpose*

As has been observed very early on in thinking about this issue,[150] the third hurdle on the way to the recognition of a general principle of online exhaustion lies in the fact that redistribution of copyrighted works through online networks inevitably entails the need to make copies (even if only temporary ones) in such a way as to interfere with the right holder's exclusive right of reproduction.

In this regard, we should start by observing that if users who have legitimately purchased a copy of a work are recognized—as I stated earlier—as being legally entitled to redistribute that copy online, then it appears unduly formalistic to distinguish and isolate the act of reproduction through which such redistribution takes place from the act (or complex of acts) of redistribution itself—considering, too, that this act of reproduction comes about as a necessity dictated by the specific technical workings of online networks.[151] This conclusion, it seems to me, also finds support in the *Donner* case, where the CJEU took a holistic approach to the notion of distribution under Article 4(1) of the InfoSoc Directive, arguing that distribution is "characterised by a series of acts going, at the very least, from the conclusion of a contract of sale to the performance thereof by delivery to a member of the public."[152] Therefore, although in this context there is no doubt that the online redistribution of a work technically entails its reproduction,[153] this reproduction does not appear to amount to an independent act of exploitation of the work subject to the right holder's consent but is merely a technical step necessitated by an act of online distribution, which ought to be recognized as including such reproduction within its scope.[154]

On the other hand, like all the other exclusive rights granted to a right holder, the right of reproduction is intended to enable this person to receive a remuneration for each use of the protected works that can be deemed reasonable in view of the actual or potential number of persons who enjoy the work. Therefore, insofar as a copy of the work has been sold by the right holder or with his consent, the proper aim of the exclusive right of reproduction is to prevent the purchaser from multiplying the copies out in the market in such a way as to increase the number of users: the aim is

---

copy by email, for in this case we do not have the indeterminate plurality of individuals by which a public is defined, and accordingly the act could not be deemed one of communication to the public.

[150] See Lehman and Brown (1995), pp. 92 ff.

[151] This issue has been specifically addressed, among others, by Sieman (2006–2007), pp. 885 ff., who has proposed to extend the scope of the implied license doctrine to bridge the gaps between copyright law and current practices on the Internet.

[152] Cf. para. 26 of the *Donner* decision.

[153] Which is true independently of whether the online redistribution is legally characterized as an act of distribution or one of communication to the public.

[154] Cf. Torremans (2014), p. 10, observing that the reproduction made in the context of digital redistribution is "nothing but ancillary."

not to make it so that a lawful acquirer is prevented from using the work according to its purpose just because such use means that the work for technical reasons will necessarily be reproduced.[155] Even though the InfoSoc Directive contains no specific provision to that effect, it seems to me that a general principle so conceived can be extracted from Article 5.1 and the related Recital 13 of the Software Directive, as well as from Article 6.1 and the related Recital 34 of the Database Directive.[156] Then, too, the question has been addressed, albeit only indirectly, by the CJEU in the *Dior/Evora* case, upholding the view that a copyright holder may not prevent a reseller from using a protected good for the purpose of the further commercialization of such good,[157] nor can copyright holders attempt to do so by using their exclusive right of reproduction. The Court, in other words, seems to have upheld the principle under which copyright holders may not invoke their exclusive rights for the purpose of preventing legitimate purchasers of a protected good from reselling that good and thus may not prevent purchasers from reproducing the work or making any other use of it as long as that use is only functional to the purpose of reselling the good. Indeed, a broader interpretation of the right holder's monopolistic power would act as an obstacle to the free movement of goods (in whose definition, it was being argued earlier, we also ought to include services enjoyed "as goods")—and that would violate the principles enshrined in the EU Treaty.

Furthermore, the legitimacy of the acts through which a work is reproduced by virtue of its being redistributed online can be probably argued not only on the basis of the systematic considerations previously made but also on a more analytical basis, by bringing those acts under the exception to the reproduction right set forth in Article 5(2)(b) of the InfoSoc Directive.

Indeed, consider that in the civil law tradition, a sale is a typical consensual contract.[158] The real effect of a sale (namely, transfer of ownership) comes into being the moment the parties agree to the terms of the contract. The sale then gives rise to obligatory effects as well, in that when the contract is executed, the purchaser comes under an obligation to pay the agreed upon price to the vendor, who in turn comes under an obligation to make the purchased goods available to the purchaser, who is already deemed to be its owner by virtue of the sale contract.[159]

According to the reconstruction offered in this contribution, the moment a copy of the work is sold by the right holder or with the right holder's consent, the

---

[155] In this sense, see also Musso (2008), p. 213.

[156] Which state that an act of reproduction performed by a lawful user of a software or a database shall not require authorization by the right holder where it is necessary "for the use of the computer program [...] in accordance with its intended purpose" or "for the purposes of access to the contents of the databases and normal use of the contents."

[157] Cf. CJEC, 4 November 1997, case C-337/95, *Parfums Christian Dior/Evora*, para 59.

[158] It is worth noting that the remarks that follow may be different in those legal systems where the consent of the parties to the sale has no immediate real effect, i.e., where the sale is not deemed to be a consensual contract.

[159] See Galgano (1993), p. 5.

exclusive right to control any further circulation of that copy is exhausted, regardless of whether the copy is tangible or intangible. This means that the first purchaser should be free to resell that copy to a subsequent purchaser while deleting his own copy, without having to obtain the right holder's consent.[160]

Now, the first purchaser's online redistribution of intangible copies can happen through a variety of technical means, and these may entail acts of reproduction by both the secondary purchaser and the reseller, as well as by third parties (service providers).

When the act of reproduction is carried out directly by the secondary purchaser—who by executing the sale contract becomes the lawful owner of the digital copy put out into the market by the right holder or with his consent—then it seems to me that this can reasonably be regarded as an act of reproduction "made by a natural person for private use," pursuant to Article 5(2)(b) of the InfoSoc Directive. Indeed, that this reproduction is "private" is clearly demonstrated by the fact that it is carried out for the sole purpose of enabling the secondary purchaser to enjoy his legitimately purchased copies, and so "for ends that are neither directly nor indirectly commercial," as required under the same Article 5(2)(b).

More complex is the question of whether it is legitimate for the reseller or for third parties not involved in the resale to engage in acts of reproduction. As some legal scholars have rightly observed,[161] however, in order for the exception on reproduction for private use to apply, the copier and the user need not be identical. Indeed, as the European Commission has stated in regard to the wording of Article 5(2)(b) of the InfoSoc Directive, "the word "by" would also allow a copy to be made for and on behalf of a natural person for private use."[162] This means that the question whether the private copy exception applies depends not on the person who physically carries out the reproduction but on whether the reproduction is intended to enable a private use by a natural person who can validly assert a right to use the copy. It follows that even acts of reproduction carried out by the reseller or by third parties can, in this sense, be legitimate under Article 5(2)(b), so long as these acts are exclusively aimed at enabling a secondary purchaser to enjoy a private use of

[160] Cf. Sarti (1996), p. 83, pointing out that a sale contract normally implies the exhaustion of the distribution right over the item sold even before that item is delivered to the purchaser.

[161] See Karapapa (2012), pp. 51 ff.; and Walter and von Lewinski (2010), p. 1033.

[162] See the European Commission, *Commission opinion pursuant to Article 251 (2) (c) of the EC Treaty, on the European Parliament's amendments to the Council's common position regarding the proposal for a Directive of the European Parliament and of the Council on the harmonisation of certain aspects of copyright and related rights in the information society amending the proposal of the Commission pursuant to Article 250 (2) of the EC Treaty*, COM(2001) 170 final, Brussels, 29 March 2001, available at http://eur-lex.europa.eu/LexUriServ/LexUriServ.do?uri=COM:2001:0170:FIN:EN:PDF p. 3. Tuttavia and Xalabarder (2009), p. 113, has critically observed that "this explanation seems to be more purposeful (so as not to further delay the adoption of the Directive) than really substantive." The same author has further pointed out that differences may be perceived at the level of domestic legislation where, depending on the country, copies may be done by the copier only (e.g., Italy) or also by someone else on his behalf (e.g., Germany).

the copy. It remains a matter for evaluation, however, whether these acts of reproduction carried out by such third parties—and especially by resellers—are to be considered as having commercial ends.[163] It must be noted in this regard that some Member States have expressly ruled out that copies made by third parties can fall under the private copy exception.[164] On the other hand, it has been observed that those Member States that have not specifically addressed the issue will potentially face difficulties in distinguishing between "agency type" situations and situations in which a legal entity provides services on the basis of remuneration, i.e. for direct or indirect commercial purposes. In this case, courts will be faced with the delicate task of distinguishing whether a charge paid for such service constitutes an indirect commercial aim and, if so, whether this is alleviated if the copy is made upon request by a beneficiary.[165]

Now, without entering into the features of the different national provisions, it seems to me that in the specific context of Article 5(2)(b) of the InfoSoc Directive, the problem of the commercial ends of the acts of reproduction needs to be solved on the basis of the premise that such negative requirement is intended to delimit the legitimate aims, not of the person who materially makes a private copy but of the person in whose interest such a copy is made (the person who will actually be *using* the copy).[166] In other words, the negative requirement that commercial ends should not be present ought to be read in combination with the positive requirement that the copy be made for personal use in such a way that the moment we rule out the former use as inapplicable, we have thereby outlined the boundaries of the latter use (thus, if a use is deemed commercial, however much indirectly, we won't be able to qualify it as "personal").

In conclusion, when a reseller (or a third party) reproduces a work for, and on behalf of, a secondary purchaser, that act of reproduction ought to be legally imputed to the latter and not to the reseller (or to the third party). From which it follows that it is by reference to the secondary purchaser that we have to evaluate whether the act of reproduction is compliant with Article 5(2)(b). And since the reproduction is carried out for the sole purpose of enabling secondary purchasers to use their legitimately purchased copies—i.e., reproduction is carried out for ends that are neither directly nor indirectly commercial—those copies can be deemed

[163] As has been pointed out by Dreier and Hugenholtz (2006), p. 375, Directive 29/2001 does not clarify what is meant by "ends that are neither directly nor indirectly commercial."

[164] For national implementations of the directive's provision, see Westkamp (2007b), pp. 19 f.

[165] Westkamp (2007b), p. 19.

[166] But see *contra* Walter and von Lewinski (2010), p. 1033, arguing that the only restriction for copies made by third parties for the private use of a different person is that the copier must not act for commercial purposes and, in particular, not ask for a payment that goes beyond the costs of material or production.

legitimate under Article 5(2)(b) of the InfoSoc Directive,[167] even if in technical terms they have been made by the reseller.

There is finally the problem of the need for the copy in the first purchasers' possession to be deleted once they transfer ownership. The problem here is twofold, having a legal aspect and a practical one, but neither aspect seems to pose too many difficulties. Indeed, on one hand, first purchasers who fail to delete the copy will be found to have done an illegitimate act as they have no longer a right to use the work;[168] on the other hand, as pointed out by the CJEU, it must also be noted that the way in which to verify such deletion is not essentially different from the way in which we would verify deletion of a work fixed in a material support:[169] in either case, whether the copy is digital or material, copyright holders can enforce deletion by recourse to technological protection measures.[170]

Conclusions

The principle of exhaustion has traditionally proved to be a fundamental tool in guaranteeing an appropriate balance between two conflicting sets of interests: those of copyright holders and those of the users of copyrighted works. But even more important, perhaps, is that the principle can be effectively used in combination with competition rules in guaranteeing the competitive structure of the European single market, thus helping to counteract a trend the European Commission has recently once more pointed out as a concern, namely, the trend toward the fragmentation of the European online market into "a patchwork of national online markets."[171]

In December 2013, the Commission launched a "Public Consultation on the Review of the EU Copyright Rules," asking whether the principle of exhaustion can be extended so as to cover the acts of transmission of digital

(continued)

---

[167] As evidence in support of the conclusion I argue in the text, consider a copy center: while the aims of its owners are undoubtedly commercial and their activity may give rise to specific obligations (such as the obligation to pay a fair compensation to the right holders), it does not necessarily follow that clients using the services offered by the copy center are thereby also engaging in a commercial activity—at least, in those Member States where copy centers are allowed to copy protected works, clients are still deemed to be pursuing noncommercial aims if the copies they are making are for private use only, in which case those copies will be deemed legitimate. On this issue, see Sarti (1996), p. 378.

[168] Cf. Perzanowski and Schultz (2010), p. 939, who further pointed out that "the burden to show exhaustion will fall squarely on the shoulders of the reseller, forcing him to prove that all remaining copies were deleted after resale."

[169] In this sense, see also Tjong Tjin Tai (2003), pp. 209 f.

[170] See, in this sense, CJEU, 3 July 2012, *cit.*, para. 79.

[171] Cf. European Commission, *Communication from the Commission to the European Parliament, the Council, the European Economic and Social Committee and the Committee of the Regions – A Single Market for Intellectual Property Rights. Boosting creativity and innovation to provide economic growth, high quality jobs and first class products and services in Europe*, *cit.*, 9.

copies "equivalent in its effect to distribution." The issues the Commission raised in this regard seem to be more practical and economic than legal,[172] and although these latter issues do come up, they do not seem intractable.[173]

It is true that, in recent years, the EU legislator has tended to marginalize the principle of exhaustion in online markets. But for one thing it has done so with some ambiguity, and for another scholars and courts seem to have the power to breathe new life into it, in such a way that an active role can be played in ensuring that the EU copyright regulatory framework stays fit for purpose in the digital environment. This is indeed a complex challenge, and it definitely cannot be overcome by clinging to a formalist and textualist approach to the interpretation of legal norms. This can be clearly appreciated in the *UsedSoft* case, where the CJEU demonstrated that, even taking the specificities of the case into account, substance can be put ahead of form in applying the principle of exhaustion to the digital environment, grounding its decision on consequentialist and economic arguments that seem to point the way for the near future.

References

Baggs S, Hansson S (2013) What's the catch? The CJEU judgement in ITV v TVCatchup. Eur Intellect Prop Rev 363 ff

Bateman A (2007) The use of televisions in hotel rooms. Eur Intellect Prop Rev 22 ff

Bently LA, Derclaye E, Dinwoodie GB, Dreier T, Dusollier S, Geiger C, Griffiths C, Hilty R, Hugenholtz PB, Janssens M-C, Kretschmer M, Metzger A, Peukert A, Ricolfi M, Senftleben M, Strowel A, Xalabarder R (2013) The reference to the CJEU in Case C-466/12 Svensson (February 15, 2013). Research Paper No. 6/2013, Faculty of Law, University of Cambridge. http://ssrn.com/abstract=2220326

Bercovitz A (2008) Copyright and related rights. In: Correa CM, Yusuf AA (eds) Intellectual property and international trade: the TRIPS agreement. Kluwer Law International, Alphen aan den Rijn

Bertani M (2000) Impresa culturale e diritti esclusivi. Giuffre, Milan

Bertani M (2011) Diritti d'autore e connessi. In: Ubertazzi LC (ed) La proprietà intellettuale, in Tratt. dir. priv. Un. eur. directed by G. Ajani, G.A. Benacchio, Turin

---

[172] Cf. European Commission, *Public Consultation on the review of the EU copyright rules*, *cit.*, 13, where the questions raised by the expansion of the exhaustion principle in the online environment are limited "to the practical application of such an approach (how to avoid re-sellers keeping and using a copy of a work after they have 're-sold' it – this is often referred to as the 'forward and delete' question) as well as to the economic implications of the creation of a second-hand market of copies of perfect quality that never deteriorate (in contrast to the second-hand market for physical goods)."

[173] And significant in this regard is what the UK government has underscored in its answer to the public consultation (available online at http://www.ipo.gov.uk/response-eucopyrightrules.pdf), noting that in view of the positive effect the exhaustion rule has on markets for physical items, there "seems to be no reason why this should not be the case for digital copies" too, so long as the previously mentioned "forward and delete" problem is adequately addressed.

Boschiero N (2007) Il principio di territorialità in materia di proprietà intellettuale: conflitti di leggi e giurisdizione. AIDA 34 ff
Capobianco G (2013) Rethinking ReDigi: how a characteristics-based test advances the "Digital First Sale" doctrine debate. Cardozo Law Rev 35:391 ff
Carver BW (2010) Why license agreements do not control copy ownership: first sales and essential copies. Berkeley Technol Law J 25:1920 ff
Clifton M-J (2011) The publican's dilemma: the legality of showing the premiership using an imported satellite decoder card. Eur Law Rep 2:38 ff.
Cohen Jehoram H (1973) Le regole di concorrenza nella CEE prima e dopo il caso Deutsche Grammophon. Riv Dir Ind I:345 ff
Cohen Jehoram H (1994) The EC copyright directives, economics and authors' rights. Int Rev Intellect Prop Competition Law 25:821
Cohen Jehoram H (1996) International exhaustion versus importation right: a murky area of intellectual property law. GRUR Int 40:280 ff
Cook T (2010) Exhaustion – a casualty of the borderless digital era. In: Bently L, Suthersanen I, Torremans PLC (eds) Global copyright. Three hundred years since the statute of Anne, from 1709 to cyberspace. Edward Elgar, Cheltenham
Correa CM (2007) Trade related aspects of intellectual property rights. Oxford University Press, Oxford
Daly A (2013) E-book monopolies and the law. Media Arts Law Rev 18:350 ff
Dreier T (2013) Online and its effect on the "Goods" versus "Services" distinction. Int Rev Intellect Prop Competition Law 40:137 ff
Dreier T, Hugenholtz PB (2006) Concise European copyright law. Kluwer, Alphen aan den Rijn
Drexl J (2012) EU competition law and parallel trade in pharmaceuticals: lessons to be learned for WTO/TRIPS? In: Rosen J (ed) Intellectual property at the crossroads of trade. Edward Elgar, Cheltenham
Dreyfus RC, Zimmerman DL, First H (eds) (2001) Expanding the boundaries of intellectual property: innovation policy for the knowledge society. Oxford University Press, Oxford
Edelman B (2001) La CJCE et la télédiffusion dans les chambres d'hôtel. Rec Dall 1094 ff
Efroni Z (2010) Access-right: the future of digital copyright law. Oxford University Press, New York
Fairfield J (2007) Virtual property and the overextension of copyright licensing online. In: Yu PK (ed) Intellectual property and information wealth: copyright and related rights. Preager, Westport
Feldman Y, Nadler J (2006) The law and norms of file sharing. San Diego Law Rev 43:587 f
Ficsor M (1995) International harmonization of the protection and management of copyright and neighboring rights. Naples Forum Book
Ficsor M (2002) The law of copyright and the internet. Oxford University Press, Oxford
Fisher WW (2004) Promises to keep: technology, law, and the future of entertainment. Stanford University Press, Stanford
Françon A (1990) Le conflit entre la SACEM et les discothèques devant la Cour de justice des Communautés européennes. RIDA 144:50 ff
Galgano F (1993) Diritto civile e commerciale. Cedam, Padova
Geiger C (2008) The constitutional dimension of intellectual property. In: Torremans PLC (ed) Intellectual property and human right. Kluwer Law International, Alphen aan den Rijn
Geiger C, Griffiths J, Hilty RM (2008) Declaration on a balanced interpretation of the "Three-Step Test" in copyright law. Int Rev Intellect Prop Competition Law 39:707 ff.
Gendreau Y (2006) The image of copyright. Eur Intellect Prop Rev 209 ff
Gervais D (1998) The TRIPS agreement: drafting history and analysis. Sweet and Maxwell, London
Ghidini G (2006) Intellectual property and competition law: the innovation nexus. Edward Elgar, Cheltenham
Ginsburg JC (2002) How copyright got a bad name for itself. Columbia J Law Arts 26:61 ff

Glusman LJ (1995) It's my copy, right? Music industry power to control growing resale markets in used digital audio recordings. Wisconsin Law Rev 709 ff
Goldsmith J, Wu T (2006) Who controls the internet?: illusions of a borderless world. Oxford University Press, New York
Goldstein P (2001) International copyright: principles, law, and practice. Oxford University Press, New York
Goodenough OR, Decker G (2009) Why do good people steal intellectual property? In: Freeman M, Goodenough OR (eds) Law, mind and brain. Ashgate, Burlington
Harris B (1980) The Coditel case – diffusion of broadcasting rights. Eur Intellect Prop Rev 163 ff
Hartmann T (2012) Weiterverkauf und "Verleih" online vertriebener Inhalte – Zugleich Anmerkung zu EuGH, Urteil vom 3. Juli 2012, Rs. C-128/11 – UsedSoft/Oracle. GRUR Int 980 ff
Hess E (2013) Code-ifying copyright: an architectural solution to digitally expanding the first sale doctrine. Fordham Law Rev 81:1965 ff
Hilty RM, Nérisson S (eds) (2012) Balancing copyright – a survey of national approaches. Springer, Berlin
Hilty RM, Köklü K, Hafenbrädl F (2013) Software agreements: stocktaking and outlook – lessons from the UsedSoft v. Oracle case from a comparative law perspective. Int Rev Intellect Prop Competition Law 44:263 ff
Hoeren T, Försterling M (2012) Onlinevertrieb "gebrauchter" Software, Hintergründe und Konsequenzen der EuGH Entscheidung "UsedSoft". MMR 642 ff
Hugenholtz PB (2000) Why the copyright directive is unimportant, and possibly invalid. Eur Intellect Prop Rev 11:499 ff
Jani O (2012) "Secondhand" software: does European copyright law permit the sale of secondhand files? ELR 1:21 ff
Kamenetz D (2011) Ninth circuit welcomes copyright-holders to bypass the "First Sale Doctrine" by crafting new rule for establishing licenses. Univ Baltimore Intellect Prop Law J 155 ff
Karapapa S (2012) Private copying: the scope of user freedom in EU digital copyright. Routledge, Oxford
Katz A (2011) What antitrust law can (and cannot) teach about the first sale doctrine. Working Paper, 2011. http://ssrn.com/abstract=1845842
Klatt M, Meiste M (2012) The constitutional structure of proportionality. Oxford University Press, Oxford
Kupferschmid K (1998) Lost in cyberspace: the digital demise of the first-sale doctrine. J Marshall J Computer Info Law 848
Landes WM, Posner RA (2003) The economic structure of intellectual property law. Harvard University Press, Cambridge
Lauterbach T (2013) Copyright law trumps free movement of unlawfully distributed goods. J Intellect Prop Law Pract 8:13 ff
Lehman BA, Brown RH (1995) Intellectual property and the national information infrastructure: the report of the working group on intellectual property rights. DIANE Publishing
Liebowitz SJ (2005) Pitfalls in measuring the impact of file-sharing on the sound recording market. CESifo Econ Stud 51:439 ff
Linklater E (2012) A European perspective on agency agreements for the sale of ebooks: happily ever after or the end of the story? May 2012. http://ssrn.com/abstract=2052119, pp 20 ff
Linklater E (2013) E-books distinguished from software, not exhausted. J Intellect Prop Law Pract 8:685 f
Litman J (2006) Digital copyright. Springer, New York
Longdin L, Lim PH (2013) Inexhaustible distribution rights for copyright owners and the foreclosure of secondary markets for used software. Int Rev Intellect Prop Competition Law 541 ff
Lucas A (2010) International exhaustion. In: Bently L, Suthersanen I, Torremans PLC (eds) Global copyright. Three hundred years since the statute of Anne, from 1709 to cyberspace. Edward Elgar, Cheltenham

Mattioli MR (2010) Cooling-off & secondary markets: consumer choice in the digital domain. Va J Law Technol 15:246 ff
Merges RP (2000) One hundred years of solicitude: intellectual property law, 1900–2000. Calif Law Rev 88:2236 ff
Minero G (2014) Videogames, consoles and technological measures: the Nintendo v PC Box and 9Net Case. Eur Intellect Prop Rev 36:335 ff
Moon K (2013) Resale of digital content: Usedsoft V Redigi. Entertainment Law Rev 6:193 ff
Musso A (2008) Diritto d'autore sulle opere dell'ingegno, letterarie e artistiche. Zanichelli, Bologna-Roma
Netanel NW (2007) Why has copyright expanded? Analysis and critique. In: Macmillan F (ed) New directions in copyright law, vol 6. Edward Elgar, Cheltenham
Olivier DA (1971–1972) The exercise of an industrial property right to partition markets within the EEC is violative of the basic policy providing for free movement of goods embodied in the Treaty of Rome. Tex Int Law J 516 ff
Overdijk T, Van der Putt P, De Vries E, Schafft T (2011) Exhaustion and software resale rights. CRi 2:36 f
Patry W (2009) Moral panics and the copyright wars. Oxford University Press, New York
Patry W (2012) How to fix copyright. Springer, New York
Peitz M, Waelbroeck P (2006) Piracy of digital products: a critical review of the economics literature. Inf Econ Policy 18:449 ff.
Perzanowski AK, Schultz J (2010) Digital exhaustion. UCLA Law Rev 58:894
Peters M (2010) The legal perspective on exhaustion in the borderless era: consideration of a digital first sale doctrine for online transmission of digital works in the United States. In: Bently L, Suthersanen I, Torremans PLC (eds) Global copyright. Three hundred years since the statute of Anne, from 1709 to cyberspace. Edward Elgar, Cheltenham
Peukert A (2012) Why do "Good People" disregard copyright on the internet? In: Geiger C (ed) Criminal enforcement of intellectual property: a handbook of contemporary research. Edward Elgar, Cheltenham
Pino G (2010) Diritti e interpretazione. Il ragionamento giuridico nello Stato costituzionale. Il Mulino, Bologna
Reese RA (2003) The first sale doctrine in the era of digital networks. Boston College Law Rev 44:583 ff
Regnell B, van De Weerd I, De troyer O (eds) (2011) Software business. Springer, Berlin
Reinbothe J, von Lewinski S (2002) The WIPO treaties 1996. Butterworths, London
Ricolfi M (2002) Comunicazione al pubblico e distribuzione. AIDA 48 ff
Ricolfi M (2004) Software e limitazioni delle utilizzazioni del licenziatario. AIDA 358 ff
Ricolfi M (2006) Is there an antitrust antidote against IP overprotection within TRIPS? Marq Intellect Prop Law Rev 10:305 ff
Riziotis D (2013) The application of exhaustion on services revisited. ZWeR 72 ff
Rognstad O-A (2008) The exhaustion/competition interface in EC law – is there room for a holistic approach? In: Drexl J (ed) Research handbook on intellectual property and competition law. Edward Elgar, Cheltenham
Rub GA (2013) The economics of Kirtsaeng v. John Wiley & Sons, Inc.: the efficiency of a balanced approach to the first sale doctrine. Fordham Law Rev 41 ff
Sacco R (1991) Legal formants: a dynamic approach to comparative law (installment II of II). Am J Comp Law 39:385 ff.
Samuelson P (2003) The constitutional law of intellectual property after Eldred v. Ashcroft. J Copyright Soc U S A 50:547 ff
Santini G (1979) Commercio e servizi. Bologna
Sarti D (1996) Diritti esclusivi e circolazione dei beni. Milan
Schovsbo J (2012) The exhaustion of rights and common principles of European intellectual property law. In: Ohly A (ed) Common principles of European intellectual property law. Mohr Siebeck, Tübingen

Senftleben M (2012) Die Fortschreibung des urheberrechtlichen Erschöpfungsgrundsatzes im digitalen Umfeld. NJW 2924 ff

Serra R (2013) Rebalancing at resale: Redigi, royalties, and the digital secondary market. Boston Univ Law Rev 1753 ff

Sieman JS (2006–2007) Using the implied license to inject common sense into digital copyright. N C Law Rev 85:885 ff

Smith J, Silver J (2011) FA premier league down at half-time in European championship: advocate general finds that territorial exclusivity agreements relating to the transmission of Football matches are contrary to EU law. Eur Intellect Prop Rev 399 ff

Spedicato G (2011) Digitalizzazione di opere librarie e diritti esclusivi. Aedon, n. 2, § 5. http://www.aedon.mulino.it/archivio/2011/2/spedicato.htm

Spedicato G (2013) Interesse pubblico e bilanciamento nel diritto d'autore. Giuffré, Milan

Streitfield D (2013) Imagining a swap meet for E-books and music. New York Times, 7 March 2013. http://www.nytimes.com/2013/03/08/technology/revolution-in-the-resale-of-digital-books-and-music.html?pagewanted=all&_r=0

Targosz T (2010) Exhaustion in digital products and the "Accidental" impact on the balance of interests in copyright law. In: Bently L, Suthersanen I, Torremans PLC (eds) Global copyright. Three hundred years since the statute of Anne, from 1709 to cyberspace. Edward Elgar, Cheltenham

Targosz T (2014) The court of justice on links: it is allowed to link. At least in principle. Kluwer Copyright Blog, 14 February 2014. http://kluwercopyrightblog.com/2014/02/14/the-court-of-justice-on-links-it-is-allowed-to-link-at-least-in-principle/

Tjong Tjin Tai E (2003) Exhaustion and online delivery of digital works. Eur Intellect Prop Rev 207 ff

Torremans PLC (2014) The future implications of the Usedsoft decision. CREATe Working Paper 2014/2, February 2014. http://www.create.ac.uk/wp-content/uploads/2014/01/CREATe-Working-Paper-2014-02.pdf

Von Lewinski S (2009) Gedanken zur Cassina-Entscheidung des Europäischen Gerichtshofs. In: Hilty RM, Drexl J, Nordemann W (eds) Schutz von Kreativität und Wettbewerb: Festschrift für Ulrich Loewenheim zum 75. Geburtstag, München

Walter MM, von Lewinski S (eds) (2010) European copyright law. A commentary. Oxford University Press, Oxford

Westkamp G (2007) Intellectual property, competition rules, and the emerging internal market: some thoughts on the European exhaustion doctrine. Marquette Int Prop Law Rev 11:291 ff

Westkamp G (2007) The implementation of directive 2001/29/EC in the Member States. http://ec.europa.eu/internal_market/copyright/docs/studies/infosoc-study-annex_en.pdf

Wiebe A (2009) The principle of exhaustion in European copyright law and the distinction between digital goods and digital services. GRUR Int 114 ff

Winston EI (2006) Why sell what you can license?: Contracting around statutory protection of intellectual property. Geo Mason Law Rev 14:93 ff

WIPO (1978) Guide to the Berne convention for the protection of literary and artistic works (Paris Act, 1971). Geneva

WIPO (2002) Intellectual property on the internet: a survey of issues. Geneva. http://www.wipo.int/export/sites/www/copyright/en/ecommerce/pdf/survey.pdf

WIPO (2003) Guide to the copyright and related rights treaties administered by WIPO and glossary of copyright and related rights terms. Geneva

Xalabarder R (2009) Study on copyright limitations and exceptions for educational activities in North America, Europe, Caucasus, Central Asia and Israel. Geneva

Zentner A (2006) Measuring the effect of file sharing on music purchases. J Law Econ 49:63 ff

Effects of Culture on Judicial Decisions: Personal Data Protection vs. Copyright Enforcement

Federica Giovanella

Contents

Abstract This work is based on a number of selected lawsuits, where copyright holders tried to enforce their rights against Internet users suspected of illegal file sharing. In so doing, copyright enforcement collided with users' information privacy.

In fact, in the analyzed controversies, users were normally only partially identifiable through their pseudonymous or IP address. In order to obtain their real identities, copyright holders required the intervention of Internet service providers (ISPs) supplying users with Internet connection. ISPs have sometimes refused to collaborate, forcing copyright holders to sue them with the aim of obtaining a

---

This paper summarizes an ongoing research, which I began during my Ph.D. I would like to thank all those who have given fruitful comments on this work and on the main research of which this paper is part. I am especially grateful to Prof. Roberto Caso for encouraging me to study this subject, for our reflections on the issue, as well as for the opportunity to publicly discuss my thesis. Usual disclaimer applies.

F. Giovanella (✉)
Faculty of Law, University of Trento, Trento, Italy
e-mail: federica.giovanella@unitn.it

R. Caso, F. Giovanella (eds.), *Balancing Copyright Law in the Digital Age*,
DOI 10.1007/978-3-662-44648-5_3

judicial provision ordering the disclosure of users' data. Here arose an animated conflict between users' data protection and copyright holders' enforceable rights.

Employing a comparative and interdisciplinary (sociocultural) approach, my case study tries to understand the way judges solve the mentioned conflict. The comparison involves the European system (with particular regard to Italy) and the North American ones (US and Canada).

My hypothesis is that, in addition to the features of each country as considered through a "traditional" comparative approach, judges may be influenced in their decisions by culture. In fact, judges do not live a secluded life but operate within a society. Therefore, it is at least plausible, if not necessary, that their decisions reflect the values of that society.

The paper has two goals, which are strictly intertwined one with the other.

The primary goal is to analyze different indicators relating to both the case studies and the considered systems, in order to understand if the decisions were the by-products of different policy conceptions and cultural perceptions of the two conflicting rights in the three mentioned systems.

The secondary goal refers to the methodology applied. From this point of view, another aim of the paper is to develop, in the wake of existing literature, an interpretative approach to examine judges' decisions from a sociocultural perspective.

Both aims will help in shedding some light on the relationship between judges and society.

1 Introduction

The existence of conflicting rights is *the* ontological characteristic of law. Law itself elaborates the necessary criteria to decree which of the conflicting rights should prevail. When there is no legal predetermination, judges are in charge of determining the prevalence of one right over the other, applying a balancing judgment. This judgment can be particularly thorny when there are fundamental rights at stake, which gain the highest rank among all other rights (at least at first sight).[1]

This work represents a first analysis of the mentioned balancing, with the aim of understanding if, besides the method of balancing applied, judges can be influenced by cultural factors relating to the perception of the conflicting rights. Moreover, the work investigates whether policies—meant as main lines of intervention followed

[1] It cannot be denied that, at least for the Italian context, the classification of copyright as fundamental right is disputed (the opposite is true for information privacy, for which see *infra*). Although more than one international treaty declares the indispensable protection of copyright (for example, art. 27.2 of the Universal Declaration of Human Rights of 1948 or art. 17.2 of the Charter of Fundamental Rights of the European Union), a lot of criticisms remain. This is particularly true when copyright, as the prince of intellectual property rights, is compared, if not assimilated, to physical property. See, for example, the work of Reyman (2009). See also the paper of Caterina Sganga in this book.

by the legislator for the protection of a given right—could affect these judicial decisions as well.

In order to answer these questions, the research is based on some case studies. These have been chosen among decisions relating to a scenario that has been highly modified by the advent of digital technology. A paradigmatic case of conflict between fundamental rights is in fact represented by the infringement of copyrighted works on the Internet. The analyzed cases concern the enforcement of copyright against illegal file sharing made through peer-to-peer platforms, where every user is at the same time both server and client and can upload and download files through the network.

Music (and later, movie) industries have been trying to stop this phenomenon for many years and in different ways.[2] In the controversies here analyzed, the target of the music industry's legal action was users. In the latter controversies, in order to sue final users, copyright holders needed to follow a particular path. In fact, Internet users are usually only partially identifiable, meaning that only their pseudonymous or IP addresses are known.[3] To match these data to users' real identities, copyright holders required the intervention of Internet service providers (ISPs) supplying users with Internet connection. ISPs sometimes refused to collaborate, forcing copyright holders to ask for judicial provisions ordering the disclosure of users' data.

In so doing, copyright holders sought to obtain data that are users' personal data.[4] Judges found themselves confronting the dilemma of making copyright

---

[2] The first step was to sue the producers of the software used for the exchange of files. See, for example, the USA Napster case: *A&M Records, Inc., v. Napster, Inc.*, 114 F. Supp. 2d 896, 900 (N.D. Cal. 2000); *A&M Record Inc. v. Napster, Inc.*, 239 F.3d 1004 (2001); the most important case probably remains the Grokster one, decided by USA Supreme Court: *MGM Studios, Inc., v. Grokster, Ltd*, 259 F.Supp. 2d 1029 (C.D. Cal. 2003); *MGM Studios, Inc., v. Grokster, Ltd*, 380 F.3d 1154 (9th Cir. 2004); *MGM Studios, Inc., v. Grokster, Ltd*, 545 U.S. 913 (2005). It seems that these controversies against software producers did not take place outside the USA.

[3] An IP number is "a unique number that identifies the precise location of a particular node on the Internet. The address is a 32-bit number usually written in dotted decimal format, i.e. in the form '123.33.22.32', and it is used by the TCP/IP protocol"; see, Collin (2004), *sub verbo*: "Internet Address."

[4] Even though the characterization of IP numbers as personal data is still controversial, they have been considered as such by the Privacy Authorities of Canada and Italy, as well as by Article 29 Data Protection Working Party. See the opinion of the Canadian Privacy Commissioner, PIPEDA Case Summaries n. 25/2001—A Broadcaster Accused of Collecting Personal Information via Web Site, at http://www.priv.gc.ca/cf-dc/2001/cf-dc_011120_e.cfm; n. 2005/315—Web-centered company's safeguards and handling of access request and privacy complaint questioned, at http://www.priv.gc.ca/cf-dc/2005/315_20050809_03_e.cfm; n. 2005/319—ISP's anti-spam measures questioned, available at http://www.priv.gc.ca/cf-dc/2005/319_20051103_e.cfm: "an IP address can be considered personal information if it can be associated with an identifiable individual." The same interpretation is made by Article 29 of the Data Protection Working Party, which explains that "IP addresses attributed to Internet users are personal data and are protected by EU Directives 95/46 and 97/66"; cf. Opinion 2/2002 on the use of unique identifiers in telecommunication terminal equipment: the example of IPv6, adopted on May 30, 2002, at 3. The document can be found at http://ec.europa.eu/justice/data-protection/article-29/documentation/

prevail—and therefore ordering the disclosure of users' identities—or making informational privacy prevail[5]—frustrating copyright holders' expectations.

These lawsuits took place in different countries, but I shall here consider and compare only some cases that took place in the USA, Canada, and Italy. I have chosen to analyze the USA and EU, of which Italy is clearly part, since they represent two important and often very different legal systems. Canada represents a middle ground between these two "blocks," given that it is inevitably influenced both by the bordering US and by the older dominance of EU.

With this work, I would like to shed some light on the possible influence that national culture plays on judges. More precisely, this paper analyzes if in the illustrated conflict, besides the method of balancing applied, judges can be affected by cultural factors relating to the perception of the battling rights. Furthermore, the work investigates whether policies—meant as main lines of intervention of the legislator for the protection of a given right—could affect judicial decisions as well. I therefore apply a sociocultural approach, in which the concept of "legal culture" becomes central.

I am totally aware that this study presents some limits, which will emerge in the following pages. In order to simplify my research, I was forced to leave in the background many different variables, isolating other ones. It would otherwise have been almost impossible to manage the entire range of variables, and I would not have been able to reach the results I was aiming for. This work is not intended to be an all-embracing explanation of the phenomenon or of all the variables existing in the chosen cases. It can nevertheless be one of the concurring explanations, bearing clearly in mind nonetheless the undoubtable differences among the considered systems.[6]

The paper starts with a brief analysis of the case studies (Sect. 2). Then it illustrates legislation on file sharing (Sect. 3) and personal data protection (Sect. 4) in the three systems. Finally, some conclusions are drawn, considering

opinion-recommendation/index_en.htm#h2-11. There seems to be still some uncertainty on the characterization of IP addresses as personal data by some scholars. See, for example, Coudert and Werkers (2008), p. 50 at 57 ff.

[5] Although the cases here analyzed affect primarily personal data protection, judicial decisions often apply the term "privacy." For decades, scholars have tried to supply an exhaustive definition of "privacy," frequently overlapping this latter concept with personal data protection (for a recap of the most famous and shared definitions, see McNairn and Scott 2001, pp. 4 ff.). I shall therefore apply the terms privacy and informational privacy interchangeably and both with "personal data protection." This indistinct application is justified also by the fact that the three countries examined do not have the same system of protection and of classification for these rights.

[6] Just to mention a couple of divergences: the classical juxtaposition between common law and civil law systems and the differences existing in the recruitment of judges or in the organization of judicial power.

the possibility of a cultural and "political" influence on judicial decisions relating to the balancing of conflicting rights (Sect. 5).[7]

2 Solutions Applied by Judges: Case Studies

Despite taking place in different countries, or even continents, the cases considered are very similar to one another. In each of them, copyright holders relied on the collaboration of companies specializing in the acquisition of online information. These companies detected the existence of an illicit exchange of music files through peer-to-peer networks and collected the IP addresses of users who allegedly participated in this exchange.[8]

Through the acquired IP addresses, it was potentially possible for record companies to identify the names of the users/alleged infringers. To achieve this aim, the collaboration of ISPs was needed. Since some of them did not collaborate, record companies sued ISPs or requested their intervention as third parties, asking for injunctions that would oblige ISPs to disclose the data of those customers suspected of illegal file sharing. The idea behind recording companies' strategy was to later sue final users directly, in the hope of reaching an early settlement, at the same time creating a deterrent effect on other users.

In these lawsuits between the music industry and ISPs, the latter denied their collaboration, also arguing that their customers' privacy had to be protected.

Judges reacted differently in the three considered systems.

2.1 Italian Cases

The Italian case considered took place between 2006 and 2008 and involved the recording company "Peppermint Jam Records GmBH" and the ISP "Wind Telecomunicazioni Spa."[9]

Peppermint is a German recording company that holds the rights to musical works of different artists. With the collaboration of a Swiss company (called Logistep), Peppermint ascertained that musical works of which it owned the rights

[7] It is not possible to give a complete illustration either of the legislation or of the cases here. I shall therefore supply sufficient information to understand the case studies, the different approaches to privacy and copyright, and the interpretation of the judicial solutions.

[8] These companies usually utilize specific software that distributes inoperative or bug files through the same peer-to-peer system accessed by "normal" users. Users access the network and download the inoperative files, as if these were normal music files. In this way, it is possible to trace who is looking for and downloading the files to which the copyright holder has right.

[9] The case is here only briefly illustrated. For a deeper analysis, see Blengino and Senor (2007), p. 835; Caso (2007), p. 471; De Cata (2008), p. 404; Foglia (2007), p. 585; Gambini (2009), p. 509.

were illegally shared through peer-to-peer networks. Logistep traced users sharing those musical works and registered their IP addresses.

Peppermint then sued Wind on the basis of a specific intellectual property enforcement tool (art. 156*bis* of Italian copyright statute, L. 22.4.1941, n. 633), which was implemented in Italy due to the European Directive called "IPR Enforcement."[10] According to this provision, if a party gives serious elements from which it can be inferred that its claims are sound, that party can ask the judge to order the counterparty to give information for the identification of the individuals involved in the production and distribution of the goods or services that constitute a violation of the copyright. Through art. 156*bis*, Peppermint asked the Tribunal of Rome to order Wind to disclose its customers' identification data associated with the IP numbers suspected of illegal file sharing collected by Logistep.

The illegality of file sharing is linked to arts. 171, 171*ter*, and 171*quater* of the Italian law on copyright.[11] Art. 171, letter a-*bis*) imposes a fine from 50 to 2,050 euros for making a copyrighted work completely or partially available to the public, by uploading the work on a telecommunication network, without having the right to do so, regardless of the aim and of the method used.[12]

Art. 171*ter*, co. 2, letter *a-bis*) punishes the infringer with imprisonment from 1 to 4 years and with a fine between 2,500 and 15,500 euros. The punishable conduct consists in communicating a complete or partial copyrighted work to the public, through its introduction into telecommunication networks, using whichever kind of connection. This conduct shall be made in violation of the right to

[10] This provision was introduced by d.lgs. 16.3.2006, n. 140, implementing Directive 2004/48/EC of the European Parliament and the Council, of 29 April 2004, on the enforcement of intellectual property rights, so-called Enforcement Directive, which, in turn, implemented the TRIPS (Trade-Related Aspects of Intellectual Property Rights) Agreements. More precisely, this provision is the implementation of art. 47 of the agreement. The nature of the tool provided by art. 156*bis* is debated. In its orders, the Tribunal of Rome classifies art. 156*bis* sometimes as a precautionary measure and sometimes as a discovery tool. Some Italian authors believe the latter interpretation is the most correct one, such as Marchetti and Ubertazzi (2012), pp. 1849 ff. as well as Sirotti Gaudenzi (2012), p. 450.

[11] See Marchetti and Ubertazzi (2012), pp. 1915–1916; Sirotti Gaudenzi (2012), p. 167. These three provisions have undergone various modifications, especially in connection with the aims for which the sharing activities is made. Initially, the text asked for the existence of a "profit-making aim" ("a fini di lucro" in the Italian text). Later on, this aim was substituted with the aim of "gaining a benefit" ("per trarne profitto" in the original wording), but then it was modified again, returning to the original version. This led to fluctuating interpretations and decisions by Italian judges and by the Italian Corte di Cassazione; cf. Terracina (2007), p. 259.

[12] This provision undoubtedly refers to peer to peer, but it considers only the introduction of the copyrighted work into the web and not the consequent sharing and diffusion (see Marchetti and Ubertazzi 2012, p. 1916).

communicate to the public (art. 16 of the Italian copyright law) and with profit-making aims.[13]

Lastly, art. 174*bis* prescribes that parallel to the criminal punishment, those who violate art. 171, co. 1, letter a*bis*) are also subject to a fine.

The long controversy between Peppermint and Wind gave rise to more than one injunction.[14] In the first ones, the Tribunal of Rome ordered the ISP to disclose users' data.[15] One of the injunctions stated that the collection of IP addresses made by Logistep was "reliable, acceptable and above all licit, given that a person who uses a file-sharing program shows, by this activity alone, the will to accept that her IP address can be known by all the other users using the same program."[16] This would have been a sort of noncodified exception to the principle of a data subject's consent to art. 23 of the Italian "Codice in materia di protezione dei dati personali," also called "Privacy Code" (d.lgs. 30.6.2003, n. 196).[17]

According to the Tribunal, another applicable exception was the one introduced by art. 24, co. 1, letter f) of the Code, which provides that consent is not required when data are necessary "to judicially enforce or defend a right."[18]

The decision taken by the Tribunal of Rome was followed in other orders by the same Tribunal until 2007,[19] when the scenario started to change. Let us take as an example the order of July 16, 2007.[20]

A very important difference between this decision and the previous ones is the presence of the Privacy Authority (so-called *Garante per la protezione dei dati personali*) in the controversy. In fact, although it had been notified by the Tribunal already in the first lawsuit, the Authority spontaneously intervened only in the lawsuit ending with the order of July 16, 2007. Its intervention in support of the

---

[13] The relationship between this provision and the one contained in art. 171, co. 1, letter a-bis) is that the former considers the right of "communication to the public" and the latter the right to "make available." See again Marchetti and Ubertazzi (2012), p. 1939.

[14] Trib. Roma, ord., 18.8.2006, Riv. dir. Ind., n. 4–5/2008, II, 328, annotated by De Cata [*Trib. Roma, ord., 18.8.2006*]; Trib. Roma, ord., 19.8.2006, Dir. Informatica, n. 4–5/2007, 815; Il civilista, n. 5/2008, 30, annotated by Valerini. This latter decision was confirmed also in Trib. Roma, ord., 22.9.2006, and the same conclusion was reached in Trib. Roma, ord., 9.9.2007.

[15] See *supra* note 14.

[16] Cf. *Trib. Roma, ord., 18.8.2006, supra* note 14, at par. 5.1.

[17] Exceptions to this principle are provided by the same Code at art. 24 and in other articles, which indicate when consent can be presumed or is anyway not needed. The solution given by the Tribunal of Rome would have been an exception not explicitly provided.

[18] See *Trib. Roma, ord., 18.8.2006, supra* note 14, at par. 6.2.

[19] V. *supra* note n. 14.

[20] Cf. Trib. Roma, ord., 16.7.2007, Dir. informatica, n. 4–5/2007, 828, with commentary by Blengino and Senor. See also, with the same contents, Trib. Roma, ord., 14.7.2007, Riv. dir. ind., n. 4–5/2008, II, 330, annotated by De Cata.

protection of users' personal information undoubtedly affected the decisions of the Tribunal of Rome.[21]

Indeed, the Authority observed that the collection of data made by Logistep had been done infringing arts. 37 and 13 of the Privacy Code. Art. 37, letter d) provides that the collection of data has to be communicated to the Authority when its purpose is to monitor electronic communication services. Art. 13 requires prior information to and specific consent by the data subject to whom the collected data refer. Furthermore, differently from what the Tribunal of Rome had stated, art. 24, co. 1, letter f) had to be interpreted as an exception applicable *in* the controversy and not to acts predestined to a possible subsequent trial.[22]

Another fundamental point stressed by the Authority is that users' privacy and the confidentiality of their communications are fundamental values in the Italian legal system, protected by arts. 2 and 15 of the Constitution. Therefore, only other fundamental values of the same degree can constrict them. Moreover, such constriction can be determined only after an effective balancing judgment, which in the specific case the judge had not made.[23]

After these orders, some others with the same content followed.[24]

It is worth mentioning another (last) decision, taken on March 17, 2008, since it considered a judgment by the European Court of Justice.[25] The case "Productores de Música de España (Promusicae) v. Telefónica de España SAU" is a European decision concerning a request for preliminary ruling by the Juzgado de lo Mercantil

---

[21] Many authors believe so: Blengino and Senor (2007), p. 836; Scorza (2007), p. 466; Foglia (2007), p. 599. Actually, the Tribunal itself states that the decision was taken that way also considering the significant intervention of the Privacy Authority.

[22] On this case and, more precisely, on the collection of data made by Logistep, the Italian Privacy Authority issued a specific decision on February 28, 2008, published in Bulletin n. 91/February 2008 and can be read at http://www.garanteprivacy.it/garante/doc.jsp?ID=1495246. See also the resolution of September 19, 2007, published in Bulletin n. 86/September 2007 (http://www.garanteprivacy.it/garante/doc.jsp?ID=1442463—spec. par. 5) and the provision on the security of telephone and online traffic data of January 17, 2008, published in Bulletin n. 30/February 2008 (http://www.garanteprivacy.it/garante/doc.jsp?ID=1482111), where the Authority explicitly excluded that ISPs can comply with requests of users' data if these requests are made in civil, administrative, or accounting controversies.

[23] It is the same Code that predetermines when the processing of data is allowed, with logic of "prior balancing." See, for example, arts. 36, co. 4, letter c); 60; and 71, co. 2 of the Code, where the law talks of rights with the same grade of the right to personal data protection or other personality rights or other fundamental and inviolable rights or freedoms.

[24] Trib. Roma, ord., 17.3. 2008, Giur. it., n. 7/2008, 1738, annotated by Sirotti Gaudenzi.

[25] C-275/06, decided on January 29, 2008 [*Promusicae*]. For an analysis and a comment of the decision, see Trotta (2008), p. 76; Caso (2008), p. 459; De Cata (2008); Di Mico (2010), p. 1 (concerning also a subsequent order of the European Court of Justice relating to an identical case that took place in Austria); Coudert and Werkers (2008), p. 37; Groussot (2008), p. 1745; Brimsted and Chesney (2008), p. 275. In 2012, the ECJ decided another case coming from the Supreme Court of Sweden, which originated in a lawsuit very similar to the Italian cases and to Promusicae v. Telefónica; see "Bonnier Audio AB et al. Vs. Perfect Communication Sweden AB" (C-461/10) decided on April 19, 2012.

n. 5 of Madrid. Promusicae, a nonprofit organization acting on behalf of its associated musical authors, asked a Spanish ISP—Telefónica—some data to identify final users suspected of illegally sharing musical works, the rights to which belonged to Promusicae's associates. The controversy was very close to the Italian ones here summarized. Based on Spanish legislation of European derivation, the Juzgado could not give prevalence to one of the conflicting rights and therefore requested the intervention of the Court of Justice. The question was whether EU law permitted member states to limit the duty of ISPs to retain and make available connection and traffic data for the purposes of criminal investigations or to safeguard public security and national defense, thereby excluding civil proceedings. The decision stated that European Directives do not obligate member states to provide a legal obligation to communicate personal data in order to ensure effective protection of copyright in civil proceedings in situations like those here described.[26] The Court further stated that when transposing European directives, member states have to rely on an interpretation of European laws that allows a fair balance among the various fundamental rights protected by the Community legal order.

Moreover, in implementing the measures transposing the directives, authorities and courts must interpret their national law in a way consistent with those directives. In the meantime, they must make sure that they do not rely on an interpretation of the directives that would conflict with the mentioned fundamental rights or with other general principles of Community law, among which is the principle of proportionality.[27]

In its decision, the EJC referred to copyright as a fundamental right, since it is considered as a right of property, and consequently as a general principle of Community law. However, the Court itself stressed that the protection of privacy and of private life is a fundamental right as well.[28] The decision faces the "need to reconcile the requirements of the protection of different fundamental rights, namely the right to respect private life on one hand and the rights to protection of property [...] on the other."[29] The Court, which considered the mechanisms to allow this reconcilement to be found in European Directives, clearly claimed that copyright has to be balanced against other rights.

[26] In particular, Directive 2000/31/EC of 8 June 2000 on certain legal aspects of information society services, in particular electronic commerce, in the Internal Market (Directive on electronic commerce); Directive 2001/29/EC of 22 May 2001 on the harmonization of certain aspects of copyright and related rights in the information society; Directive 2004/48/EC of 29 April 2004 on the enforcement of intellectual property rights; and Directive 2002/58/EC of 12 July 2002 concerning the processing of personal data and the protection of privacy in the electronic communications sector (Directive on privacy and electronic communications).

[27] I believe that the European decision, even if harshly criticized by a number of scholars for its ambivalence (see fn 25), suggests a slight prevalence of data protection on copyright.

[28] *Promusicae, supra* note 25, at pars. 61–63.

[29] *Promusicae, supra* note 25, at par. 64.

From the wording of this decision, it can be clearly inferred that copyright is not an absolute right. The ECJ proclaimed that a fair balance needs to be struck between the numerous fundamental rights protected by Community law.[30]

2.2 US Cases

The US decisions on copyright enforcement against Internet users are numerous. In order to give a complete picture of the situation, I shall illustrate two controversies in which two different mechanisms were applied.

I shall first briefly sketch the regulation of file sharing.

In the US, file sharing of copyrighted material through peer-to-peer networks seems to be sanctioned by multiple provisions, none of which however explicitly refers to file sharing. Indeed, the 1978 Copyright Act has been frequently modified since its enactment[31] as a response to the increasing need for copyright protection due to the diffusion of technological innovations. Many different bills have been proposed to punish file sharing, but no single one has become law yet.[32] Despite the absence of a specific punitive provision, there are very few doubts on the illegality of file sharing of copyrighted materials. File sharing can be considered an act of copying, therefore infringing the author's right of reproduction. Indeed, despite the existence of limitations and exceptions to copyright, under current interpretations, file sharing does not fit into them.[33]

The first case to be analyzed originated from the refusal of an ISP (Verizon) to comply with the *subpoena* requested by the *Recording Industry Association of America* (RIAA), the trade organization that represents recording industry distributors in the United States.[34]

---

[30] *Promusicae, supra* note 25, at pars. 66–68.

[31] The present Copyright Act was issued on October 19th, 1976 (Pub. L. No. 94-553) and came into force at the beginning of 1978. It constitutes title 17 of the U.S. Code.

[32] Among some of the most recent bills still pending in Congress: Peer-to-peer Piracy Prevention Act, proposed in 2003; Inducing Infringement of Copyrights Act (INDUCE Act), Piracy Deterrence and Education Act, and Protecting Intellectual Rights Against Theft and Expropriation Act (PIRATE Act)—all of which were presented in 2004; Prioritizing Resources and Organization for Intellectual Property Act (PRO-IP Act) of 2008; Combating Online Infringement and Counterfeits Act (COICA) introduced at the Senate in September 2010 and never approved, later presented again with the name PROTECT IP Act (or PIPA—Preventing Real Online Threats to Economic Creativity and Theft of Intellectual Property Act) in 2011, together with another very similar bill introduced in House of Representatives called Stop Online Piracy Act (SOPA).

[33] Cf. LaFrance (2008), pp. 161–162.

[34] *In re Verizon Internet Services*, 240 F. Supp. 2d 24 (D.D.C. 2003) [*In re Verizon*]; *RIAA v. Verizon Internet Services, 351 F.3d 1229* (DC Cir. 2003); *In re Verizon Internet Services*, 257 F. Supp. 2d 244 (D.D.C. 2003) [*In re Verizon II*]. As already done for the Italian context, the US decisions will also be only sketched here. For a deeper analysis of the case RIAA v. Verizon, see Kao (2004), p. 405; Gorski (2005), p. 149; Dutcher (2005), p. 493; Raynolds (2005), p. 343.

Through a *subpoena duces tecum*, a court, upon request of a party, orders a third person to produce documents or other tangible forms of evidence[35]. In the US legal system, a special form of subpoena exists for the enforcement of copyright, provided by § 512(h)[36], according to which "a copyright owner or a person authorized to act on the owner's behalf may request the clerk of any United States district court to issue a subpoena to a service provider for identification of an alleged infringer in accordance with [17 USC § 512]"[37].

The RIAA meant to use this tool to obtain users' identities associable to the collected IP addresses suspected of illegal file sharing of musical contents.

The District Court for the District of Columbia stated that Verizon had to comply with the RIAA's request. Verizon appealed this decision, and the Court of Appeal reversed it. Among the reasons for the appeal, Verizon considered the contrast between § 512(h) of the Copyright Act and the First Amendment of the Constitution, protecting freedom of expression and therefore also anonymity. The subpoena was quashed for other reasons, and more specifically because of a restrictive interpretation of the hypothesis in which the subpoena tool was applicable. Nevertheless, what has to be stressed is the exception mentioned, made by Verizon with regard to anonymity of users, which can be somehow considered a form of privacy. In its defense, Verizon argued that the DMCA subpoena violated users' First Amendment rights by uncovering their anonymity, given that courts have recognized that the First Amendment also covers expression on the Internet[38].

Verizon's statements on anonymity can be considered a defense of privacy as well. Anonymity is in fact a tool to preserve or conceal someone's privacy, and at the same time, the former can enjoy some protection as a component of the latter[39]: they can somehow be seen as complementary to one other.

Given the unsuccessful results obtained through the DMCA *subpoena*, the RIAA chose another typical trial tool: the so-called ex parte discovery. In this kind of process, one of the parties is not notified of the existence of the process itself; hence, it is not present or represented.

The RIAA started a number of lawsuits against "John Doe"[40]. An "ex parte" order would permit the RIAA to obtain "immediate discovery," which is an

---

[35] Black (1979), *sub verbo* "Subpoena duces tecum" [*Black's Law Dictionary*].

[36] This paragraph was introduced by the Digital Millennium Copyright Act (DMCA) of 1998, implementing the World Intellectual Property Organization (WIPO) Copyright Treaty (WCT) and the WIPO Performances and Phonograms Treaty (WPPT) undersigned by USA in 1996.

[37] Some problematic questions have been raised with reference to the fact that this subpoena is issued by a clerk, whose functions are administrative and not judiciary. This means that the warranties linked to the evaluation of the judiciary fail. Cf. *In re Verizon II*, *supra* note 34, at 248 ff.

[38] *Reno v. ACLU*, 521 U.S. 844 at 870 (1997).

[39] Kerr et al. (2009), p. 438.

[40] "John Doe" is a fictional name given to a male party of a process when his real name is not known or must remain unknown for legal reasons. *Black's Law Dictionary*, *sub verbo* "John Doe." The female corresponding is "Jane Doe."

authorization to issue a subpoena to the ISPs as third parties, requesting them to supply the information on their clients[41].

As an example, let us take the decision *Arista Records, LLC v. Does 1-16*[42]. Again, the ISP objected that the First Amendment was violated, even though the District Court held that sharing files through peer-to-peer technologies could not be considered an "expression" for the purposes of the First Amendment. Moreover, the Court observed that there was a scarce expectation of privacy[43]: users who share files through peer-to-peer networks accept that their personal data can be spread through the same networks[44].

The most interesting part of the decision is the application of a specific test in order to understand which of the conflicting rights—meaning, privacy/copyright—should prevail[45].

The factors considered are the following:

1. concrete showing of a prima facie claim of actionable harm,
2. specificity of the discovery request,
3. absence of alternative means to obtain the subpoenaed information,
4. central need for the subpoenaed information to advance the claim, and
5. the party's expectation of privacy.

This test was followed in the majority of the decisions here illustrated and resulted, in most of the cases, in a victory for copyright enforcement.

As we will see, a similar test is applied also in the Canadian decisions, while it does not exist in the Italian context, even though, in the case of interpretation of art. 156*bis* as a precautionary measure, the requirements of *fumus boni iuris* and *periculum in mora* must be evaluated[46].

---

[41] Backerman (2008).

[42] *Arista Records, LLC v. Does 1-16*, 2009 U.S. Dist. LEXIS 12159.

[43] Expectation of privacy refers to a test born in the concurring opinion of Justice Harlan in the case *Katz v. United States*, 389 U.S. 347 (1967) [*Katz*], to be applied in cases referred to privacy as protected by the Fourth Amendment. The test consists of two steps: the first is to investigate whether the subject demonstrated an actual subjective expectation of privacy; the second is whether her expectation is one that society is prepared to recognize as reasonable. As often happens with tests implying these types of evaluation, the test has been the source of many doctrinal debates, also because it does not give directions to follow in practical cases. On this test, see Wilkins (1987), pp. 1077 and 1089; Ashdown (1981), p. 1289; Libeu (1985), p. 849.

[44] It is the same argumentation made by the Tribunal of Rome in one of the analyzed sentences (see Peppermint vs. Wind, *Trib. Roma, ord., 18.8.2006, supra* note 14, at par. 5.1).

[45] See, for example, the following cases: *Sony Music Entertainment, Inc. v. Does 1-40*, 326 F. Supp. 2d 556 (S.D.N.Y. 2004); *UMG Recording, Inc. v. Does 1-4*, 2006 U.S. Dist. LEXIS 32821 (N.D. Cal. 2006); *Elektra Entertainment Group, Inc. v. Does 1-9*, 2004 U.S. Dist. LEXIS 23560 (S.D.N.Y. 2004).

[46] A summary finding that (1) the claim is founded and (2) the danger that the right may be impaired by the lapse of time. As an example, consider the decision of *Trib. Roma, ord., 18.8.2006, supra* note 14, at par. 5.1. Some scholars do not share the interpretation of art. 156*bis* given in this sentence: De Cata (2008), p. 411.

2.3 Canadian Cases

There are very few Canadian decisions relating to the enforcement of file sharing against final users. The case here considered is *BMG v. Does*[47], the first and most important decision of this kind in the Canadian legal system. The case is a copy of the US ones, promoted by the *Canadian Recording Industry Association* (CRIA), the Canadian correspondent of the RIAA.

In Canadian copyright law, there is no tool such as the subpoena provided by §512(h) of the U.S.C. or art. 156*bis* of Italian law on copyright. Hence, CRIA used the tool of the John Doe processes since the beginning, following rules 233 and 238 of the Federal Court Rules. These rules, concerning the discovery phase, aim at revealing the existence of documents and at obtaining the subsequent showing of the same documents by people who are not part of the lawsuit.

In *BMG v. Does*, five different ISPs were involved: four of them refused to comply with the requests of plaintiffs, arguing that the privacy of users/clients had been violated. These arguments were based on the applicability to the case of the Personal Information Protection and Electronic Documents Act (PIPEDA) of 2001.

Unlike what happens in the US and in Italy, when the Canadian decisions were taken, there was no legislative provision from which one could infer with certainty that file-sharing activities were illegal. The CRIA argued that users infringed authors' exclusive rights: Sections 18 and 27 of the Canadian Copyright Act protecting reproduction and distribution of copyrighted works[48]. Nevertheless, in this case, the Court stated that "downloading a song for personal use does not amount to infringement in the light of Section 80(1) of the Copyright Act" providing an exception to copyright for personal use[49].

This interpretation, as well as the absence of specific provisions punishing file sharing, was an effect (also) of the late implementation of World Intellectual Property Organization Treaties by the Canadian government[50]. These international agreements introduced a new right for the copyright holder: the exclusive right to make available, which can be seen as a way to stop file sharing and other similar activities[51].

---

[47] *BMG Canada Inc. v. John Doe*, [2004] 3 F.C.R. 241 and *BMG Canada Inc. v. John Doe*, [2005] 4 F.C.R. 81. For further details see Kerr and Cameron (2006), p. 269; Wilkinson (2008), p. 227.

[48] The current Copyright Act was enacted in 1921 and is the sole copyright legislation applicable, although it has been frequently and substantially amended since its appearance. The last amendment was made with the "Copyright modernisation act" of 2011.

[49] See *BMG Canada Inc. v. John Doe*, [2004] 3 F.C.R. 241, paras. 21–25.

[50] I am referring to the mentioned World Intellectual Property Organization (WIPO) Copyright Treaty (WCT) and the WIPO Performances and Phonograms Treaty (WPPT) undersigned by Canada in 1997.

[51] Canada tried to modify its Copyright Act and to implement the WIPO Treaties with many bills starting from 2005, but due to government collapses, these bills never became law. Only in 2012, the bill C-11 titled "Copyright Modernisation Act" was released. With this Act, Canada implements the mentioned treaties, including the right to make available, as well as other important pieces of legislation (including ISPs' liability and technological protection measures).

In the Canadian case, as happened in the US ones, in order to decide which right had to prevail, the court applied a test made of five steps:

a) "the applicant must establish a prima facie case against the unknown alleged wrongdoer;
b) the person from whom discovery is sought must be in some way involved in the matter under dispute, he must be more than an innocent bystander;
c) the person from whom discovery is sought must be the only practical source of information available to the applicants;
d) the person from whom discovery is sought must be reasonably compensated for his expenses arising out of compliance with the discovery order in addition to his legal costs;
e) the public interests in favour of disclosure must outweigh the legitimate privacy concerns"[52].

The judge stated that since file sharing could not be univocally considered illicit, and privacy was "of utmost importance to Canadian society"[53], the interest of privacy protection had to prevail[54].

The CRIA appealed[55]. In the opening words of the Federal Court of Appeal's decisions, the "case illustrate[d] the tension existing between the privacy rights of those who use the Internet and those whose rights may be infringed or abused by anonymous Internet users"[56].

The Court of Appeal specified that, although the lower court erred in judging file sharing as legal, CRIA's request had to be rejected, even only for the time passed between the collection of IP addresses and the request for users' identification[57].

2.4 Some Preliminary Thoughts

Even if only briefly illustrated, the selected case law shows the conflict springing from the introduction of a new technology (*i.e.*, file sharing) in the existing legal scenario. Indeed, looking closer, both rights (privacy and copyright) seem to sprout

---

[52] *BMG Canada Inc. v. John Doe*, [2004] 3 F.C.R. 241, paras. 13–14.

[53] Cf. *BMG Canada Inc. v. John Doe*, [2004] 3 F.C.R. 241, par. 36.

[54] *BMG Canada Inc. v. John Doe*, [2004] 3 F.C.R. 241, paras. 36–42.

[55] *BMG Canada Inc. v. John Doe*, [2005] F.C.J. No. 858. See *supra* note n. 47 for bibliographical references.

[56] *BMG Canada Inc. v. John Doe*, [2005] F.C.J. No. 858, par. 1.

[57] In fact, IP addresses are usually "dynamic," meaning that the addresses assigned are changeable, and not fixed, as static IP addresses would be. ISPs can reallocate the same address to different users in different moments, allowing the intermediaries to manage a number of IP addresses that is inferior to the number of users. Since users linked to an IP address vary with time, the more time passes, the more difficult it becomes to trace the user behind a given IP address.

exactly from the introduction of a technological innovation, whether revolutionary or not[58].

Facing a new situation, judges, who cannot avoid making a decision, have to understand which of the two conflicting legal spheres has to prevail. The judge finds herself in need of balancing rights whose prevalence is not predefined by the system. Each of the countries examined lacks a norm indicating clearly which road has to be taken: in all the systems, the two rights seem to have the same rank.

Data protection is usually considered part of the right to privacy, either as an interpretation of it or as a way to protect privacy itself. In each of the three countries examined, both courts and scholars have made efforts to trace back the right to privacy to national constitutions, despite the fact that none of the constitutions explicitly mentions privacy. As for the US, privacy is usually linked to the First, Fourth, Fifth, and Fourteenth Amendments of the Constitution[59]. In the Canadian system, the protection of privacy comes from the Charter of Rights and Freedoms of 1982, and in particular from Sections 7 and 8[60]. In the Italian context, a right to privacy has been retraced to arts. 2, 3, 13, 14, and 15 of the Constitution, as can be read in the famous "Soraya" decision[61]. Furthermore, the European Convention on Human Rights (art. 8) and the Charter of Fundamental Rights of the European Union (art. 7) sanction in the same way the need to respect private and family life.

As for copyright, the US system explicitly protects it through Clause 8, Section 8 of article 1 of the Constitution, which includes the so-called copyright clause. As is well known, according to this section, Congress "shall have the power to promote the Progress of Science and useful Arts, by securing for limited Times to Authors and Inventors the exclusive Right to their respective Writings and Discoveries." Through this section, Congress acquires the competence to legislate on this subject, and meanwhile, copyright is consecrated as an exclusive right of authors, even though limited in time. In Canada, legislative power on copyright is exclusively given to the Congress as well. This can be inferred from Section 91(23) of the

---

[58] On the one hand, the introduction of movable types generated interests that resulted (also) in the birth of copyright (see, for example, the considerations by Izzo 2010); Deazly et al. (2010). On the other hand, it was a portable camera that causes in two American jurists' minds the sensation of being the target of yellow journalism: I am clearly referring to the seminal work of Warren and Brandeis (1890), p. 193.

[59] Solove and Schwartz (2011), pp. 34–36; Solove and Rotenberg (2003), pp. 33–34; see also the following leading cases: *Olmstead v. United States*, 277 U.S. 438 (1928); *Griswold v. Connecticut*, 381 U.S. 479 (1965); *Katz, supra* note 43; *Roe v. Wade*, 410 U.S. 113 (1973), and more recently: *Kyllo v. United States*, 533 U.S. 27 (2001) and *U.S. v. Jones*, 132 S. Ct. 945 (2012).

[60] The following leading cases explain the link between privacy and the Charter: *R. v. O'Connor*, [1995] 4 S.C.R. 411; *M. (A.) v. Ryan*, [1997] 1. S.C.R. 157; *R. v. Mills*, [1999] 3 S.C.R. 668; *Hunter v. Southam Inc*., [1984] 2 S.C.R. 145, introducing the expectation of privacy (for which see also *R. v. Tessling*, [2004] 3 S.C.R. 432) and explicitly referring to the US case *Katz, supra* note 43. See also McIsaas et al. (2007), spec. pp. 2–9. In 1987, the Justice Committee of the Canadian House of Common unsuccessfully suggested introducing a constitutional right to privacy (cf. Flaherty 1991, p. 831, spec. pp. 843 ff., for a deeper analysis).

[61] Cass. civ., 27.5.1975, n. 2129, Foro it., 1976, I, 2895.

Constitution Act of 1867, nowadays part of the Canadian Constitution. This section considers copyright a constitutionally recognized right, even though the same section does not give a definition. In the Italian context, copyright is traced back to arts. 9 (on the development of culture and scientific and technical research), 21 (freedom of expression), and 33 (freedom of arts and science). It is also connected to arts. 2 and 4, which consider the protected work an activity concurring in the spiritual or material progress of society. Finally, art. 17, co. 2 of the mentioned Charter of Fundamental Rights of the European Union states that "Intellectual property shall be protected."

Looking at the results of the illustrated cases, it is possible to make the following observation[62]: in the US, the majority of the cases results in a win for copyright holders; in Canada, even if the sample is very limited, one can say that the protection of information privacy prevailed on copyright. This last statement is true also for the Italian context.

It often happens that the context in which judges work does not allow a clear predetermination of the prevailing interest, and on the contrary, that same context puts the judge in front of provisions that allow a certain degree of discretion. Which parameters should judges follow to determine the prevalence of one or the other right in these situations? And which parameters did in fact judges adopt in the concrete cases?[63]

There are a number of different mechanisms, which judges follow in their decisions. "Classical" balancing mechanisms concern the techniques used by courts to weigh different rights and interests against each other. These methods, which have been analyzed by many scholars, are applied especially by the highest courts,

[62] It is important to note that more case studies were analyzed than those illustrated here, but they were not recalled due to space limitations. The other cases are the following—for the US system: *Universal City Studios, Inc. v. Sony Corp. of America*, 480 F. Supp. 429 (C.D. Cal. 1979); *Universal City Studios, Inc. v. Sony Corp. of America*, 659 F.2d 963 (9th Cir. 1981); *Sony Corp. of America v. Universal City Studios*, 464 U.S. 417 (1984); *A&M Records, Inc. v. Napster*, 114 F. Supp. 2d 896, 900 (N.D. Cal. 2000); *A&M Record Inc. v. Napster, Inc.*, 239 F.3d 1004 (2001); *MGM Studios, Inc. v. Grokster, Ltd*, 259 F. Supp. 2d 1029 (C.D. Cal. 2003); *MGM Studios, Inc. v. Grokster, Ltd*, 380 F.3d 1154 (9th Cir. 2004); *MGM Studios, Inc. v. Grokster, Ltd*, 545 U.S. 913 (2005); *In re Charter Communications, Inc., Subpoena Enforcement Matter*, 393 F.3d 771, 773 (8th Cir., 2005); *In re Subpoena to University of North Carolina at Chapel Hill*, 367 F. Supp. 2d 945 (M.D.N.C., 2005); *Arista Records, LLC v. Does 1-12*, 2008 U.S. Dist. LEXIS 82548; *Arista Records, LLC v. Lime Group, LLC*, 715 F. Supp. 2d 481 (2010); *Sony Music Entertainment, Inc. v. Does 1-40*, 326 F. Supp. 2d 556 (S.D.N.Y. 2004). For Canada, the cases are *Glaxo Wellcome PLC v. Minister of National Revenue*, [1998] 4 F.C. 439; *Irwin Toy Ltd. v. Doe*, [2000] O.T.C. 561; *CCH Canadian Ltd. v. Law Society of Upper Canada*, [2004] S.C.R. 339; *SOCAN Statement of Royalties, Public Performance of Musical Works 1996, 1997, 1998* (Tariff 22, Internet) (Re) 1 C.P.R. (4th) 417; *Voltages Pictures LLC v. Jane Doe and John Doe*, 2011 FC 1024. For the Italian context, in addition to all the orders relating to the Peppermint casa, also the "Fapav v. Telecom" case was considered (Trib. Roma, ord., 14.4.2010, Riv. dir. ind., n. 3/2010, II, 248 with commentary by Mula).

[63] It is absolutely evident and obvious that the differences among the three countries considered go well beyond what I can illustrate in the next paragraphs. As an example, let us think of the classical differentiation between common law and civil law systems.

such as constitutional courts, valuing the compatibility of a given norm *vis–à–vis* the constitution[64]. Balancing mechanisms appear to be external, meaning that they are objectively observable by reading judicial decisions. The study here proposed looks for a different approach, under the mentioned sociocultural analysis. My idea is to look through judicial decisions and see whether judges are culturally influenced, besides the actual methods of balancing applied. Judges are indeed part of the social structure by which they can be influenced[65]: culture can affect judges[66].

In my analysis, the concept of "legal culture" plays a pivotal role. Legal culture can approximately be described as a factor (or at least one of the factors) in helping to explain the differences between so-called law in the books and law in action[67]. A straightforward definition of legal culture considers it a cluster of "ideas, values, attitudes, and opinions people in some society hold, with regard to law and the legal system"[68]. The concept of legal culture is not an easy one[69], and while explaining some mechanisms, it also involves some complications.

---

[64] See, just as examples, with reference to Italy: Pino (2007), p. 219; Bin (1992), spec. pp. 56 ff. With regard to the US: Aleinikoff (1987), p. 943; McFadden (1988), p. 585, as well as the earlier seminal work by Dworking (1978). See also the book of Alexy (2002), in which the author theorized a "law of balancing," according to which "[t]he greater the degree of non-satisfaction of, or detriment to, one principle, the greater must be the importance of satisfying the other" (p. 102).

[65] Judges, as members of a society, and therefore personally and not in their institutional role, bring their own values and are guided by social norms; see the work of Pocar (1997), p. 146. See the interesting sociological research by Bianchi d'Espinosa et al. (1970).

[66] Culture is here meant as follows: "a complex of conceptions, knowledge, ideas, norms, values, by which a population is inspired in its daily life"; cf. Ferrari (2004), p. 23. Gunnar Beck believes that "[j]udges have personal values and convictions but they also share many assumptions, values and beliefs as a result of common legal education and training, reinforced by a professional lifetime working in and with the law"; cf. Beck (2012), p. 39.

In my analysis, I shall refer to what Lawrence Friedman called "external legal culture." The author recognized a distinction between external legal culture (legal culture of the entire population) and internal legal culture (legal culture of the part of the population that carries out specialized legal activities); cf. Friedman (1975), p. 223. Judges clearly represent a part of the population with specialized knowledge in law, and which can therefore have its own internal legal culture. Nevertheless, what I would like to stress is the influence of external legal culture on their decisions and not on their own legal culture. For a criticism of Friedman's idea, see Engel (2012), pp. 77 ff.

[67] This antithesis can be traced back to the essential works of Roscoe Pound, founder of judicial realism. Just to have an idea of his interest in interdisciplinarity and, in particular, of his attention to the social framework, see Pound (1907), p. 911.

[68] Friedman (1994), p. 117 at 119. According to this author, "[e]very person has a "legal culture," just as every person has a general culture, and a social culture; every person has individual, unique traits, as distinctive as his or her fingerprints; but each person is at the same time part of a collective, a group, a social entity, and shares in the ideas and habits of that group."

[69] Cf. Nelken (2004), p. 1 at 2; of the same author, see also "Using Legal Culture: Purposes and Problems," in Nelken (2012), pp. 1 ff. (the entire volume is a critical reading of the use of the concept of "legal culture").

Every state seems to have its own culture[70], even though in the time of globalization it can seem obsolete to talk of cultures enclosed within national borders[71]. This is the reason why I believe it is possible to talk, for example, of an "Internet users' culture" or a "file-sharers' culture," which necessarily go beyond national boundaries. To this extent, a person can belong to different cultures at the same time[72]. Despite not being legal cultures, these cultures affect the legal culture of judges, since judges are part of the same social context.

After making these premises, I want to stress that the present analysis does not aim to indicate which methods of interpreting the law are correct. On the contrary, this paper is intended to be a first step towards investigating the interpretation and balancing made by judges, as it will emerge from the next paragraphs.

3 "Conception" and "Perception" of File Sharing

In the previous paragraphs, I referred to some statutory provisions applied in the cases examined. Now, I would like to give a synthetic picture of these regulations, trying to describe each system's policy on copyright and file sharing. In this work, I use the term "policy," meaning the main line of legislative intervention, the organic set of laws, and policies on a particular subject matter in a country[73]: in other words, this is what I like to call the "conception" of a legal system on a specific institution.

At the same time, I would like to illustrate the reflection of file sharing on the three societies (and vice versa), as well as the existence of so-called social norms in this area. Psychological and sociological researches will allow me to sketch also the "perception" of copyright and file sharing, which I intend as the cultural feeling and social attitude towards the institution.

The first thing worth mentioning is that, unlike what happens for informational privacy, copyright benefits from a number of international treaties, which somehow uniform the disciplines of the signatory countries. Clearly, the supranational intervention deeply affects national regulations, aligning them to a greater or a lesser

[70] National culture clearly changes with time passing: cf. Nelken (2004), p. 6.

[71] But see again Nelken (2004), p. 3. The author writes: "[w]hat does seem undeniable is the extent to which legal culture is becoming ever more what we could call 'relational'. With increasing contact between societies there are ever more opportunities to define one's own legal culture in terms of relationships of attraction to or repulsion from what goes on in other societies"; *Ibidem*, p. 7.

[72] Webber (2004), p. 27 at 31. According to Ferrari (2004), p. 23, there exist many different "subcultures" of different groups.

[73] In this short paper, I can only outline some aspects of copyright in the three countries examined. In addition to the works mentioned here, for a deeper understanding of their approach, see, for Italy, Musso (2008) and Greco and Vercellone (1974). For the USA, see Merges et al. (2012), Halpern (2010), and Nimmer and Nimmer (1978–2012). For the Canadian system, see Judge and Gervais (2011), Handa (2002), McKeown (2000), and Vaver (2000).

extent. This can drift domestic policies away from national cultures and perceptions[74].

If one looks at the body of norms protecting copyright, one notices that the Italian and the US systems have adopted, up to now[75], a more protective approach than the one taken by Canada. Some examples will clarify this statement.

First of all, as illustrated in the brief reconstruction of the cases, Italy and the US have legal provisions that punish file sharing as an illegal activity. These provisions are (also) the result of the implementation of WIPO treaties, which at the time of the decisions here considered had not yet been applied by Canada. Even if the WIPO Copyright Treaty does not explicitly sanction file sharing, it introduces a right to make available through its art. 6, which undoubtedly makes room for punishing file sharing as a "making available activity"[76]. In wider terms, copyright statutes in the US and Italy have undergone endless modifications in order to keep up with technologies that ease the infringement of copyright. Canada instead chose a softer approach.

The existence—in Italy and the US—of specific provisions that help the enforcement of copyright and that are conceived specifically and exclusively for this right (art. 156*bis*, l. 633/41, and §512 (h) US *Copyright Act*) indicates the strong will to protect this right[77]. Unlike what happens in these two countries, in Canada there is no specific provision, and consequently the normal procedure applicable to any

[74] The first of these international treaties is the Berne Convention for the Protection of Literary and Artistic Works, from 1886, which obligated the signatory countries to recognize the copyright of works of authors from other signatory countries (each of the three countries examined joined the Convention in different moments). Other more recent international treaties are the WIPO Treaties of 1996: The WIPO Copyright Treaty and the WIPO Performances and Phonograms Treaty. The latest document signed by a high number of countries was the Anti-Counterfeiting Trade Agreement (ACTA), including a number of provisions aimed at protecting intellectual property rights and, more precisely, relating to their enforcement. At the moment, ACTA has been ratified only by Japan and will come into force only when at least six signatory countries will ratify it. Protests against ACTA seem to be on the rise also as a way to contrast a sort of "Americanization" of the legal solution for copyright: cf. Gracz (2013b), p. 21 at 24. This eventual expansion of the American approach affects the peculiarities of national regulation for copyright.

[75] See infra for an account of the recent reform implemented in Canada, which will change the scenario at least partially.

[76] In addition, art. 8 of the same treaty introduces a "right to communicate to the public," providing that "authors of literary and artistic works shall enjoy the exclusive right of authorizing any communication to the public of their works, by wire or wireless means, including the making available to the public of their works in such a way that members of the public may access these works from a place and at a time individually chosen by them."

[77] These provisions are a consequence of WIPO Copyright Treaty art. 14, which in its second part states that the Parties have to ensure the existence in their law of enforcement procedures to permit effective action against infringement of the rights covered by the same Treaty, including expeditious remedies to prevent infringement.

kind of controversies, to protect any other right, applies[78]. Giving copyright holders a tool that is not contemplated for other rights—privacy included—gives a privilege to copyright, providing it with a "fast track"[79].

Another important issue, which is different but closely related to what is described here, is ISPs' liability. Once again, Canada finds itself in a different position when compared to Italy and the US: up to the implementation of Copyright Modernization Act of 2012, Canada lacked a specific discipline on this subject. Courts simply applied analogically what had already been defined for similar cases in the "analogical" era, stating, for the majority of cases, no ISP liability for users' illicit activities[80]. On the opposite end, both the US and Italy, more than a decade ago, implemented a specific discipline that considers a graduation of liability for ISPs, according to their concrete functions[81].

Clearly, most of the divergences registered between Canada and the other two countries come from the delayed implementation of WIPO Treaties made by Canada. Nevertheless, the interpretation given by Canadian courts is also the most open and most malleable among the three countries. The most evident signal of this "soft" attitude is the interpretation wave of the Canadian Supreme Court, which has been applying a lenient approach to copyright, which seems to be ongoing[82]. Hence, even though international treaties on copyright exist, differences

[78] As illustrated, the tool provided by the DMCA was ineffective for the purposes of the copyright holders in the specific cases. The consequence was that RIAA had to apply the "John Doe" process, placing the subsequent US cases on the same ground of the Canadian context.

[79] Different approaches apply also to other branches of copyright law, such as Digital Rights Management (DRM) or Technological Protection Measures (TPMs). The introduction of a regulation of DRM and TPMs in Canada was postponed for years, since it was part of the aforementioned bills that never became law. Changes in these fields came, once again, with the Copyright Modernization Act, for which see *supra* note n. 51.

[80] Canadian scholars seem to give this interpretation to the leading case *CCH Canadian Ltd. v. Law Society of Upper Canada*, [2004] S.C.R.; cf. Judge and Gervais (2011), p. 184. See also the so called "Tariff 22" case: *Society of Composers, Authors and Music Publishers of Canada (SOCAN) v. Canadian Association of Internet Providers*, [2002] 4 F.C. 3; *Society of Composers, Authors and Music Publishers of Canada (SOCAN) v. Canadian Association of Internet Providers*, [2004] 2 S.C.R. 427. After the implementation of the Copyright Modernization Act, ISPs' liability discipline is included in Section 31.1 of the Canadian Copyright Act.

[81] US: Online Copyright Infringement Liability Limitation Act (OCILLA), § 512 Copyright Act. Italy: art. 14–17, d.lgs. 70/03, implementing European Directive 2000/31. Reading the case law, it comes to light that in both countries, the limitations to ISPs' liability have been conceived as a sort of compensation for the collaboration of ISPs in the fight against so-called piracy and similar phenomena. See, for USA, *In re Charter Communications, Inc., Subpoena Enforcement Matter*, 393 F.3d 771, 773 (8th Cir., 2005) and *In re Verizon*, *supra* note 34 at 37. As for Italy, see Trib. Roma, ord., 9.2.2007, Riv. dir. ind., n. 4–5/2008, II, 328, with comment by De Cata (2008) (again in the context of the controversy between Peppermint and Wind).

[82] I am referring, for example, to *BMG Canada Inc. v. John Doe*, and *CCH Canadian Ltd. v. Law Society of Upper Canada* or, again, to the mentioned case "Tariff 22." More recently, five decisions taken by the Supreme Court in July 2012 (the so-called copyright pentalogy, namely, *Entertainment Software Association v. Society of Composers, Authors and Music Publishers of Canada*, 2012 SCC 34, [2012] 2 SCR 231; *Rogers Communications Inc. v. Society of Composers,*

persist among the countries, due to implementation and application of the treaties[83].

I chose these examples as clear explanations of the way in which the three countries approach copyright.

I shall now illustrate how societies perceive the same right.

The respect of copyright laws has been declining with the diffusion of digital technologies and the Internet. But despite what one might think, this decline is not a new phenomenon[84].

Many have been analyzing the reasons of this decline. Normally, when a statute is not respected, there can be numerous concurring causes. Two of these factors are "morality" and "legitimacy." The former concerns an individual's personal feeling about what is right and what is wrong. The latter, instead, is related to one's feeling that one should obey the law. When these factors are there, voluntary compliance is promoted. People do not uniformly consider breaking the law as morally wrong: attitudes vary according to different types of illegal behavior. The findings on the scarce compliance with intellectual property law mean the lack of a public perception that breaking intellectual property law is wrong. Law can have a great symbolic function if it is in line with public views about what is fair, but it loses this power as the formal law departs from public morality[85].

Legitimacy has instead a great advantage on morality: when something is perceived as legitimate, citizens obey the law even if they do not feel that it is consistent with their personal morality. Legitimacy is closely related to the procedures through which legal authorities make rules. A central issue relates to the fairness of decision-making authorities: together with fairness, another important characteristic is trustworthiness of legal authorities; when people feel that authorities are trying to be fair towards them, they are more willing to accept and obey rules[86].

Authors and Music Publishers of Canada, 2012 SCC 35, [2012] 2 SCR 283; *Society of Composers, Authors and Music Publishers of Canada v. Bell Canada*, 2012 SCC 36, [2012] 2 SCR 326; *Alberta (Education) v. Canadian Copyright Licensing Agency*, 2012 SCC 37, [2012] 2 SCR 345; *Re:Sound v. Motion Picture Theatre Associations of Canada*, 2012 SCC 38, [2012] 2 SCR 376) greatly sustained users' rights, somehow narrowing copyright. The decisions enlarged the province of fair dealing exceptions, which according to the Supreme Court must be interpreted liberally. The Justices also stated that technology is neutral: the different types of technology through which the content is obtained and enjoyed does not modify the system of protection of copyrighted works. Furthermore, copyright cannot be an obstacle for technological progress. For a deep overview of these five decisions, see Geist (2013).

[83] Clearly, only time will tell how Canadian courts will interpret the new Act.

[84] Tyler (1997), p. 219. On the perception of copyright see also: Content Production and Perception of Copyright: Aliprandi and Mangiatordi (2013).

[85] Tyler (1997), pp. 224–227, passim. The author makes the example of "fair use": in his opinion, the public seems to be operating within a sort of implicit standard of fair use, believing that some behaviors are acceptable while others are not. As another author notes, "law will not work as law unless it seems to people to embody the basic commitments of their society"; cf. Whitman (2004), p. 1153 at 1220 (emphasis in original).

[86] Tyler (1997), pp. 229–233, passim. This is part of what can be called "procedural justice," which influences the image of copyright and its obedience; cf. Gracz (2013b), pp. 23 ff.

In the field of intellectual property, there is the perception (or, rather, the awareness) that laws, for the most part, respond to lobbies' interests[87]. There is no reason to think that this mechanism applies to each of the three countries examined here. Nevertheless, up to now, it seems that Canada is the most "lobby-proof" or is lobbied to the same extent by both sides among the three systems. This can be one of the reasons why, to date, Canada has the softest of the three copyright policies analyzed[88].

The existence of lobbies in the field of copyright seems to be in contrast with the absence of a similar phenomenon in the field of privacy protection. Or, rather, despite the existence of associations defending privacy and anonymity, lobbying potentialities appear fewer both in terms of quality and quantity[89].

Another factor affecting the respect of copyright law is the existence of so-called social norms, going in the opposite direction of the legislative provisions[90]. "Social norms are the informal social and moral standards of a particular group which regulate the behavior of individuals within that group"[91].

These norms can affect the making and enforcement of laws and are themselves influenced by the birth and enforcement of laws[92]. Social norms prescribe or forbid some behaviors to single individuals or to groups of a given community and are considered binding for the community itself or at least for a part of it[93].

---

[87] It is sufficient to take into consideration the terms extension to which the USA Copyright Act has been subjected. It is no accident that the Copyright Term Extension Act of 1998 has been called "The Mickey Mouse Protection Act" due to the lobbying efforts made by Walt Disney Company. This Act is just a single example of a consolidated practice; cf. Litman (2009), p. 313 at 314. In one sense, this is probably true since the birth of copyright as we know it. See Izzo (2010), *passim*. The entire book aims to explain the interests behind the birth of copyright and *droit d'auteur*, which in the majority of cases were not authors' interests.

[88] As an example, see the questions posed by US copyright lobbies against the entrance of Canada into the "Trans-Pacific Partnership" (a free trade agreement that includes nations of both sides of the Pacific, which can be found at http://fpc.state.gov/documents/organization/145583.pdf): Geist (2012).

[89] Lobbies on privacy work in the opposite direction to the protection of privacy of users. Let us think of big companies such as Google, Yahoo!, Facebook, and so on, whose businesses are based on information as commodity.

[90] On this issue, see Schultz (2006), p. 202; Jensen (2003), p. 531. See Gracz (2013b), spec. pp. 23–26; and Gracz (2013a), p. 39 at 41 ff.

[91] Quotation from Neri (2005), p. 733 at 746. For a general review of sociological theories on social norms, see Horne (2001), pp. 3 ff.

In the last years, social norms on copyright infringement have been studied widely. I will here just mention them in order to illustrate my point. For further bibliography, see the contributions mentioned here.

[92] Schultz (2006), p. 202.

[93] See Pocar (1997), pp. 29 ff. A more complete definition given by Luciano Gallino: variously articulated and codified statement prescribing to an individual or to a community, as a stable element characterizing its culture or subculture (or another foreign culture or subculture to which it is exposed at that moment), the conduct or behavior that is the most appropriate (i.e., "right") to comply with. This prescription is made taking into account the subject's characteristics, the actions

Empirical studies have been carried out to demonstrate the existence of social norms on file sharing[94]. These researches show how, especially among youngsters, there is the sensation that sharing copyrighted content online is not a wrongful behavior[95]. On the contrary, there seems to be mutual support upon this practice within the Internet community[96]. In addition to this, let us consider the persistence of this phenomenon in which millions of people take part every day: they illicitly share copyrighted content online[97], despite antipiracy campaigns and legal actions begun in different ways by copyright holders[98].

This perception is homogeneous among the three considered systems, and it actually goes well beyond their national boundaries. Therefore, one could maybe talk of an "Internet culture," or of a "file-sharers" culture, considering the wide diffusion of the phenomenon[99].

It might be hypothesized that, in the decisions here briefly illustrated, judges were influenced by the social (negative) perception of copyright. Indeed, if we

she possibly endures, and the resources she has. It also prescribes, in many cases, which action must be avoided, even if this implies sacrifices or other nature costs: see Gallino (2006), *sub verbo* "Norma sociale."

[94] I shall take these empirical studies as "given": the aim of this work is not to judge methodological approaches and results of these researches. These studies are mainly concentrated on US society. However, I believe that their results can be generalized with reference to Canada and Italy. Indeed, file sharing is a common activity in each of the three systems, and P2P users can be conceived as a single "population." In addition to this, socioeconomic characteristics of the three countries are very close.

[95] Moore and McMullan (2004), p. 1. The results of this study show that 71 % of the participants in the survey do not consider equivalent sharing copyrighted works through peer-to-peer networks and stealing copyrighted material from "physical" shops. Aliprandi and Mangiatordi (2013).

[96] Wingrove et al. (2011), p. 261 at 271.

[97] Researches relating this phenomenon are innumerable. See as an example, for the Canadian context, Associated Press (2009) and CIPPIC. For the US, although recent researches show that file sharing is decreasing, it remains around 9 % of the population: see Graham (2011). See also the interesting study conducted by Columbia University: http://piracy.ssrc.org/wp-content/uploads/2011/11/AA-Research-Note-Infringement-and-Enforcement-November-2011.pdf.

[98] See again the contribution by Schultz (2006).

[99] In the last few years, the aversion to the regulations incrementing the protection of copyright has resulted in real political movements, such as the Pirate Party (born in Sweden as an antagonist to copyright and patents and then spread into many other countries also outside Europe). There have been also other reactions as an answer to the introduction of new statutes that would have incremented the protection of copyright: I am referring, for example, to the US bills SOPA (Stop Online Piracy Act) and PIPA (PROTECT IP Act) and to the displeasure they generated in the Internet context, not only among users but also among some important actors. These protests have taken place worldwide, moving away from the place where the contested statutes were born (this is clearly linked also to the inner structure of the web, where decisions taken in a given country can have a deep impact also in geographically very distant places). The movement against the adoption of ACTA by the European Union should also be mentioned. Both in the case of SOPA/PIPA and of ACTA, the countries stopped the process of adoption of the new legislation also due to the protests that had taken place. For a deeper understanding of these phenomena, see Milan and Hintz (2013), p. 7. See also, for a reconstruction of the anti-ACTA protests and their meaning, Gracz (2013b).

consider the existence of a common perception of copyright and of specific social norms, we can infer that judges can feel these factors as important and can therefore be influenced in their decisions.

4 "Conception" and "Perception" of Informational Privacy

As far as the concept of privacy is concerned, the first assertion that can be made is that the regulations of Italy and Canada are quite close to each other, while they deeply differ from the US legislation[100].

I shall start by saying that at the international level, there are no treaties or conventions on the regulation of privacy or data protection. The only international text that can be mentioned is the OECD Guidelines of 1981. Even though not binding, these guidelines were the basis for the regulation in Europe and in the US[101].

In fact, US legislation is based on a number of different acts that are normally not linked to each other: they are often a response to temporal needs or scandals[102] or are introduced to regulate specific and narrow sectors[103]. Hence, the protection of privacy is delegated to a fragmented, sectorial legislation, which is not able to face all the situations: the result is that, contrary to what happens in Canada or Italy, in

[100] I shall here only briefly illustrate the legislations of the three countries on data protection. For a deeper analysis, see the works already cited in this paper, as well as the following references. For Italy, see Pardolesi (2003), Giannantonio et al. (1999), and Buttarelli (1997). For a historical overview, see the works of Stefano Rodotà, among which Rodotà (1973). As for the USA, see Solove and Schwartz (2009, 2011) and Solove and Rotenberg (2003). For a historical perspective, see the masterpiece by Westin (1967). As far as Canada is concerned, see McIsaas et al. (2007) and Perrin et al. (2001).

[101] Solove and Rotenberg (2003), pp. 713–714. An effect of internationalization (or of globalization) is constituted by the measures that non-EU countries have taken in order to properly trade with the European Union. In fact, Directive 95/46 (arts. 25 and 26) provides that European citizens' personal data can be transferred to third countries only when they are adopting a regulation that is consistent with the protection aims of the EU or when they negotiate specific agreements. The first case is Canada: with the enhancement of PIPEDA; the second case is the US: they negotiated with the EU the so-called "safe harbors principles." A complete study on the influence of a country's privacy policy on another's is Bennett (1992), *passim*. See also the recent contribution of Schwartz (2013), p. 1966. Schwartz believes that the delicate balance between the US and EU approach made of safe harbors, model contractual clauses, and binding corporate rules could crumble if the current draft for the new European regulation on data protection should pass.

[102] Think of the Privacy Act of 1974, which was a sort of answer to the Watergate scandal: cf. Solove and Schwartz (2009), p. 304. For a list of all the statutes protecting privacy and their different subject matters, see Solove and Schwartz (2011), pp. 23–24.

[103] See, for example, the Telephone Consumer Protection Act of 1991, the CAN-SPAM Act of 2003, the Driver's Privacy Protection Act of 1994, the Children's Online Privacy Protection Act of 1998.

the US, in most daily situations implying privacy issues, there is no specific protection[104].

In addition, legislative interventions are mainly focused on the regulation of the intrusion of the state in citizens' lives (broadly speaking)[105].

Finally, there is a peculiar aspect of the conception of privacy in the US. Some rights and freedoms, which in other systems would be considered as autonomous, in the US are traced back to the right to privacy[106]. This right becomes therefore much broader and is able to cover a high variety of circumstances. This perspective strengthens and weakens at the same time the right itself: if, on one hand, privacy is strengthened by the fact that it is often pleaded to protect a situation, on the other hand its omnipresence makes it more evanescent, feebler[107]. Moreover, in the US, some freedoms, such as freedom of expression or of the press, are considered sacred: privacy has been sometimes treated as an obstacle to them[108].

The Canadian and Italian scenarios are different from the US one and are closer to one other[109]. Both systems have at least one important and all-embracing regulation on privacy (i.e., PIPEDA and the Italian *Codice in materia di protezione dei dati personali*). Canada also has the Privacy Act of 1985, relating to the public sector. Strict rules apply in both countries, where the data subject's consent is at the center of the regulation, and is meant as a cornerstone.

This approach is in contrast with the US one, where there is mostly an opt-out regime (vis-à-vis the Italian and Canadian opt-in)[110]. In an opt-out system, the

---

[104] Apart from a specific contract or from the existence of an action in tort (which is not present in each of the confederation states). Cf. Soma and Rynerson (2008), p. 48. For an analysis of the reasons for this sectorial approach and the consequences of the possible adoption of a federal omnibus law, see the close examination by Schwartz (2009), p. 902.

[105] As an example, take again the Privacy Act of 1974 or the Privacy Protection Act of 1980 or the Computer Matching and Privacy Protection Act of 1988. For some authors, this is the main difference between the US and the European approaches: Whitman (2004). Cf. also Rotenberg (2001) at par. 27; Pagallo (2008), pp. 70 ff.

[106] Think, for example, of the famous case *Roe v. Wade*, 410 U.S. 113 at 153 (1973). In that case, the Supreme Court struck down a Texas law on abortion. To reach this conclusion, the Court made an analysis of the right to privacy. The Court found that the Fourteenth Amendment due process clause was to be considered an expression of personal liberty, a right to privacy. Furthermore, it stated that "the Ninth Amendment's reservation of rights to the people, is broad enough to encompass a woman's decision whether or not to terminate her pregnancy"; cf. *Ibidem*, 153.

[107] According to Pagallo (2008), p. 99, it is (even) unclear if in the US privacy *is* a right (and a fundamental one) or if it is more an interest that, in relations between private parties, does not assume a value itself: it rather has to be funded or justified by something else (emphasis added). A critical view on the ability of courts and policy makers to recognize the interest beyond privacy is made by Solove (2006), p. 477 at 480.

[108] Whitman (2004), p. 1209; Bennett (1992), p. 137. As an example, see the well-known "Sidis case": *Sidis v. F-R Publishing Corp.*, 113 F.2d 806 (1940).

[109] According to Paul Schwartz, the current divide could further widen if the proposed Data Protection Regulation of January 2012 would come into force; see Schwartz (2013), pp. 18 ff.

[110] Many discussions have been made on the dichotomy opt-in/opt-out, and the debate is still going on, especially from an economic point of view. As mere examples, I shall here mention Sovern (1999), p. 1033; Bouckaert and Degryse (2006).

processing of personal data can be made regardless of the data subject's consent: it is the subject herself who explicitly opposes the processing.

Another sign of the juxtaposition between Canada and Italy on one side and the US on the other is the presence in the former two of a privacy authority with a fundamental role and provided with specific powers as a jurisdictional organ. In Italy, the authority is called *Garante per la protezione dei dati personali* and was introduced as l. 675/1996, implementing the European Directive 95/46. Its structure and powers were confirmed in the *Codice della Privacy* of 2003. As for Canada, the Privacy Commissioner was created in 1985 with the Privacy Act: when PIPEDA was introduced in 2001, the authority's powers were broadened in order to include the situations covered by PIPEDA itself.

The US does not have an autonomous authority specifically created for and devoted to the safeguard of privacy. Only in 2006, a dedicated division was created inside the Consumer Protection Bureau of the Federal Trade Commission, called "Division of Privacy and Identity Protection." Taking into account its recent introduction and the fact that this Bureau is only a division of a bigger institution, I believe that there is a different idea of privacy authority in the US when compared to the Italian and Canadian ones. This contributes to the overall picture of the US as the country, among the three examined, giving the least importance to the protection of privacy.

The existing divergences can be the reflection of a different perception of privacy as a value. Indeed, although privacy is a value that exists in every society, the way in which it is perceived and demonstrated changes deeply among cultures[111]. The European privacy legislation was undoubtedly a response to the needs of the internal market, at least in part[112]. On the other hand, US regulation on privacy remains focused on the relation between the state and citizens, with the aim of limiting the intrusion of the former in the lives of the latter. The Canadian approach can be told as a "middle-ground" between the Italian and the US ones:

[111] See, for example, the anthropological studies of Altman (1977), p. 66. Consider also the already mentioned work of Whitman (2004). The author argues that Europe demonstrates an idea of privacy based on the importance of human dignity and human rights. This is in contrast with an American idea of privacy as liberty, especially from the intrusion of the state. As another example of the diversity of perception of privacy, consider the scenario of Japan, even if not involved in the present work: Adams et al. (2009), p. 327.

[112] European Directive 46/95 mentions many times the need to protect personal data as a way to improve the functioning of the internal market (see, for example, recitals 3, 5, 8). Nevertheless, the important efforts of the European Council need to be taken into account. Indeed, it adopted two fundamental resolutions in the 1970s (one on September 26, 1973 relating to private databases and one on September 20, 1974 relating to public databases). The principles contained in these resolutions were included in Strasbourg Convention n. 108 of 28.1.1981, for the Protection of Individuals with regard to Automatic Processing of Personal Data (ratified in Italy with L. 21.2.1989, n. 98). The Convention aimed (art. 1) at ensuring in the territory of each state the respect of privacy for each individual with reference to the automatic processing of personal data. This Convention posed therefore a primary uniformity among the undersigning states, even though in reference to the sole automatic processing of personal data.

indeed, it places high importance on the aspect of dignity without forgetting the necessity of freedom from the state[113].

Empirical studies demonstrate that privacy regulation reflects, among other values, also the cultural perception of it[114]. More precisely, there is a correlation between the national regulation and the population's concerns on privacy[115]. When a state regulation is perceived as inadequate by citizens, it is plausible that their pressure affects normative interventions, giving an incentive to the production of new or better laws[116].

Even if the cultural aspect cannot be considered a sufficient factor in explaining the way in which every state created its privacy regulation, it is nevertheless highly probable that a correlation between the perception of the need for privacy protection and the way in which it is regulated exists.

This correlation might be perceived also by the same judges, both directly and indirectly: directly, since judges are part of a given society and live inside it, and indirectly, as a consequence of the policies adopted by the state in which the judges operate. These policies are in fact, in turn, born and/or shaped by citizens' perceptions.

5 An Interpretation for the Judicial Solutions Adopted

At the end of this brief paper, I shall try to give an interpretation of the solutions adopted by judges and to illustrate not only the aim of this work but also the future research developments I would like to follow.

As mentioned, my scope is to approach balancing methods under a sociocultural point of view. Classical legal comparison would underline the structural differences among legal systems and how these differences can affect judicial decisions. My approach instead aims at a further development, meaning investigating beyond appearance and formalities, taking into account the cultural context in which judges operate.

My hypothesis is that a circle of perceptions and thought exists. To put it simply, this circle springs from society, goes through lawmakers and policymakers, and reaches judges. Through the activity of judges, it goes back to society. But judges

---

113 Cf. Levin and Nicholson (2005), p. 357. The authors claim that Canadians are not concerned with disclosing their data; rather, they are concerned with the way in which their data are handled: see *Ibidem*, pp. 391–393.

114 Again, as already said, I shall not discuss the methodology or the results of these researches.

115 Bellman et al. (2004), p. 313 at 320. See also Whitman (2004), p. 1219, who states: "[p]rivacy law is not the product of logic [...] It is the product of local social anxieties and local ideals." Valuable information can be found also in the study by Milberg et al. (2000), p. 35.

116 Milberg et al. (2000), pp. 47–50.

themselves can be directly influenced also by the society in which they live[117]. There is a sort of virtuous circle among these factors, and judges are somewhere in the middle[118]. Legislative interventions can modify or at least influence the perception that society has of a particular issue. In the meantime, the same perception that citizens have of a given institution can be the source from which a regulation originates or be affected by it. The opposite is also true: judges, as well as the other lawmakers, can affect society, in this way closing the circle previously mentioned[119].

It must immediately be clarified that my hypothesis applies to judges meant as a category, even if I am well aware that there can be differences, and very strong ones, among them. However, what is relevant for this research is that judges, as one could intuitively argue, think and act exactly as all other individuals. This demonstrates that they are subject to the same cognitive biases[120] and that they can bring to the bench their personal beliefs, values, and interests[121]. This, in turn, means that they can be influenced by the culture in which they live. Some interdisciplinary studies that I shall now illustrate can help explain these statements.

Foremost, the concept of social norms needs to be considered. Judges are in fact exposed to the tension between what the law orders and what social norms prescribe, given that judges can share social norms as a "normal citizen"[122]. More precisely, cognitive researches showed that when decision makers—a category to which judges undoubtedly belong—believe that a social norm is particularly deep-rooted, they will find it difficult to apply a statute aimed at modifying that social norm[123].

---

[117] In fact, judges are clearly part also of the two categories (lawmakers/policy makers). From a sociological point of view, Friedman explains that a technological change (for example, the introduction of personal computers) does not automatically result in a change in the juridical order. Rather, the technological change modifies the social configuration, the way in which things are in a given society. This, in turn, modifies the way in which people see their society and what they expect from it. This finally modifies also their orientation toward law. See Friedman (1994), pp. 118–119. On the influence that end users have or can have on laws in the field of copyright, see the work of Gracz (2013b), spec. pp. 28 ff.

[118] Actually, the circle can also be "vicious." Think, for example, of those pieces of legislation enacted as a response to mass panic.

[119] It is with reference to this influence of judges on society that many legal theory researches have been developed. See, as an example, the work of Rosenberg (1991). The interpretation provided by law professionals supports legislation in a fundamental task: making adaptation of law to social change possible. According to Valerio Pocar, these two aspects of judicial change are always present at the same time. The prevalence of one over the other depends on the higher or lower congruence among laws, social norms, and culture, meaning on the greater or lesser sharing of common values. Cf. Pocar (1997), pp. 159–160.

[120] On this issue, see the following works: Sherwin (2010); Guthrie et al. (2007), p. 1; Guthrie et al. (2001), p. 777; Wrightsman (1999).

[121] Beck (2012), p. 42.

[122] Pocar (1997), p. 133.

[123] I am referring to the study by Kahan (2000), p. 607.

This stems from the fact that individuals are more willing to consider a conduct worthy of condemnation when other people also do. Conversely, when a norm is the result of lobbying, people tend to consider that norm not representative of a general consensus[124]. In this latter case, then, decision makers will be reluctant to apply the new law trying to modify the social norm[125].

Given the existence of social norms on Internet file sharing and considering judges as decision makers, the mechanism I just illustrated seems to also apply to them. Making reference to the concrete cases, this rule appears to apply to all the three contexts examined here, where social norms in contrast with/against copyright are anyway present, even if with different depth and nuances.

To support these statements, let us consider some psychological surveys: researchers proved that when judges have to decide a case where there is no law and must therefore identify the best outcome for the dispute, they apply a "moral reasoning"[126]. If the population of a given country demonstrates strong affection for a particular right—such as the right to privacy—and intense dislike for another right—as copyright—it appears morally better to support the former over the latter. Simply put: there is a cultural influence on judges[127].

What I defined as "conception" of each of the two rights also needs to be considered so as to better understand the solutions given in the cases. Canadian judges found themselves in front of a coherent, consistent, and strong regulation for the right to privacy and a weaker, even if consistent, regulation for copyright. In Italy, there is a solid and systematic regulation of the protection of personal data. Even though copyright enjoys high protection, privacy is more strongly protected than copyright[128]. In the US, judges found themselves *vis-a-vis* two very different legislative frameworks: on one side, there is a strong and complete protection of copyright; on the other, privacy is protected by a fragmented and incomplete legislation.

---

[124] According to Robert Ellickson, when a law is perceived to be the product of lobbyism relating to special interests, this law would not influence the existing norms on the same subject matter: people would not consider that law to be a credible product of a social consensus. See Ellickson (2001), p. 61.

[125] Kahan (2000), pp. 614–620, *passim*. There is a clear correlation between these cognitive theories and the theory of procedural justice.

[126] Cf. Sherwin (2010), p. 122. It is possible to consider also the research conducted by Lin (1999), p. 739, spec. pp. 769 ff. Even if the context is clearly very different, this study gives strength to my hypothesis that, when norms are not clearly defined, judges can more easily be affected by cultural perceptions.

[127] According to Pocar: "the interpretation of legal norms and their application is the result (also) of the effect of other social norms"; cf. Pocar (1997), p. 138. This reasoning, which appears to be evident when there are "open" norms, can anyway be applied every time a judge carries out her interpreting functions. Furthermore, in the word of G. Beck, "the protection of fundamental individual rights in almost all legal systems curbs the influence of public opinion on judicial decision-making"; cf. Beck (2012), pp. 35–36.

[128] In this sense, as mentioned, the Privacy Authority intervention in the lawsuit played a fundamental role.

These premises assumed, it is plausible that a judge can be influenced in giving prevalence to one or the other right, taking into consideration also the indications that the legislator *de facto* offers when supplying a different legal framework for the two rights.

Conception and perception strengthen each other: policies are the result *also* of social and cultural perceptions. When judges find it hard to reach a clear solution and need to apply general principles emerging from policies, they are taking inspiration from social and cultural perceptions. In this sense, judges can be the "mouth" through which societal feeling can be expressed.

It derives from this picture that plausibly the preponderance of one or the other right in the analyzed decisions is dictated by the influence that culture and perceptions, policy and conception can have—and indeed had—on judges.

At the end of this paper, I would like to stress again my research question. This work starts analyzing the reasons behind different judicial orientations in the systems compared.

Even though the paper is mostly a descriptive work, it also has a prescriptive implication, which is linked to the methodology applied: I believe that jurists should pay more attention to the social and cultural externalizations of law. Therefore, my aim is to illustrate the benefits of such an analysis in better understanding law and its functioning, especially in a comparative perspective.

The analysis offered and its possible developments do not pretend to explain the phenomenon in its entirety. The observations made here do not constitute a valid explanation for each judicial decision, nor do they intend to explicate the way in which judges should decide. Nor does the research claim that judges should approve and promote social perceptions[129].

Moreover, my analysis is not grounded on specific and direct empirical researches tailored to this work. It is rather based on works by scholars of other fields of study, on related subjects. This is a limit of my work of which I am conscious: further developments of this research include setting specific surveys to obtain empirical data, for a better understanding of the phenomena and for a stronger explanation of my hypothesis.

The cultural influence I try to demonstrate is anyway only one of the factors that can affect judicial decisions. It would be *naïve* to consider cultural influence as the sole factor having an effect on those decisions or to believe that this is the only interpretation for the balancing of rights.

The aim of this study is to foster a discussion and to start tracing a path from a methodological point of view: a path that seems promising. Shedding some light on the relationships between society and judges is a way to better understand this phenomenon and to offer an alternative reading for the balancing of rights, which at the same time would be complementary to the predominant interpretations.

---

[129] I share the vision of an Italian scholar, who some years ago wrote roughly what follows: "I do not know if a theoretical analysis needs to be able to give solutions to the problems analyzed: certainly, its task is to clarify the real nature of these problems and, when possible, to dissolve them. Sometimes a theoretical analysis can also show that a given problem does simply not have a solution or that the rise of a certain problem is inevitable." Cf. Pino (2007), p. 221.

References

Adams AA, Murata K, Orito Y (2009) The Japanese sense of information privacy. AI Soc 24:327

Aleinikoff TA (1987) Constitutional law in the age of balancing. Yale Law J 96:943

Alexy R (2002) A theory of constitutional rights (trans: Rivers J). Oxford University Press, Oxford

Aliprandi S, Mangiatordi A (2013) An Analysis of habits and beliefs of Internet users. Eur J Law Technol 4. http://ejlt.org//article/view/257

Altman I (1977) Privacy regulation: culturally universal or culturally specific? J Soc Issues 33:66

Ashdown GA (1981) Legitimate expectation of privacy. Vand Law Rev 34:1289

Associated Press (2009) Canada on U.S. copyright piracy watch list. CBSnews.com, 30 April 2009. http://www.cbc.ca/news/technology/story/2009/04/30/copyright-piracy.html

Backerman R (2008) How the RIAA litigation process works. http://beckermanlegal.com/howriaa.htm

Beck G (2012) The legal reasoning of the Court of Justice of the EU. Oxford-Portland

Bellman S, Johnson EJ, Kobrin SJ, Lhose GL (2004) International differences in information privacy concerns: a global survey of consumers. Inf Soc 20:313

Bennett CJ (1992) Regulating privacy. Data protection and public policy in Europe and the United States. Cornell University Press, Ithaca

Bianchi D'Espinosa L, Celoria M, Greco E, Odorisio R, Petrella G, Pulitanò D (1970) Valori socio-culturali della giurisprudenza. Laterza, Bari

Bin R (1992) Diritti e argomenti. Il bilanciamento degli interessi nella giurisprudenza costituzionale. Giuffrè, Milano

Black HC (1979) Black's Law Dictionary. St Paul

Blengino C, Senor MA (2007) Il caso "Peppermint": il prevedibile contrasto tra protezione del diritto d'autore e tutela della privacy nelle reti peer to-peer. Dir inf e informatica 4–5:835

Bouckaert J, Degryse H (2006) Opt in versus opt out: a free-entry analysis of privacy policies. CESifo Working Paper No. 1831, October 2006

Brimsted K, Chesney G (2008) The ECJ's judgement in Promusicae: the unintended consequences – music to the ears of copyright owners or a privacy headache for the future? A comment. Comput Law Secur Rep 24:275

Buttarelli G (1997) Banche dati e tutela della riservatezza. La privacy nella società dell'informazione. Milano

Caso R (2007) Il conflitto tra copyright e privacy nelle reti Peer to Peer: in margine al caso Peppermint – Profili di diritto comparato. Dir Internet 5:471

Caso R (2008) Il conflitto tra diritto d'autore e protezione dei dati personali: appunti dal fronte euro-italiano. Dir Internet 5:459

CIPPIC. How widespread is music file-sharing? http://www.cippic.ca/en/file-sharing#faq_how-widespread

Collin SMH (2004) Dictionary of computing. Peter Collin Publishing, London

Coudert F, Werkers E (2008) In the aftermath of the Promusicae case: how to strike the balance? Int J Law Inf Technol 18:50

De Cata M (2008) Il caso "Peppermint". Ulteriori riflessioni anche alla luce del caso "Promusicae". Riv dir industriale 4–5:404

Deazly R, Kretschmer M, Bently L (2010) Privilege and property. Essays on the history of copyright. Open Book Publishers, Cambridge

Di Mico L (2010) Il rapporto tra diritto di autore e diritto alla riservatezza: recenti sviluppi nella giurisprudenza comunitaria. Il diritto di autore 1:1

Dutcher TA (2005) A discussion of the mechanics of the DMCA safe harbor and subpoena power, as applied in RIAA v. Verizon Internet Services. Santa Clara Comput High Technol Law J 21:493

Dworking R (1978) Taking rights seriously. Harvard University Press, Cambridge

Ellickson RC (2001) The evolution of social norms: a perspective from the legal academy. In: Hechter M, Opp KD (eds) Social norms. Russell Sage Foundation, New York, p 61

Engel DM (2012) The uses of legal culture in contemporary socio-legal studies. In: Nelken D (ed) Using legal culture. Wildy, Simmonds and Hill Publishing, London
Ferrari V (2004) Diritto e società. Elementi di sociologia del diritto. Bari
Flaherty DH (1991) On the utility of constitutional rights to privacy and data protection. Case Western Res Law Rev 41:831
Foglia G (2007) La privacy vale più del diritto d'autore: note in materia di filesharing e di sistemi peer-to-peer. Dir industriale 6:585
Friedman L (1975) The legal system: a social science perspective. Russell Sage Foundation, New York
Friedman L (1994) Is there a modern legal culture? Ratio Juris 7:117
Gallino L (2006) Dizionario di Sociologia. Torino
Gambini M (2009) Diritto d'autore e tutela dei dati personali: una difficile convivenza in Rete. Giur it 2:509
Geist M (2012) US copyright lobby wants Canada out of TPP until new laws passed, warns of no cultural exceptions, 16 January 2012. http://www.michaelgeist.ca/content/view/6243/125/
Geist M (ed) (2013) The copyright pentalogy. How the Supreme Court of Canada shook the foundations of Canadian Copyright Law. University of Ottawa Press, Ottawa. http://www.press.uottawa.ca/sites/default/files/9780776620848.pdf
Giannantonio E, Losano MG, Zeno Zencovich V (eds) (1999) La tutela dei dati personali. Commentario alla L. 675/1996. Cedam, Padova
Gorski D (2005) The future of the Digital Millennium Copyright Act (DMCA) subpoena power on the internet in light of Verizon cases. Rev Litigation 24:149
Gracz K (2013a) Bridging the gaps between social and legal norms concerning the protection of intellectual and artistic creations: on the crisis of copyright law in the digital era. J World Intellect Prop 16:39
Gracz K (2013b) On the role of copyright protection in the information society. JIPITEC 4:21
Graham L (2011) With Limewire shuttered, peer-to-peer music file sharing declines precipitously. NPD.com, 23 March 2011. www.npd.com/press/releases/press_110323.html
Greco P, Vercellone P (1974) I diritti sulle opere dell'ingegno, in Trattato di diritto civile italiano redatto da diversi giureconsulti sotto la direzione di Filippo Vassalli. Torino
Groussot X (2008) Rock the KaZaA: another clash of fundamental rights. Common Mark Law Rev 45:1745
Guthrie C, Rachlinski JJ, Wistrich AJ (2001) Inside the judicial mind. Cornell Law Rev 86:777
Guthrie C, Rachlinski JJ, Wistrich AJ (2007) Blinking on the bench: how judges decide cases. Cornell Law Rev 93:1
Halpern SW (2010) Copyright law: protection of original expression. Carolina Academic Press, Durham
Handa S (2002) Copyright law in Canada. Butterworths, Markham
Horne C (2001) Sociological perspectives on the emergence of norms. In: Hechter M, Opp KD (eds) Social norms. Russell Sage Foundation, New York, p 3
Izzo U (2010) Alle origini del copyright e del diritto d'autore. Tecnologia, interessi e cambiamento giuridico. Carocci, Roma
Jensen C (2003) The more things change, the more they stay the same: copyright, digital technology, and social norms. Stanford Law Rev 56:531
Judge EF, Gervais DJ (2011) Intellectual property: the law in Canada. Carswell, Toronto
Kahan D (2000) Gentle Nudges vs. Hard Shoves: solving the sticky norms problem. Univ Chic Law Rev 67:607
Kao A (2004) RIAA v. Verizon: applying the subpoena provision of the DMCA. Berkeley Technol Law J 19:405
Kerr I, Cameron A (2006) Nymity, P2P & ISPs: lessons from BMG Canada Inc. v. John Doe. In: Standburg KJ, Stan Raicu D (eds) Privacy and technologies of identity: a cross disciplinary conversation. New York, p 269

Kerr I, Steeves V, Lucock C (eds) (2009) Lessons from the identity trail: anonymity, privacy and identity in a networked society. Oxford University Press, New York
Lafrance M (2008) Copyright law in a Nutshell. Thomson West, St Paul, pp 161–162
Levin A, Nicholson MJ (2005) Privacy law in the United States, the EU and Canada: the Allure of the Middle Ground. Univ Ottawa Law Technol J 2:357
Libeu A (1985) What is a reasonable expectation of privacy? Western State Univ Law Rev 12:849
Lin TE (1999) Social norms and judicial decisionmaking: examining the role of narratives in same-sex adoption cases. Columbia Law Rev 99:739
Litman J (2009) The politics of intellectual property. Cardozo Arts Entertainment Law J 27:313
Marchetti P, Ubertazzi LC (2012) Commentario breve alla leggi su proprietà intellettuale e concorrenza. Cedam, Padova
McFadden PM (1988) The balancing test. Boston College Law Rev 29:585
McIsaas B, Shields R, Klein K (2007) The law of privacy in Canada. Carswell, Toronto
McKeown JS (2000) Fox on Canadian law of copyright and industrial designs. Thomson Carswell, Scarborough
McNairn CHH, Scott AK (2001) Privacy law in Canada. Butterworths, Markham
Merges RP, Menell PS, Lemley MA (2012) Intellectual property in the new technological age. Wolter Kluwer, New York
Milan S, Hintz A (2013) Networked collective action and the institutionalized policy debate: bringing cyberactivism to the policy arena? Policy Internet 5:7
Milberg SJ, Smith HJ, Burke SJ (2000) Information privacy: corporate management and national regulation. Organ Sci 11:35
Moore R, McMullan EC (2004) Perceptions of peer-to-peer file sharing among university students. J Crim Justice Popular Cult 11:1. http://www.albany.edu/scj/jcjpc/vol11is1/moore.pdf
Musso A (2008) Diritto di autore sulle opere dell'ingegno letterarie e artistiche. Zanichelli, Bologna
Nelken D (2004) Using the concept of legal culture. Aust J Legal Philos 29:1
Nelken D (2012) Using legal culture: purposes and problems. In: Nelken D (ed) Using legal culture. Wildy, Simmonds and Hill Publishing, London
Neri G (2005) Sticky fingers or sticky norms? Unauthorized music downloading and unsettled social norms. Georgetown Law J 93:733
Nimmer MB, Nimmer D (1978–2012) Nimmer on copyright: a treatise on the law of literary, musical and artistic property, and the protection of ideas. Matthew Bender, New York
Pagallo U (2008) La tutela della privacy negli Stati Uniti d'America e in Europa. Giuffrè, Torino
Pardolesi R (ed) (2003) Diritto alla riservatezza e circolazione dei dati personali. Giuffrè, Milano
Perrin S, Black HH, Flaherty DH, Murray Rankin T (2001) The Personal Information Protection and Electronic Documents Act: an annotated guide. Irwin Law, Toronto
Pino G (2007) Conflitto e bilanciamento tra diritti fondamentali. Una mappa dei problemi. Ragion Pratica
Pocar V (1997) Il diritto e le regole sociali. Lezioni di sociologia del diritto. Guerini Scientifica, Milano
Pound R (1907) The need of a sociological jurisprudence. Annu Rep Am Bar Assoc 31:911
Raynolds K (2005) One Verizon, two Verizon, three Verizon, more? – a comment: RIAA v. Verizon and how the DMCA subpoena power became powerless. Cardozo Arts Entertainment Law J 23:343
Reyman J (2009) The rhetoric of intellectual property: copyright law and the regulation of digital culture. Routledge, New York
Rodotà S (1973) Elaboratori elettronici e controllo sociale. Il Mulino, Bologna
Rosenberg G (1991) The hollow hope: can courts bring about social change? University of Chicago Press, Chicago
Rotenberg M (2001) Fair information practices and the architecture of privacy (what Larry doesn't get). Stanford Technol Law Rev 2001:1. http://stlr.stanford.edu/2001/02/fair-information-practices-and-the-architecture-of-privacy

Schultz MF (2006) Copynorms: copyright and social norms. In YU PK (ed) Intellectual property and information wealth. Westport, p 202
Schwartz PM (2009) Preemption and privacy. Yale Law J 118:902
Schwartz PM (2013) The EU–US privacy collision: a turn to institutions and procedures. Harv Law Rev 126:1966. http://www.harvardlawreview.org/media/pdf/vol126_schwartz.pdf
Scorza G (2007) Il conflitto tra copyright e privacy nelle reti Peer to Peer: il caso Peppermint – Profili di diritto interno. Dir Internet 5:466
Sherwin E (2010) Features of judicial reasoning. In: Klein D, Mitchell G (eds) The psychology of judicial decision making. New York, p 122
Sirotti Gaudenzi A (2012) Il nuovo diritto d'autore. La tutela della proprietà intellettuale nella società dell'informazione. Maggioli editore, Sant'Arcangelo di Romagna
Solove DJ (2006) A taxonomy of privacy. Univ Pa Law Rev 154:477
Solove DJ, Rotenberg M (2003) Information privacy law. Aspen, New York
Solove DJ, Schwartz PM (2009) Privacy, information, and technology. Wolters Kluwer, New York
Solove DJ, Schwartz PM (2011) Information privacy law. Aspen, New York
Soma JT, Rynerson SD (2008) Privacy law in a Nutshell. Thomson West, St Paul
Sovern J (1999) Opting in, opting out, or no options at all: the fight for control of personal information. Wash Law Rev 74:1033
Terracina D (2007) Lucro e profitto nella giurisprudenza della Corte di Cassazione in materia di violazione del diritto d'autore e dei diritti connessi. Dir Internet 3:259
Trotta A (2008) Il traffico telefonico fra la tutela del diritto d'autore e quella della privacy. Dir Industriale 1:76
Tyler TR (1997) Compliance with intellectual property laws: a psychological perspective. N Y Univ J Int Law Policy 29:219
Vaver D (2000) Copyright law. Irwin Law, Toronto
Warren SD, Brandeis LD (1890) The right to privacy. Harv Law Rev 4:193
Webber J (2004) Culture, legal culture and legal reasoning: a comment on Nelken. Aust J Legal Philos 29:27
Westin A (1967) Privacy and freedom. New York
Whitman JQ (2004) The two western cultures of privacy: dignity versus liberty. Yale Law J 113:1153
Wilkins G (1987) Defining the "Reasonable Expectation of Privacy": an emerging tripartite analysis. Vand Law Rev 40:1077, 1089
Wilkinson MA (2008) Battleground between new and old orders: control conflicts between copyright and personal data protection. In Gendreau Y (ed) Emerging intellectual property paradigm: perspectives from Canada. Cheltenham, p 227
Wingrove T, Korpas AL, Weisz V (2011) Why were millions of people not obeying the law? Motivational influences on non-compliance with the law in the case of music piracy. Psychol Crime Law 17:261
Wrightsman LS (1999) Judicial decision making: is psychology relevant? Wolters Kluwer, New York

Academic Freedom, Copyright, and Access to Scholarly Works: A Comparative Perspective

Valentina Moscon

Contents

Abstract The right to academic freedom protected both under international treaties and national constitutions is at the very heart of social, cultural, and economic development. As far as scientific research and teaching are concerned, copyright has to be considered within the context of a proper balancing of rights. This issue will be addressed taking into account the traditional publication model in light of the peculiarities of scientific research, including the mechanisms of evaluating research and the relevant stakeholders's interests that differ from those characterizing other sectors of content production. We will analyze whether the current practice in academic content dissemination and legal framework are compliant with academic freedom principles, considering the role of copyright in science. Since effective protection of academic freedom also depends on the possibility of access to knowledge, we will examine whether and how the open access model can achieve a proper balance between the rights at stake, looking at legal instruments recently issued by Italian, German, and US legislatures.

V. Moscon (✉)
Faculty of Law, University of Trento, Trento, Italy
e-mail: valentina.moscon@unitn.it

R. Caso, F. Giovanella (eds.), *Balancing Copyright Law in the Digital Age*,
DOI 10.1007/978-3-662-44648-5_4

Proposal for copyright provisions tailored to specific needs of the scientific field will be considered as well.

1 Introduction

Construing copyright law as a tool to serve the common good, creative results are something that should be bestowed on society.[1] In keeping with this, Article 27 of the Universal Declaration of Human Rights (hereinafter UDHR) gives everyone "the right freely to participate in the cultural life of the community, to enjoy the arts and to share in scientific advancement and its benefits."[2] Needless to say, granting access to knowledge while balancing author's and users' interests fosters the knowledge ecosystem[3] that is based on the "incremental and transformative" nature of information.[4] This is especially true in the academic field where the *rationale* of copyright for several reasons must be considered with even greater attention being paid to the peculiarity of scientific production.[5] Copyright assumes a prominent role in the circulation of scientific knowledge and information since these are embedded in scholarly works and databases. However, the relevant stakeholders's interests significantly differ from those in other sectors of content production. Therefore, in order to design a balanced regulation in this field, a number of peculiarities need to be considered. First, the academic community is governed by a core of specific social values such as "universalism, disinterestedness, originality, organized scepticism and communalism."[6] According to them, what matters most of all is the advancement of scientific knowledge, which must be evaluated by both individuals and the scientific community through open exchange of ideas and intellectual debate.[7] Re-use of knowledge and knowledge sharing are at the heart of

[1] Hilty (2006), p. 103.

[2] At the international level, the need for societal development inspires the Agreement on Trade-Related Aspects of Intellectual Property Rights (TRIPS Agreement) April 15, 1994, Art. 28.1 Marrakesh Agreement Establishing the World Trade Organization, Annex 1C, Legal Instruments—Results of the Uruguay Round, vol. 31, 33 I.L.M. 81 (1994); Word Intellectual Property Organization Copyright Treaty, December 20, 1996, 36 I.L.M. 65 (1997).

[3] The term "ecosystem," as used in this paper, refers broadly to the system that facilitates the conception, production, dissemination, commercialization, consumption, usage, and enjoyment of creative works in society. See Kaufman (2012).

[4] See Netanel (2008); Torremans (2008), p. 197. From a "law and economics" perspective, see Farell and Shapiro (2004); Landes and Posner (2003), pp. 66 ff. In U.S. case law, see *Campbell v. Acuff-Rose Music, Inc.*, 510 *U.S.* 569, 575 (1994).

[5] See Reichman and Okediji (2012), p. 1362.

[6] See Merton (1942), p. 1973.

[7] Robertson (1977–1978), p. 1204.

scientific methods. Furthermore, scientists have slightly different aims from those who first conceived the utilitarian approach to copyright.[8] The incentive for academic authors to publish research results is mostly reputational rather than economic,[9] bestowing only indirect gains in the way of peer esteem and professional advancement.[10] In fact, ever since the first scientific journals were founded (in the seventeenth century), publishers have rarely paid authors for their articles.[11] This is also where the scientific publishing industry is distinguished from the traditional one,[12] as the interests of commercial publishers and other information providers differ from those of scholarly authors, with the former usually pursuing a profit-maximizing strategy. Furthermore, the vast majority of academic research is publicly funded. Indeed, rewarding scientists *ex ante* and ensuring job security[13] is aimed at allowing development in all fields of science,[14] achieving objective findings and disseminating these whenever and however researchers like.[15] This is closely bound up with the protection of academic freedom that, as we are about to see, is promoted also by granting broad access, free dissemination, and re-use of scientific outcomes. In this respect, copyright law and academic freedom are in a robust and complex relationship that would likely need to be settled considering the nature of the various rights at stake.[16] When dealing with scientific knowledge and academic freedom, what is relevant is the extent to which copyright is considered a right constitutionally protected and the role of copyright in fostering academic freedom as a social interest. To this aim, whether the interest of academic authors in "owning" their works, and commercially exploiting them has an impact on other collective interests, such as accessing and sharing scientific findings, is a relevant question.

In most EU Member States, unlike in the US, copyright is not itself listed as a constitutional right. However, it does enjoy protection as being attached to other fundamental rights. Moreover, at European level the Charter of Fundamentals

---

[8] Some scholars argue in favor of abolishing copyright; see Shavell (2010), p. 301; Breyer (1970), pp. 281–355. See also Mueller-Langer and Scheufer (2013).

[9] Some form of compensation may be provided for certain genres, such as teaching material, handbooks, etc.

[10] See Suber (2012), pp. 29 ff.

[11] There is no empirical evidence that copyright increases authors' earnings. See Towse (2001).

[12] Guedòn (2001).

[13] This is also pointed out in the US "Statement on Academic Freedom and Tenure": "Tenure is a means to certain ends; specifically: (1) freedom of teaching and research and of extramural activities, and (2) a sufficient degree of economic security to make the profession attractive to men and women of ability. Freedom and economic security, hence, tenure, are indispensable to the success of an institution in fulfilling its obligations to its students and to society."

[14] See Tartari and Breschi (2012), p. 1117.

[15] Ludington (2011), pp. 397–432.

[16] On this point, see Hilty et al. (2009), p. 309. According to the EU Commission, the mentioned authors speak about "a Fifth Freedom" that would set a new paradigm regarding the free circulation of knowledge. This is particularly relevant for scientific information and knowledge.

Rights of the European Union (2000/C 364/01—CFREU—Article 17)[17] expressly protects intellectual property (IP), referring to it as "property" ("Intellectual property shall be protected" as a "property right"). Nevertheless, neither the CFREU nor the Court of Justice of the European Union (CJEU) defines any ranking among rights and liberty as being protected,[18] delegating to national authorities and the courts the task to "... strike a fair balance between the protection of copyright and the protection of the fundamental rights of individuals [...]."[19] What "property" refers to in the European framework with regard to copyright law should be clarified also in light of the principle of "proportionality" as affirmed in Article 52 (1) of the CFREU and in several EU Directives.[20] Nevertheless, the legislature currently seems to care more about right holders' than users' interests. For example, the InfoSoc Directive is based on the general assumption that, particularly in the online environment, right holders need effective and rigorous control over widespread forms of mass usage. While this paradigm may be more adequately employed in the areas of art and entertainment, it is applied in an unmodified way to the area of scientific research when the Internet offers the technological opportunities to constitute a comprehensive representation of knowledge.[21]

In this picture, one of the first questions we should answer is whether in today's scholarly publishing environment the traditional proprietary model complies with academic freedom, including the freedom of authors to choose where, when, and how to publish their works while accessing previous research results. In this respect, we may also take into account current mechanisms of evaluating research and scientific careers including citation rules, that have a significant impact on scholarly publishing. At least two aspects are to be considered here: first, researchers "have to" publish only in journals that are deemed as prestigious; second, in exchange for the reputation associated with publication in a prominent journal, scientific authors are willing to freely hand over to publishers their

[17] Article I, Section 8, Clause 8 of the US Constitution, known as the Copyright Clause, empowers the United States Congress to secure "for limited times to Authors and Inventors the exclusive Right to their respective Writings and Discoveries."

[18] For an introduction on the balancing of fundamental rights with respect to intellectual property, see Brown (2012).

[19] CJEU, 16 February 2012, case C-360/10 (Netlog), para 43; CJEU 24 November 2011, case C-70/10 (Scarlet), para 45.

[20] The principles of proportionality and "fair balancing" are mentioned in several decisions of the Court of Justice of the European Union (CJEU) dealing with the clash between copyright and fundamental rights. See, *inter alia*, CJEU, 18 July 2007, case C-275/06 (Promusicae); CJEU 24 November 2011, case C-70/10 (Scarlet); CJEU, 16 February 2012, case C-360/10 (Netlog); CJEU, 13 February 2014, case C-466/12 (Svensson and Others). For an extensive look at this subject in this book, see the chapters by C. Sganga and G. Spedicato, this volume.

[21] Hilty et al. (2009).

exclusive rights in a work under copyright law. This leads to the "propertization" of scientific findings.

In contradistinction to the traditional scholarly publishing model relying on protections restricting access and imposing high costs to users, the open access model arises, (hereinafter OA) aiming at disseminating research outputs and granting free access to information. OA is developing also through policies and legislative tools raising a number of questions: on one hand, whether the OA itself fulfills academic freedom principles and, on the other, whether OA mandates comply with freedom of scientific research.

We will thus address the above-mentioned issues focusing in the next section on the relationships between academic freedom and intellectual property in the German, Italian, and US legal systems. In the third section, we will take a look at the traditional scholarly publishing model and the way in which technological development have changed communication methods.

We will then examine whether and how open access may endorse academic freedom, also analyzing the legal instruments recently issued by some legislatures, including the ones in Italy, Germany and the US. In disseminating research outputs and granting free access to information, OA indeed offers new standards and publishing models assuming that academic authors for the most part are concerned with moral rights. Since several communication channels in science might foster academic freedom, we defend the idea of a more open access to research and also endeavor to point out that the "open" and "proprietary" models are not mutually exclusive. On this basis, some proposal for copyright provisions tailored to the specific needs of the academic field will be considered in conclusion.

2 Academic Freedom and Intellectual Property: Clash or Merge?

Freedom of arts and science and the right to teach them are considered a means of ensuring cultural and social growth.[22] While academic freedom is recognized as a fundamental right by several national constitutions and international treaties, there is little consensus as to what academic freedom means: What rights, responsibilities, and necessary limitations it entails. In the following pages, we will try to define it by describing the connections with IP rights in the light of German, Italian, and US laws.

[22] See Dershowitz (2005).

The content of this right as well as of its legal protection is closely connected with freedom of thought, expression, and information[23]; the right to education,[24] to participate in cultural life,[25] to enjoy the benefits of scientific progress and its application.[26] Academic freedom, however, enjoys proper protection relating to both researchers' independence from any external influence and the autonomy of research entities and universities from political and economic power. These features help to reinforce one another: institutional autonomy fortifies the individual one and vice versa.[27]

Academic freedom in its broader meaning, which includes freedom of research and teaching, serves the common good by fostering independent thought and expression among researchers and students, who are free to spread ideas, arguments, and conclusions that may be reached in any studies or investigations.[28] Objectivity, systematic research and scientific rigor are all aspects of this freedom, which are strengthened by communication of scientific outcomes.[29] Indeed, starting from international law, a first concern with regard to scientific research has to do with access to findings. Article 27 (1) of the UDHR mentioned above focuses on the beneficiaries of science, as does Article 15 (1–3) of the International Covenant on Economic, Social and Cultural Rights (1966), which states that "(1) The States Parties to the present Covenant recognize the right of everyone: [. . .] (b) to enjoy the benefits of scientific progress and its applications; (c) To benefit from the protection of the moral and material interests resulting from any scientific, literary or artistic production of which he is the author [. . .] (3) The States Parties to the present Covenant undertake to respect the freedom indispensable for scientific research and creative activity."

In the European context, Article 13 of the CFREU strengthens the international framework establishing that "The arts and scientific research shall be free of constraint. Academic freedom shall be respected." According to the explanatory memorandum[30] of the CFREU, that right "is deduced primarily from the right to freedom of thought and expression," and it may be subject only to the limitations authorized by Article 10 of the European Convention on Human Rights (ECHR).

The ECHR does not contain any explicit definition and guarantee of academic freedom. However, as like artistic freedom, academic freedom enjoys the protection

---

[23] As Connolly observes, "academic freedom is a kind of cousin of freedom of speech" Connolly (2000), p. 71. In the same direction, Daughtrey (1991), pp. 213–271. See also Turner (1988).

[24] International Covenant on Economic Social and Cultural Rights (ICESCR), Article 13.

[25] ICESCR, Article 15 (1)(a). A right to share in cultural life is also found in Article 30, Convention of the Rights of Persons with Disabilities, 2007.

[26] ICESCR Article 15 (1)(b).

[27] For a comparative analysis of academic freedom in terms of both individual and institutional independence, see Karran (2007).

[28] See Robertson (1977–1978), p. 1204.

[29] Monotti and Ricketson (2003).

[30] "Explanations relating to the charter of fundamental rights" (2007/C 303/02).

provided by the above mentioned Article 10 (1) ECHR "...This right shall include freedom to hold opinions and to receive and impart information and ideas without interference by public authority and regardless of frontiers...." According to paragraph 2,[31] this freedom is limited only to the extent reasonable in the public interest.

Academic freedom also figures prominently in the activities of the European Council. In 2000, the Committee of Ministers adopted a recommendation underlining aspects of academic freedom,[32] while the Parliamentary Assembly of the Council of Europe in 2006 adopted a recommendation exhorting the Committee of Ministers to "strengthen its work on academic freedom and university autonomy as a fundamental requirement of any democratic society."[33] Of practical importance in the EU are Articles 179–190 of the Treaty on the Functioning of the European Union (TFEU), according to which the EU is required to support research through funding policies. Pursuant to Article 179 TFEU, European research funding may promote the establishment and strengthening of the "European Research Area" in which research results may be freely and quickly shared.

At the European national level, academic freedom, with a view to fostering scientific progress and transferring the benefits of this to society, is usually afforded separate protection in the Constitution, as is the case in both the German[34] and the Italian[35] Constitutions (Germany: *Gruendgesetz für die Bundes Republik Deutschland*—GG; Italy: *Costituzione della Repubblica Italiana*—Cost).[36] By contrast, the US Constitution does not expressly mention that right, which is, however, certainly recognized by scholars and case law as a specific aspect of freedom of expression in the wider context.

---

[31] See Article 10 (2) ECHR: "The exercise of these freedoms, since it carries with it duties and responsibilities,may be subject to such formalities, conditions, restrictions or penalties as are prescribed by law and are necessary in a democratic society, in the interests of national security, territorial integrity or public safety, for the prevention of disorder or crime, for the protection of health or morals, for the protection of the reputation or rights of others, for preventing the disclosure of information received in confidence, or for maintaining the authority and impartiality of the judiciary".

[32] Recommendation (2000) 8 of the Committee of Ministers of 30 March 2000 on the research mission of universities, adopted at the 705th meeting of the Ministers' Deputies.

[33] Recommendation (2006) 1762 of the Parliamentary Assembly of 30 June 2006 on academic freedom and university autonomy, adopted by the Assembly on 30 June 2006.

[34] Grundgesetz für die Bundesrepublik Deutschland vom 23. Mai 1949, Art. 5 (3): "Kunst und Wissenschaft, Forschung und Lehre sind frei. Die Freiheit der Lehre entbindet nicht von der Treue zur Verfassung." The constitutional provisions that explicitly proclaim the freedom of research in European countries are directly related to the events of the Second World War. See Santosuosso et al. (2007), p. 342.

[35] See Costituzione della Repubblica Italiana (GU n. 298 del 27-12-1947) Art. 9 (1) "La Repubblica promuove lo sviluppo della cultura e la ricerca scientifica e tecnica" and Article 33 (1): "Art and science are free and teaching them is free.

[36] For a comprehensive analysis of the law governing protection of academic freedom in European countries, see Karran (2007), p. 289.

2.1 The German and Italian Approaches

The German Constitution establishes in Article 5 (3) that "Art and scholarship, research, and teaching shall be free . . .." The constitutional legislature upholds any scientific research regardless of the source of funding and of who conducts the research activity. The expression "research freedom" (*Wissenschaftsfreiheit*) is interpreted as a general phrase referring to both research and teaching,[37] and which are at the interface of IP law, right of ownership (*Eigentumfreiheit*),[38] freedom of information (*Informationsfreiheit*),[39] and to exercise a trade and profession (*Berufsfreiheit*).[40] Article 5 (3) protects both the freedom of individuals to practice research and teaching and the public interest in the advancement of knowledge. Indeed, outputs achieved by methodological, systematic, and verifiable research means are conveyed to the community through teaching and publishing.[41] Therefore communication means including publication process are also protected under Article 5 (3) GG. Since scientific knowledge and progress are not the work of a single scientist, sharing results seems to be also constitutionally protected.[42] From this perspective, Article 5 (3) by granting the right to disseminate research outcomes gives authors the right to choose the place, time, and manner of their publication and publishers should be at the services of this constitutional right.[43]

Academic freedom affords scientific authors a special protection in conjunction with intellectual property law whose patrimonial aspect, which includes the right of commercial exploitation, is grounded in principle in Articles 14 GG (right of ownership) and 12 GG (freedom to exercise a trade and profession). According to the prevailing view,[44] then, the commercial use of research results does not fall within the scope of academic freedom. Indeed, researchers pursue interests other than commercial ones: first and foremost for scientists are exchange of knowledge, research development, and the reputational impact of their works. These aspects, which are uncontested and in some ways proven by empirical research,[45] are thus protected by Article 5 (3) GG. Meanwhile, in areas concerning both commercial interests and research freedom, Articles 12, 14, and 5 GG should be applied in a

---

[37] BVerfGE 35, 79, 112 ff.—*Hochschulurteil*. See Mangolt and Klein, Starck (2010); Pernice (2004); Epping and Hillgruber (2009); Jarass and Pieroth (2014).

[38] See Art. 14 (1) of the German Constitution.

[39] See Art. 5 (1) of the German Constitution.

[40] See Art 12 (1) of the German Constitution.

[41] See Lutz (2012); Leinemann (1998), 53 ss.

[42] Pernice (2004), pp. 28 ff.

[43] Steinhauer (2010), pp. 43 ff.; Fehling (2010), p. 74; Jarass and Pieroth, pp. 122 ff.; Sanberger (2006), pp. 818 and 820; Krasser and Schricker (1998), pp. 128 and 152.

[44] Pflueger and Ertmann (2004), pp. 436 and 441.

[45] This also emerged from a study of the Commission of the European Communities, Brussels, 14 January 2002, in which the potential conflicts between "publishing" and "patenting" strategies were considered.

balanced way.[46] This matter also emerges, for example, with regard to Article 42 of the German Employee Inventions Act (*Arbeitnehmererfingungsgesetz—ArbEG*[47]), as amended in 2002, which regulates the economic rights of patentable scholarly works. According to it and contrary to the prior approach that provided for a privilege for researchers and professors (*Hochschullehrerprivileg*),[48] all inventions by employees have been equally regulated since 2002, without any privilege for professors.[49] Allocation depends on whether such an invention is an "independent invention" (*freie Erfindung*) or a "job-related invention" (*Diensterfindung*), with universities being able to claim inventions and exploit them commercially. The legitimacy of this provision has been criticized on the basis of its inconsistency with Article 5 of the German Constitution.[50] University lecturers have observed that their inventions are not directly qualified as job-related inventions since the principle of freedom of research would apply and their work is largely independent. However, the view taken by the legislature is that, while provision has to be made to reward authors for their creative efforts,[51] the right to commercialize IP rights is likely not protected as an aspect of academic freedom. In support of this rule, the legislature pointed out that "The fundamental right recognized by Article 5 of the Constitution does not require research results to be attributed to the researcher, since freedom of research does not include the right to commercial exploitation of the invention."[52] On the other hand, publishing research outputs is recognized by the legislature as being independent from their commercialization. In fact, the German Employee Inventions Act contains special provisions for both the "positive" and "negative" freedom to publish assuming that the right of "whether and when" to publish is in the hands of scientists. Article 42 of the Act provides for the "freedom not to publish work": if employees do not want to publish their

[46] Fechner (1999), pp. 288 ff. and 328; Bethge (2009), 220 ff.

[47] See Art. 42 of the ArbEG.

[48] An overview of this topic is found in Guarda (2013).

[49] "Änderung des Gesetzes über Arbeitnehmererfindungen," Bundesgesetzblatt Teil I, Nr. 4, January 24th 2002. The initiative of the Federal Government is published as Bundestags-Drucksache 14/7565, November 23rd, 2001, at http://www.ipjur.com/data/1407565.pdf, which is identical to the document by the parties that support the Federal Government (Social Democrats, Green): Bundestags-Drucksache 14/5975, May 5th, 2001, http://www.ipjur.com/data/1405975.pdf.

In amending the German Employee Inventions Act, policy makers were concerned that individual researchers might be unwilling or unable to pursue the commercial application of their ideas through patenting and licensing activities. Dedicated technology transfer offices (TTOs) were seen as better suited to fulfilling these tasks.

[50] In the literature, see Leistner (2004), pp. 859 ff.; von Falck and Schmaltz (2005), p. 912.

[51] See Art. 42 (4) of the ArbEG.

[52] "Das Grundrecht des Artikels 5 Abs. 3 GG gebietet zwar nicht die Rechtsinhaberschaft des Hochschullehrer an seinen Forschungsergebnissen, denn die Forschungsfreiheit umfasst nicht das Recht auf kommerzielle Nutzung von Wissenschaft-Erfindungen," BT-Dr 14/5975 of 9 May 2001; BR-Dr 583/01 of 17 August 2001.

inventions, they are not obligated to report the invention to the employer (s.c. notification obligation) pursuant to Article 5 of the Act.[53] As regards the positive right to publish, the provision tries to balance the university's interests in commercial exploitation of the invention and the author's right to publish, shortening the period within which universities must claim an invention.

At this juncture, having clarified that in the German legal system the commercial exploitation of the patrimonial rights in academic works is not an object of academic freedom but instead concerns the IP law, we should take a closer look at this body of law, giving due regard to its constitutional basis and *rationale*.

German scholars[54] and a number of decisions by the German Constitutional Court (*Bundesverfassunggericht*—BVerfGE) have broadened the category of constitutional property to include IP, applying Article 14 GG.[55] Property is defined as a fundamental right linked to the concept of "social function."[56] Hence, the "propertization" of IP lays the foundation for the legislative limitation of authors' rights in light of the social function of the right of ownership, affording an adequate balancing of IP with the interests of equal and higher hierarchical rank. Also from this perspective, the right of commercial exploitation is subordinate to the social function of IP, which is certainly represented by the advancement of knowledge and cultural development. This is also consistent with Article 7 of the TRIPS agreements, according to which "the protection and enforcement of intellectual property rights should contribute to the promotion of technological innovation and to the transfer and dissemination of technology, to the mutual advantage of producers and users of technological knowledge and in a manner conducive to social and economic welfare, and to a balance of rights and obligations."[57] This provision makes it clear that IPs are not an end in themselves, clearly establishing that the protection and enforcement of intellectual property rights do not exist in a vacuum. They are meant to benefit society as a whole and are not aimed at the mere protection of private rights.[58]

In the German legal system, the role of the courts has been crucial in defining the boundaries between IP rights and other fundamental rights, highlighting the social function of IP law, namely patent and copyright law.[59] A seminal precedent in the

[53] "[b]erücksichtigt werden muss aber das aus der Forschungsfreiheit herzuleiten Recht auf negative Publikationsfreiheit, also das Recht des Wissenschaftlers, Ergebnisse seiner Arbeiten der Öffentlichkeit nicht mitzuteilen. Auch muss gewährleistet werden, dass die positive Publikationsfreiheit nicht in unzumutbarer Weise beschränkt wird." BT-Dr 14/5975 of 9 May 2001, at 5; same wording BR-Dr 583/01 of 17 August 2001, at 5.

[54] Braegelmann (2009–2010), p. 99.

[55] See Pernice (2004), pp. 1439 f.; Dreier (2013), p. 94.

[56] See the chapter by C. Sganga, in this volume; Fechner (1999), pp. 186 ff.

[57] See Yu (2009), pp. 979 ff.

[58] Council for Trade-Related Aspects of Intellectual Property Rights (2001), Submission by the African Group, Barbados, Bolivia, Brazil, Cuba, Dominican Republic, Ecuador, Honduras, India, Indonesia, Jamaica, Pakistan, Paraguay, Philippines, Peru, Sri Lanka, Thailand and Venezuela', IP/C/W/296, para. 18.

[59] As for the patent law, this emerges clearly in the Klinische Versuche leading case Klinische Versuche 1 BVerfG, 1864 (1995). See Niioka (2001).

field of copyright law is represented by the *Schoolbook* case.[60] In 1965, the German parliament amended the German Copyright Act to permit already published "literary and musical works of small extent, single artistic works, or single photographs" to be published in a collection "that assembles the works of a considerable number of authors and is intended, by its nature, exclusively for religious, school, or instructional use." Several authors filed constitutional complaints alleging that the amendment violated their property rights under Article 14. The Court found that the right of access to copyrighted works properly served society's interests as secured by Article 14 (2), establishing that "in defining the content of copyright according to Article 14 GG [the legislature], should provide rules adequate to assure an exploitation of the work which is coherent with the nature and social relevance of copyright." On the other hand, the German Constitutional Court also found that the attribution of a fair compensation is required since denial of any compensation for the prescribed use of copyrighted works violates the copyright holder's interests in property under Article 14 (1).[61] A few years later, in the leading *Church music* case (1971),[62] the Court was again concerned with the tension between the private and social dimension of copyright. Several composers of church music challenged provisions of the Copyright Act of 1965, which allowed the reproduction of a musical score without authorization or payment of royalties if played at a state-sponsored non-profit public event in a church or in connection with a religious event. The Court ruled that the performance of a musical piece without authorization at a public event may be justified by a "social character of IP."

In this scheme of things, given that academic freedom protects a social interest, it seems reasonable that copyright and the academic publishing system should be established in a way that dissemination of and access to scientific knowledge are effectively ensured.

The Italian case deserves attention from this perspective since, after establishing that "The arts and sciences as well as their teaching are free . . .,"[63] it also explicitly requires the Italian legislature not only to protect but also to promote and support freedom of research and cultural development: " . . . The Republic promotes the development of culture and of scientific and technical research."[64] This obligation is not literally provided by the German Constitution, but the legal literature and case law attribute to Article 5 (3) the same broad meaning.[65]

---

[60] Schoolbook, 31 BVerfGE 229 (1971).

[61] In those years, the Federal Constitutional Court was involved in this topic on numerous occasions. See, *inter alia*, the *Broadcast Lending* case 31 BVerfGE 248 (1971). For further analysis, see Kommers (1997), pp. 651 ff.; Geller (2010), p. 907.

[62] 49 BVerfGE 382 (1978).

[63] See Article 33, Italian Constitution.

[64] An overview of the Italian scenario in light of the constitutional provisions is found in Merloni (1990).

[65] See Mangolt and Klein, Starck (2010) Pernice (2004), Epping and Hillgruber, (2009) Jarass and Pieroth, (2014)

The Italian guarantee is developed in the precedents of the Constitutional Court, emphasizing the autonomy of universities and research institutions from external economic and political forces.[66] According to the Court definition, independence means self-government through the community of academic members.[67] This is consistent with the fundamental principle of the Magna Charta of European Universities, which states that "[t]he university produces, examines, appraises and hands down culture by research and teaching. To meet the needs of the world around it, its research and teaching must be morally and intellectually independent of all political authority and economic power. Freedom in research and training is the fundamental principle of university life. Governments and universities, each as far as in them lies, must ensure respect for this fundamental requirement."[68]

In terms of researchers' autonomy with regard to the Italian legislative framework, academic freedom does enjoy even a high level of protection, given that, for instance, the Italian Industrial Property Code grants what is referred to as "professor's privilege."[69] Article 65 establishes that "... when the employment relationship exists with a university or a public body which has research among its institutional purposes, the researcher is the holder of exclusive rights to the patentable invention he has authored." The fifth paragraph of Article 65 also stipulates that "the provisions of this article shall not apply in the case of research funded, in whole or in part, by private persons or implemented within specific research projects funded by public bodies other than the university, institution or administration of the researcher." Leaving aside critical issues such as the transaction costs relating to the system established by law,[70] what is remarkable is that Italy, by applying the principle of "academic privilege" to the invention, emphasizes the researcher's independence also from the institution or university.[71]

As pointed out above, when attempting to define content and the scope of the right to academic freedom, we also deal with the nature of IP rights and, as for our concern, particularly of copyright. Since the Italian Constitution does not expressly

---

[66] This is also in Germany; see 1 BVerfG, 333 (1975). 1, 1864 (1995). On this subject, see Ruffert and Steinecke (2011).

[67] See Corte Cost. 9. 11. 1988, no. 1017, available at http://www.giurcost.org/decisioni/1988/1017s-88.html.

[68] The Magna Charta of European Universities is the final outcome of the proposal put forward by the University of Bologna, in 1986, to the oldest European universities. The document, drafted in Barcelona in January 1988, was signed by several universities. The document is available at http://www.magna-charta.org/cms/cmspage.aspx?pageUid={d4bd2cba-e26b-499e-80d5-b7a2973d5d97}.

[69] Law No. 383 of 18 October 2001 added a new Article 24 to the law on invention, which is now transposed in Article 65 of the Industrial Property Code, Law of 10 February 2005, No. 30.

[70] For an in-depth discussion on this profile, see Guarda (2013).

[71] Probably the legislature also aims to provide incentives for authors, although it is debatable whether this legislative model responds to the real need to incentivize research activity. On this point it is worth considering a precedent of the Constitutional Court establishing the right of scientists to be recognized as authors of their invention. The Court highlights the need to provide incentives for authors even in the academic context. See Corte cost. 20 March 1978, n. 20. See *ex plurimis*, Ubertazzi (2003b), p. 1109.

provide for a specific discipline of copyright as a constitutional right,[72] the Italian Constitutional Court has enshrined copyright in several fundamental rights. Hence, the protection of intangible goods represents the "balanced summary" of different values. Of significance here are thus Article 2, which introduces the protection of fundamental human rights; Articles 9 and 33, both promoting the development of culture and science; and Article 21, which protects freedom of expression. No one of these provisions attributes to the author the right to an economic monopoly on the creative work, but the Constitution does ascribe it to freedom of economic activity and protection of competition (Art. 41).[73] Scholars have also highlighted the relevance of Article 35, which legitimizes the remuneration of authors for their work.

Basing copyright on a number of constitutional interests appears to justify different protection techniques, thereby giving priority to the most important value on a case-by-case basis.[74] Consequently, although organic regulation - especially for the academic field - would be desirable, the controversial overlaps between IP and academic freedom may be interpreted in light of these considerations.[75]

2.2 *Legal Nature and Scope of Academic Freedom in the United States*

In some countries, academic freedom does not enjoy any specific constitutional safeguard. This is the case in the United States. However, American scholars who had studied in Germany brought back with them the concept of freedom of teaching and research.[76] The first explicit document about academic freedom was issued in 1915 by the American Association of University Professors (A.A.U.P.) and is a cornerstone of the US academic system. This is the "Statement on Academic Freedom and Tenure."[77] Another step forward was achieved by the 1940 Declaration of the A.A.U.P. The new Declaration greatly differed from the first one, not only in the sense that it redefined some of the principles of the 1915 Declaration but also in that the later Declaration is the result of a joint work of the A.A.U.P. and the American Association of Colleges (which would later become the American Association of Colleges and Universities). Academic freedom was accepted then

[72] See Moscarini (2006), pp. 162 ff.; Ubertazzi (2003a), p. 1054.

[73] Among others, see the above mentioned Corte Cost., 20 March 1978, n. 20, in *Giur. Cost.*, 1978, 446; Corte Cost., 23 March 1995, n. 108, in *AIDA*, 1995, 297.

[74] Scaccia (2005), p. 198.

[75] Orsi Battaglini (2007), p. 1399.

[76] Commager (1963), p. 361.

[77] The Statement is available at http://www.aaup.org/report/1940-statement-principles-academic-freedom-and-tenure.

as a major principle of academic life and achievement by employers and employees alike. Indeed, colleges and universities take up not only the cause of teachers and institutions but also that of the community as a whole, and this is a responsibility that is shared by both the institution and faculty. The A.A.U.P. principles created a "soft law" that to a certain extent was absorbed into judicial concepts of common law. Academic freedom is considered as one aspect of the wider concept of freedom of expression. That said, although the First Amendment is indiscriminate in the sense that it equally provides for freedom of speech for all American citizens, academic freedom is bestowed on researchers and academic teachers so that they can conduct their legitimate academic activities under optimal conditions, notably without constraints and limitations.

The substance of this right is still a controversial issue[78]; nevertheless, it is often applied by the courts in reference to the First Amendment.[79] The notion of academic freedom is defined in some leading cases such as *Sweezy v. State of New Hampshire*[80] and *Griswold v. Connecticut*: "The right of freedom of speech and press includes [...] freedom of inquiring, freedom of thought and freedom to teach."[81]

Despite the cultural and historical distinguishing factors between the European and US academic system[82] and the lack of explicit constitutional protection, academic freedom is highly regarded in the US case law also at the interface with IP. Indeed, in the US IP is clearly defined as a pendant of scientific progress, as stated in the US Constitution in Art. I, 8 § 8: "The Congress shall have the power [...] to promote the progress of science and useful arts, by securing for limited times to authors and inventors the exclusive right to their respective writings and discoveries [...]." The US Constitution highlights the need to ensure access to knowledge as an engine of scientific progress. Therefore, both copyright and academic freedom are means by which a community's learning and knowledge can be continually enhanced. Freedom to publish and access both the processes and results of scientific research promotes further investigation by informing other scholars and researchers of the results achieved, as well as communicating these ideas to a wider nonacademic audience.

---

[78] Oldaker (1992).

[79] Strauss (2011), p. 4.

[80] Sweezy v. State of N.H. by Wyman, 354 U.S. 234 (1957).

[81] Griswold v. Connecticut, 381 U.S. 479 (1965).

[82] In the US, research and teaching management respond to partly different paradigms. In addition, relationships between professors and research institutions or universities are mostly based on private contracts and university policy, while all US universities are governed by a board composed by external members.

2.3 Academic Exceptionalism in Copyright Ownership

Carrying on with the comparative reasoning we have started above, a reference to copyright ownership regulation is concerned and will follow hereafter.[83]

In the Italian legal system,[84] the creator, pursuant to Article 6 of the Copyright Act, is the holder of the copyright in creative intellectual works.[85] As regards works created in the course of an employment relationship, there are some exceptions. In cases where the creative activity is performed in the fulfillment of contractual obligations, copyright belongs to the employer, while the author is only entitled to moral rights. As regards academic written works, Articles 11 (2) and 29 of the Italian Copyright Act provide for a special regulation. A systematic interpretation of the aforementioned Articles shows that the allocation of ownership in scholarly works to the university is exceptional: it occurs only under the conditions specified by these rules. Precisely, Article 11 grants copyright to universities for collections of documents or publications prepared on their behalf and at their expense. These rules in any case apply unless otherwise agreed with the authors of the published works. Moreover, according to Article 29, the economic rights in documents or publications relating to the normal activities of public administration, which include universities (i.e., communication on activity progress, reports of results, proceedings), are granted to the public entities for a limited period of time (20 years after the first publication). After that the authors recover their rights. Furthermore, for the original works created by authors affiliated to the university, it is only when the public entity undertakes publications and assumes costs that the author is free to fully exploit his writings for up to 2 years after the first publication. In any other case, authors own copyright in their works.

This exception, which falls in line with an informal rule, ensures academic freedom through recognition of copyright ownership on behalf of the scientist. Needless to say, research might otherwise be influenced by the economic and cultural leanings of the university.[86]

Similarly, in the German legal system pursuant to Article 7 of the Copyright Act, the creator is the author of the work (i.e., *Schöpferprinzip*). However, when authors are employees and produce the work in accordance with their employment obligations, Article 43, as construed by literature and case law, and Article 69 (b), in the case of computer programs, stipulate that the exploitation rights are normally allocated to the employer.[87] The holder of the moral rights is always the author, although their use might be limited. While the decision concerning who is regarded

[83] For a thorough treatise, see Guarda (2013).

[84] See Lorenzato (2009), p. 47.

[85] Law of 22 April 1941, No 633.

[86] Pila (2010), p. 609.

[87] We stake an in-depth look here at the issue regarding the interpretation of Article 43 of the German Copyright Act, which has been a debated rule in the literature and case law. See Wandtke and Bullinger (2014), pp. 30–36; Dreier and Schulze (2013), pp. 1–39; Nordemann et al. (2008).

as an employee is left to labor law, the regulation applies to employees in the private sector, as well as civil servants employed in the public sector.

For works created by faculties given the nature of employment and the constitutionally protected freedom of research, the situation is different. The general view held is that copyright is allocated to the author.[88]

Under the US legal system, while the Copyright Act does not contain specific provisions for academic works, the implementation of general rules relating to works created in the scope of an employment relationship has been a subject of discussion. As in the Italian and German systems, the question is whether the rights in the researcher's work belong to the author or to the research institute as the employer.[89] Under Section 201 of the US Copyright Act, ownership of IP rights is granted to the creator of the work. However, an issue looked at in the US is the "work for hire" doctrine, whereby the work is created by a person "within the scope of his or her employment." Section 201 (b) of the Copyright Act (1976) states that "In the case of a work made for hire, the employer or other person for whom the work was prepared is considered the author for purposes of this title, and, unless the parties have expressly agreed otherwise in a written instrument signed by them, owns all of the rights comprised in the copyright." Copyright law provides no definition for key terms such as employee or "scope of employment." Hence, case law serves to identify the standard to be applied, to decide whether an intellectual work was created in a work-for-hire situation.[90]

At the university level, it is debatable whether the work-for-hire doctrine is applicable[91] and, if so, whether the criteria devised by the courts for its definition are appropriate and should be used in that situation. Even in the US, an informal rule defined as "teacher exception"[92] appears to be what is in force and is being applied by the courts.[93] The basis cited for this exception is that it ensures "academic freedom" for professors and researchers. According to Posner, one of the judges in the Hays leading case, this exception was rooted in academic tradition

[88] Herrera Diaz (2010), p. 95; Ulrici (2008), pp. 205 ff.; Pramann (2007), pp. 46 ff.; Schricker and Krasser (2004), 419 ss.; Heerman (1999), p. 468; Haberstumpf (2001), pp. 819 and 826.

[89] With respect to the US System, see Priest (2012), p. 377; Denicola (2006); Daniel and Pauken (1999), p. 1; Laughlin (2000), pp. 549 and 567; VerSteeg (1990), pp. 381 and 407.

[90] A leading case on this matter is *Community for Creative Non-Violence v. Reid* 490 *US* 730 (1989).

[91] The subject is fiercely debated, especially with regard to teaching which is more measurable for research institutions from an economic viewpoint. See Townsend (2003).

[92] See Packard (2002), p. 275; Centivany (2011), p. 385.

[93] In favor of the teacher exception, see Weinstein v. Univ. of Ill., 811 F.2d 1091, 1094 (7th Cir. 1987); Hays and Macdonald v. Sony Corp. of Am., 847 F.2d 412, 416–17 (7th Cir. 1988). More recently Shaul v. Cherry Valley-Springfield Cent. Sch. Dist., 363 F.3d 177, 186 (2d Cir. 2004); Bosch v. Ball-Kell, 80 U.S.P.Q.2d (BNA) 1713, 1719–20 (C.D. Ill. 2006). Contra: Vanderhurst v. Colo. Mountain Coll. Dist., 16 F. Supp. 2d 1297 (D. Colo. 1998); Univ. of Colo. Found. v. Am. Cyanamid, 880 F. Supp. 1387 (D. Colo. 1995), 902 F. Supp. 221 (D. Colo. 1995); Rouse v. Walter & Assocs., 513 F. Supp. 2d 1041 (S.D. Iowa 2007).

and then absorbed into the judicial concepts of common law based on the nature of the researcher's activity[94] that needs to be "free."[95] It is remarkable that in implementing this rule, the US case law makes explicit reference to academic freedom, although extensions of academic freedom as propounded by private associations have not matured into legal regulations.[96]

Moreover, given the lack of clarity in formal law, institutional policies and contracts regulate, among other things, the management of IP rights and become highly relevant.[97] Even though the situation concerning policies is quite varied, exclusive rights in scientific publications are generally granted to their authors in the majority of cases.[98] Sometimes, in line with academic tradition, applicability of the "teacher exception" is explicitly stated and the author is assumed to be the copyright owner.[99] In other institutional regulations the university is required to transfer ownership to the author in the event that copyright has been granted to it in the first place.[100]

What emerges from this short comparative analysis is that formal legislation is mainly focused on the creation of economic incentives, assigning exclusive rights to those subjects that support the production of creative works economically. No specific comprehensive regulation for academic works is provided. In this environment, however, a kind of "privilege" is applied: within the academic context, informal rules grant ownership in a publication to the author.

Under the current publishing system, however, the rules and policies aimed at protecting academic freedom, giving the authors the entitlement to choose how to share their works, might lose their significance. Currently, the scientific ecosystem seems to be influenced by the interrelationship between copyright law, law of contract, and research evaluation systems, which, together, are strengthening the oligopolistic market of academic publishing and are leading to the private control of scientific content.

---

[94] Hays and Macdonald v. Sony Corp. of America, cit.

[95] On academic freedom in the USA, Sterckx (2012); Van Bouwel (2012); Pinxten (2012); Dupré (2001); Byrne (1989), pp. 251 and 259–260.

[96] See Metzger (1988), pp. 1265 and 1279; Byrne (2006), p. 929.

[97] Lape (1992).

[98] Daniel and Pauken (1999), p. 140. The Author pointed out that the copyright management expenses would be more than the profits deriving from the exploitation of the works. By contrast, software, audiovisual, or other materials for e-learning would be more profitable.

[99] See, for instance, the policy of the University of Harvard, available at http://www.techtransfer.harvard.edu/resources/policies/IP/; and the University of Stanford available at http://doresearch.stanford.edu/policies/research-policy-handbook/intellectual-property/copyright-policy#anchor-533.

[100] See, University of Michigan. The policy is available at http://www.lib.umich.edu/files/services/copyright/601.28%20%281%29.pdf.

3 Control of Knowledge in Scholarly Publishing

The limited concern for the scientific perspective in regulating copyright law, the weak exceptions and limitations to exclusive rights, and the general trend towards broadening copyright protection[101] are all elements conspiring against freedom of accessing and exchanging information, disseminating knowledge, and preserving research results.[102] In this scenario lies a system of scholarly publishing where few private stakeholders control research results. This situation appears unreasonable and even more irrational when scientific works are produced with public funds. It is thus worth considering how publishers rose to prominence in the field during the latter half of the twentieth century.[103]

From the 1960s, scientific publishing began to be a profitable business for commercial publishers. According to Jean Claude Guedòn,[104] the archetype of scientific journals was born as a "public registry" of discoveries, i.e. a system to assign "scientific paternity" and priority, thus resolving the issue of authorship of original ideas. The subsequent progress made in the scientific publishing industry led to a consolidation on the market to a few dozen major publications, each of them addressing a specific subject. It was then in the late 1960s that the concept of core journals emerged, and to this day all researchers still prefer their works to be published in them.[105] Hence, publishers have created markets with a broad and stable institutional customer base, also favored by the growing number of libraries and universities.[106]

The advent of digital technology and the Internet saw a radical change in the way scientific communication works. Major commercial publishers seized the opportunity to extend their control over content, also benefiting from technology and e-publishing. Thanks to digital technology, right holders can grant users access to and use of information under specific conditions protected by technological protection measures (TPM)[107] and digital rights management (DRM) systems.[108] In the scientific publishing industry, the most common contract format is the end-user license agreement (EULA),[109] which mirrors the business model produced by

[101] The literature on the trend towards a strengthening of exclusive rights, confining limitations and exceptions, is immense. Among others, see Mazziotti (2013); Torremans (2010); Gasaway (2010); Dusollier (2008), p. 569; Dusollier (2002); Drexl and von Lewinski (2007), p. 3; Hilty and Peukert (2004); Guibault (2002).

[102] See Reichman and Okediji (2012). See also Geiger (2006), p. 366.

[103] For a clear overview on this subject, see Priest (2012), pp. 9 ff.

[104] Guedòn (2001).

[105] Russel (2008).

[106] For more details, see Priest (2012), pp. 10 ff.

[107] See Moscon (2013).

[108] v. Reichman and Okediji (2012), op. cit.

[109] Among others, see Rice (1990), p. 157; M. A. Lemley, *Intellectual Property and Shrink wrap Licenses*, (August 8, 2012). Stanford Public Law Working Paper No. 2126845. Available at SSRN: http://ssrn.com/abstract=2126845.

digital technology and allows control over information. Such a powerful legal device is driven by a commercial and proprietary *rationale*, aimed at restricting access to content.[110] EULAs normally prohibit any form of redistribution of content, causing secondary markets to disappear and strengthening the oligopolistic power of major scientific publishers.[111]

It was on this basis that a small handful of international publishing companies by the 1990s came to control distribution of the most widely read and prestigious academic journals. Subscription fees for major scientific journals have seen a steep rise. Since universities and public libraries are unlikely to buy all publications, they end up investing in the most important journals according to the quality rating system for publications, thereby favoring the market concentration even further.[112] Once a journal establishes itself as a "must have" title in its subject area, libraries will continue to purchase the title even if the price increases.

The paradox is that universities themselves subsidize the production of much of the research and scholarship published in academic journals. Since scientists normally underestimate the importance of their rights while creating a work,[113] especially their economic rights, and want to publish in "good" journals, they then transfer copyright for free to the publisher, who later licenses them to research institutions at high prices and on strict terms and conditions of access and use of the content.[114] In fact, all scientists, given the evaluation system, want to publish their work in the most prestigious journals. This phenomenon is prevalent in the scientific areas that make use of periodicals and bibliometric indices (such as the impact factor and the h-index) but is also found in the humanities and social sciences, the so-called non-bibliometrics sectors, that are making increasing use of similar tools, such as listing journals according to quality categories, taking account of the publisher's prestige.[115] In the scenario described, it also happens quite often that authors offer their contribution to journals and book collections for free as members of scientific committees and as auditors to the peer review process organized by publishers.

The current trend threatens not only innovation and productivity but also scientific freedom, the latter in any case being the premise for promoting the former. Researchers who need to draw from many databases to conduct research are aware of the difficulty of dealing with a myriad of divergent and overlapping policies, agreements, and laws, as well as parsing incomprehensible fine print that often

---

[110] From a critical perspective, see Hilty (2006), pp. 180 ff.

[111] On the specific problem of the exhaustion principle, see CJEU, 3 July 2012, case C-128/11, *UsedSoft GmbH v Oracle International Corp*. On the *UsedSoft* decision, see, *inter alia*, Hilty et al. (2013), p. 263. The subject is analyzed by G. Spedicato in this volume.

[112] Horowitz (2007), p. 38.

[113] Caso (2013); Jordan (2003), pp. 15 and 92.

[114] Suber (2012), pp. 129 ff.

[115] See, Caso (2013). With specific reference to the Italian system for evaluating research in the humanities, see Galimberti (2012); Pascuzzi and Caso (2011), p. 685.

carries conflicting obligations, limitations, and restrictions. These licenses and agreements can hinder research and also potentially enable data providers to exercise "remote control" over downstream users of data, likely dictating what research can be done and by whom, what data can be published or disclosed, what data can be combined and how, and what data can be re-used and for what purposes. Imposing that kind of control imperils the very foundations of science, which is grounded in freedom of inquiry and freedom to publish.

From this perspective, the traditional scientific publishing industry appears to be neutralizing the revolutionary power of digital technology and the Internet that would help increase knowledge dissemination, improve the preservation of publications over time, and create new business models and value-added services. So while on one hand new technology has the potential to increase and accelerate access,[116] on the other it is being exploited in the market of scientific publishing to produce the opposite effect.

The dominant position of publishers on the market is due to many factors, some of which we have touched upon above. Among them is the evaluation of scientific publications, which is linked to the traditional functions of scientific journals, including quality certification, awareness, archiving and, historically, registration.[117] Certification and awareness functions are currently under discussion while still relying heavily on the traditional communication system based on the concept of core journal. This method, also known as the "gatekeeper model"—the system of deciding on the quality of works before publication based on both publisher policies and peer-review practice—raises many issues. First, it predefines its audience and disregards a series of important questions, such as how the value of the material that is pre-excluded can be fully known, given that the reviewers will likely embrace ideologies that are not always explicitly clear from their immanent position. Furthermore, it seems reasonable to wonder what value will be established by gatekeepers in the future.

In this scenario, traditional publishers are also trying to defend their position on the market by promoting accessory services for scientific product evaluation. Indeed, the method for measuring the impact of scientific production in terms of quantity is becoming increasingly powerful and sophisticated, thanks to the techniques of data analysis. Control over scientific literature, therefore, is also being strengthened by the management of the data relating to it. Data management is thus acquiring great importance both in the European and US context. One example of this is the management of databases like ISI Web of Science (Thomson Reuters) and Scopus (Elsevier).[118]

The aforementioned quality rating system for publications merges the power derived from research quality evaluation criteria and that stemming from the market,[119] creating a centralized management of scientific knowledge.

[116] On Internet developments, see Berners-Lee (1999).

[117] Roosendaal and Geurts (1997).

[118] Databases are strongly protected at a European level.

[119] Horowitz (2007), p. 38.

Copyright and contract laws, as currently regulated, are the essential lever of this system. Within this framework in the legal literature, it is nowadays almost a generally accepted opinion that one answer to the problem cited should be a partly distinct set of copyright rules for scientific research, fostering wide and efficient dissemination, also by securing competitive market conditions and thereby encouraging innovative dissemination models.[120] Second, copyright legislation without an adequate regulation of copyright contracts remains incomplete, also because of the inequality of the parties: while authors are not businessmen, their partners typically are well-organized commercial entities.[121]

4 The Open Access Model

The open access (OA) paradigm has developed in a bottom-up process,[122] thanks to initiatives promoted by some scientific communities[123] and librarian groups. Declarations,[124] policies, and contracts and the further implementation of statutes in some legal systems have shown the growing interest in the OA principles globally. The foundations of OA are provided by three main declarations: Budapest (2002), Bethesda (2003), and Berlin (2003). The latter encompasses the most comprehensive definition according to which OA grants access to all academic works, free of technological, legal, and economic barriers, thus also reducing the costs arising from the publication process. Free access to content and some basic economic rights through free, irrevocable, and worldwide licenses subject to the attribution of authorship are therefore by the user as pillars of OA. Furthermore, appropriate technological standards to ensure long-term archiving and interoperability are crucial to the development of OA.

The two main approaches to OA are the gold road and the green road. The first one is defined by the literature as "scholarly work published *ab origine* on an OA basis," while the second is referred to as "(self-)archiving in OA repositories of published, peer-reviewed articles."[125] Authors opting for the green road can publish their work through traditional channels and then disseminate it through OA reposi-

---

[120] Hilty et al. (2009).

[121] On contracts in copyright law, see Schricker (2004), p. 850.

[122] For a comprehensive review of the OA literature, see Frosio (2014).

[123] Open access principles arise from some scientific communities, such as physicists, in that sharing articles is an established practice. See the arXiv repository at http://arxiv.org/.

[124] See Berlin Declaration 2003, available at http://openaccess.mpg.de/286432/Berlin-Declaration. At the European level, see EU Recommendation 17 July 2012 (2012/417/EU) on access to and preservation of scientific information. In the U.S., *Revised Policy on Enhancing Public Access to Archived Publications Resulting from NIH-Funded Research,* available at http://grants.nih.gov/grants/guide/notice-files/NOT-OD-08-033.html.

[125] See Harnad et al. (2004).

tories, either institutional or disciplinary.[126] Currently, many journals allow OA republication, only requiring an "embargo period," i.e., the time between the first publication and the OA re-publication. How long it is depends on the discipline and the policy of the publisher.[127] Meanwhile, publishers support the so-called hybrid road allowing for the OA publication of articles (known as open choice) in closed-access journals, against payment of the article processing charges (APCs)[128] by the author or the institution financing the research.[129]

A further distinction may be made between weak forms of OA (i.e., gratis OA), which eliminate only the economic barrier to access, and strong forms (i.e., *libre* OA), which, as stated in the Berlin Declaration, also lower the legal barrier to restricted access to and use of scientific contributions.

Some scholars highlight the benefits of OA,[130] including speed, efficiency, and extent of content dissemination; strengthening of interdisciplinary research; collaboration between different scientific disciplines; transfer of knowledge to businesses; transparency towards citizens; and preservation of research results over time.

That said, OA is not against the traditional scholarly publication system[131]: it does not replace peer review, and it does not ignore the fact that any publication involves costs that must somehow be recovered by authors or research institutions. However, the role of publishers may change under the OA paradigm; they may provide a service that would be rewarded *ex ante* by the authors or research institutions. Publishers could also develop new services, related, for example, to the storage of content and the development of data mining techniques facilitating retrieval of documents and other services valorizing the technological means.

OA is a concrete alternative that enhances pluralism of information sources and perhaps also of public research evaluation. Indeed, an *ex post* peer review might work easier with OA publications: the storage of research results can lead to improvements in the research evaluation systems, creating new criteria that might serve as a basis for pluralism also in the valuation of academic works.[132] Participation by the academic community in the peer-review process offers tools that are

---

[126] See The Directory of Open Access Repositories—OpenDOAR, at http://www.opendoar.org/.

[127] See Millington (2011). A list of journals that allow OA re-publication is available at http://www.sherpa.ac.uk/romeo/PDFandIR.html.

[128] Björk and Solomon (2014), Final Report to a consortium of research funders comprising Jisc, Research Libraries UK, Research Councils UK, the Wellcome Trust, the Austrian Science Fund, the Luxembourg National Research Fund and the Max Planck Institute for Gravitational Physics. Available at http://www.wellcome.ac.uk/stellent/groups/corporatesite/@policy_communications/documents/web_document/wtp055910.pdf.

[129] Hybrid OA has met with some criticism from the literature. The risk is having to pay twice: first, when the author or the institution pays extra APCs in order to have their papers appear without the gatekeeping charges and, second, because libraries and institutions still have to pay for the journal subscription. See Adams (2007); Björk (2012), p. 1496.

[130] See Suber (2012), pp. 65 ff.; Herb (2010).

[131] On the interfacing between open and private models, see Hilty and Köklü (2013).

[132] See *Altmetric Manifesto*, on the website http://altmetrics.org/manifesto/. See Eve (2013).

different to "traditional" peer review, namely open, documented peer review that usually takes place at a post-publication stage, therefore giving readers access to a live and ongoing literature review.[133] Post-publication review through online commentary and social media in communicating published works and discussing their merits and weaknesses might play an important role. In the case of so-called interactive OA, for instance, pre-print and post-print are available for comment. The bar for peer review is raised by having preapproval by the editor, verifying that the article is relevant, and a public peer review with the article published as discussion papers open to interactive and viewable comments from the referees and the community.[134]

4.1 Developing Open Access Through Legal Tools

OA represents a collateral solution to the traditional publishing channels that are indeed still dominant. Recent empirical studies have shown that proper recognition of OA (even the green road) is slowing down and its implementation varies by country and discipline, sometimes encountering obstacles within the scientific community itself.[135] Of course, one of the difficulties in growing OA can be found in the hostility from traditional publishers to a full recognition of the OA paradigm. They contrast OA in different ways, including by adapting contracts to changes and tensions of scientific communities in a way that secures their "old" business models, actually directing the choices of authors.[136]

The best prospect for change probably lies in ethical rules and social norms through a bottom-up approach.[137] However, a top-down system may also play a key role in addressing cultural and social changes towards a broad dissemination of and access to research outputs. Among these, institutional policies adopted by many research and funding bodies in accordance with organizational and regulatory choices are crucial in promoting OA.

---

[133] For a discussion of the so-called open peer review or peer-to-peer review, see Fitzpatrick and Santo (2012).

[134] Armbruster (2005). About models that entail post-publication peer review, see Shirky (2008).

[135] Some researches show that proper recognition of full Open Access journals by the community remains a major obstacle to overcome if they are to become a viable alternative to scholarly communication. As in other social contexts that rely more on collective action and reciprocal recognition than on a top-down structure, social norms tend to prevail over laws because they seem better able to regulate social interactions. This is underlined by a wealth of literature. Furthermore, though we generally think of academics as a unified group, their social norms are actually localized and vary across disciplines and national boundaries. See Migheli and Ramello (2014); Migheli and Ramello (2013), pp. 149–167; Björk (2004), p. 1; Eger et al. (2013).

[136] See Kaufman (2008). More generally, see Albert (2006), p. 253; Stevenson (2010).

[137] See Lametti (2010), p. 309. Geiger (2013). On the role of the social norms in determining individuals' behavior, see the chapter by F. Giovanella in this volume.

The various options that have emerged can be grouped into two main categories: voluntary and mandatory policies.[138] The choice between them could be influenced by the aim to preserve academic freedom of researchers: mandatory regulation imposing obligations on authors regarding the right to freely choose whether, where, how, and when to publish the research outcomes restricts academic author's freedom.[139] As a matter of fact, most of the policies adopted by universities and research institutions in Europe are voluntary, at most, providing for incentive mechanisms to encourage faculties to publish or re-publish in OA or, at least, to deposit the published work in a repository (referred to as "dark deposit"). This is the case of the University of Liège. While this policy requires storage in the institutional repository (ORBI) of all works accepted for publication,[140] public access to works is only allowed after the university is granted a license by the right holder. The deposit guarantees the preservation of research products, indexing them and making the bibliography available to the public. The strength of this regulation is the incentive approach that is based on the evaluation procedures of curricula: for such purpose, only works deposited in the institutional archive are taken into account.

Following the US model, some European governments have taken some steps towards proper recognition of the OA principle (i.e., Spain,[141] Italy,[142] and Germany[143]). Although other countries, including Argentina, have also recently issued acts aimed at regulating the subject,[144] we will consider hereinafter the US and European systems, particularly those in Italy and Germany.

From the European perspective, the US system offers much food for thought. One reason for this can be found in its tradition of encouraging knowledge transfer to private industry,[145] an area in which Europe has been developing significant policies of late. At the same time, some major US universities, such as Harvard and the Massachusetts Institute of Technology in Boston, strongly support the OA principle through institutional regulations aimed at ensuring its full recognition. These two examples prove that research results can be appreciated in two different ways: through economic exploitation by patent licensing and OA to publishing. As for the latter, the US government in 2008 strongly promoted OA by stipulating, first in the biomedicine sector, that "all articles arising from the National Institutes of

[138] Suber (2012).

[139] With regard to the German legal system, see Lutz (2012); Krujatz (2012); E. Steinhauer (2010). On the US contest, see Priest (2012). For the Italian one, see Caso (2013).

[140] See http://orbi.ulg.ac.be/.

[141] Articulo 37 (Difùsion en acceso abierto), Ley 14/2011, de 1 de junio, de la Ciencia, la Tecnologia y la Innovacion.

[142] § 4, Law 7th October 2013, n. 112.

[143] Law 1st October 2013 (BGBl. I S. 3714).

[144] Marzetti (2013).

[145] See the Bayh–Dole Act or Patent and Trademark Law Amendments Act (Pub. L. 96-517, December 12, 1980).

Health (NIH) funds must be submitted to PubMed Central upon acceptance for publication."[146] The law[147] safeguards free access for the public, requiring all beneficiaries of public funding to republish the peer-reviewed version on PubMed Central no later than 12 months from the first publication. The fulfillment of this obligation was subject to implementation by the publicly funded entity of a policy aimed at managing copyright issues between authors and publishers. More specifically, the statement requires the research institution (e.g., the university) to prepare a regulation assisting authors in managing copyright law. The funded institution has to make sure that whoever processes the publication of an article on PubMed Central is entitled to publish or republish it.[148]

The governmental promotion of OA in the US has been progressing steadily, despite debates and the reactions also from publishers that have challenged the mandate policy.[149] On 18 January 2014, the US government adopted the Consolidated Appropriations Act 2014.[150] Section 527 of the Act requires publicly funded research from grants made by US government agencies with a funding turnaround of more than $100 million annually to be available online in OA within 12 months of publication in a peer-reviewed journal. The Act calls for open licensing, common deposit procedures among agencies, and formats that support re-use and additional uses such as computational analysis.[151] While the federal regulation strengthens the green road of OA by extending the mandate of the success achieved by the NIH to all research financed by all agencies of the federal government, OA policies are also arising at the federal state level.[152]

European countries, on the other hand, have been urged to take specific and clear measures to support OA. Since 2006, the European Commission has taken some important steps towards ensuring access to publications and scientific data (referred to as open data). The EU Commission applies this intervention to its own research programs as well (i.e., FP7 and Horizon 2020[153]) and encourages Member States to take measures aimed at promoting both open access and open data.[154] This approach has resulted in the EU Communication "Towards better access to

[146] See the "Revised Policy on Enhancing Public Access to Archived Publications Resulting from NIH-Funded Research" at http://grants.nih.gov/grants/guide/notice-files/NOT-OD-08-033.html.

[147] Division G., Title II, Section 218 of PL 110–161 (Consolidated Appropriations Act, 2008).

[148] Carroll (2008).

[149] See Snyder (2009), p. 127.

[150] See Suber (2014). The new Law is available at the URL http://www.gpo.gov/fdsys/pkg/PLAW-113publ76/pdf/PLAW-113publ76.pdf.

[151] See White House Office of Science and Technology, Memorandum for the Heads of Executives Departments and Agencies, Increasing Access to the Results of Federally funded Scientific Research (23 February 2013) http://www.whitehouse.gov/sites/default/files/microsites/ostp/ostp_public_access_memo_2013.pdf. See also Suber (2013).

[152] The California Taxpayer Access to Publicly Funded Research Legislation (AB 609). See more at http://www.sparc.arl.org/advocacy/state/ab609#sthash.bi9lAuau.dpuf.

[153] Guarda (2014).

[154] See Guibault (2013).

scientific information: Boosting the benefits of public investments in research," COM (2012) 401, and the Commission Recommendation on "Access to and preservation of scientific information" (2012/417/UE) of 17 July 2012.

The European approach promotes a multilayer system involving all lawmakers, including states, funding bodies, and research entities that manage public funds. The regulation details are to be defined by the subjects that are more familiar with each specific scientific reality.

Within this framework, the Italian legislature has been one of the first to take action, approving an Act concerning the valorization of culture (Law of October 7, 2013, n. 112, G.U. n. 236, 8.10.2013). With the new statute, the parliament is seeking to bring Italian law in line with the aforementioned EU Recommendation, addressing all the subjects involved that shall "implement the necessary measures for the promotion of Open Access" with regard to works publicly financed (at least 50 %) and published in periodical collections (at least biannual). The Law requires the research institutions to adopt policies that promote OA by following both the gold road and the green road. As for the latter, the Italian statute encourages republishing articles for noncommercial purposes in institutional or disciplinary repositories (so that they can be accessed free of charge from a place and at a time individually chosen by the user) no later than 18 months from the first publication for scientific, technical, and medical disciplines and no later than 24 months for humanities and social sciences.

While one positive aspect of the Act is to recognize and encourage the application of OA, it presents some shortcomings as well. First, the law uses several terms without defining them, even though these terms may be ascribed different meanings. One example is the notion of OA, which is defined neither in the Act nor elsewhere. Second, the new Italian law does not at all address the issue of IP rights management. Consequently, the authors may assign or license their copyright and consequently will not likely be able to republish in OA.

A further benchmark in the European context is the German model and, more particularly, the Law of October 1, 2013, amending Section 38 of the German Copyright Act (*Urheberrechtsgesetz*—UrhG) removing one of the main obstacles to OA, i.e., loss of the right to re-publish the work as a consequence of assigning the copyright to the publisher. The new law allows the author of a scientific work (*wissenschaftlicher Beitrag*),[155] published in a periodical collection (at least biannual) and created in the context of a research activity that "was at least 50 % publicly funded" (*mit oeffentlichen Mitteln gefoerdeten Forschungstaetigkeit*), to make his work publicly available for noncommercial purposes 12 months after the publication. The provision is mandatory, and any derogating agreement is invalid.

[155] The scope of this expression has still not been clarified by the legislature. According to some first comments, "scientific work" includes not only written works but also technical projects, designs, tables, three-dimensional models, etc. See Wandtke and Bullinger (2014), pp. 15–25.

Therefore this right persists even if the author has assigned all exclusive rights to an editor or publisher.

One possible shortcoming of the new provision might be the uncertainty surrounding its scope of application. Article 38 may be subject to different interpretations. While, issues could arise in calculating the minimum limit of 50 %, also considering that professors and researchers working at public research entities are remunerated with public funds, this limit is criticized by those claiming a broader scope of application to also include privately funded research.[156]

Furthermore, the law suffers from the intrinsic limitation of being a national law. Defining the scope of the application in terms of private international law is a complex question that cannot be discussed here. Consider, for example, the situation where a German author publishes with foreign publishers and they subscribe a contract choosing to govern it with foreign substantive laws. The case of a publication being held by more than one entity, with some authors being Germans and others foreigners, might also frequently arise. Several questions could arise, such as: What implications arise for a secondary publication right when authors have published in a foreign collection? Is Article 38, which is intended to protect the weaker party, applicable to contracts between German authors and foreign publishers if the parties opted for the foreign jurisdiction? Does Article 38 apply only to authors with German citizenship or to any scientific author if he wants to make a secondary use in Germany? Could Article 38 apply to a second publication visible to a worldwide web, even though the server repository is in Germany? Lastly, as the issue concerns both copyright law and the law of contract, it might be asked whether the applicable private international law refers to the copyright or law of contract.[157]

In the German legal system, the debate on the affirmation of OA is emerging not only at the federal level but also at the regional one. Although competence for copyright law belongs to the federal government, the employment relationships between faculties and universities are regulated at the regional level. Along these lines, the Federal State of Baden-Wuerttemberg is discussing a draft law intended to amend Section 44 (6) of the university regulation *Landeshochschulgesetz* (LHG-E).[158] The Act would require higher education institutions (*Hochschulen*) to provide a framework within which to compel research staff employed by a university to give a guarantee that their works arising from an institutional activity

---

[156] See the "Protest gegen die Diskriminierung der Hochschulwissenschaft im Urheberrecht," open petition available at https://www.openpetition.de/petition/online/protest-gegen-die-diskriminierung-der-hochschulwissenschaft-im-urheberrecht.

[157] See von Lewinski and Thum (2011).

[158] See the Statute at http://www.landesrecht-bw.de/jportal/;jsessionid=266382535A5E6903F880C454DA1E532F.jpa4?quelle=jlink&query=HSchulG+BW&psml=bsbawueprod.psml&max=true&aiz=true. On this issue, the Federal State of Baden-Wuerttemberg appointed a commission of experts to work on the issue, which elaborated a strategic concept available at http://mwk.baden-wuerttemberg.de/uploads/media/066_PM_Anlage_E-Science_Web.pdf.

will be available for green OA.[159] This provision would not have immediate effect, as it would first have to be transposed into university statutes. This law may have a broader scope than the above-mentioned Section 38 of the Copyright Act and probably refers to all those works produced by the authors within the scope of their employment.[160] Complementing this provision is the one contained in Section 28 (3) LHG-E, which provides for the establishment of repositories (*Repositorien*) where to publish on an OA basis. If the institutional repository is not available, research entities can encourage republication in disciplinary repositories provided by third parties.

This rule suggests requiring the author to retain the right to republish in the negotiation phase.[161]

The law has given rise to many issues in the scientific community and among publishers.[162] Here it is criticized that republishing on an OA basis could prevent publishers from profiting from sales of the journal: if the content were made freely available, nobody would purchase the journals. Scientific periodicals would no longer be primarily a place to exchange knowledge but only a means of assessing the quality of the work. It is also criticized that the draft law limiting freedom of negotiating and thus of publishing would run contrary to academic freedom as protected by the German Constitution. Moreover, according to critics, any limits on the freedom of publishing would have ultimately negative effects on the quality of universities or research institutions that adopt similar policies, since they would no longer be able to attract young researchers who, deprived of the opportunity to negotiate with prestigious journals, would opt for other research centers.

Finally, the validity of the draft law has been called into question from a strictly legal perspective as it borders on copyright legislation—the preserve of federal law.

Conclusion: Toward Academic Freedom Through a Pluralistic Model
The right to freely develop and express scientific thought implies the possibility of both publishing and accessing the results of scientific research. The OA approach, granting access to all academic works without legal, technological, and economic barriers, thus reflects the principles of community science described above. The gold road of OA, which seems to be the best way to meet the interests of all stakeholders, implies a paradigm shift in

(continued)

[159] About the critical aspects of obligations to academic authors, see Hilty et al. (2013).

[160] See Articles 9 and 10 of the *Landeshochschulgesetz. Gesetz über die Hochschulen in Baden-Württemberg (Landeshochschulgesetz—LHG) Vom 1. Januar 2005.*

[161] See Kuhlen (2013).

[162] See Sprang (2014).

which commercial publishers would no longer be the holders of the exclusive rights. Everyone would have the right to access and use the scientific content of any published article. Since scientific works should be disseminated as widely as possible, these OA journals would invoke copyright as an instrument not to restrict access to the material they publish but instead to ensure permanent OA through open licensing. Along these lines, scientific publishers would provide a service for which they would be paid, probably *ex ante* (by authors or research institutions), without the need to enforce or license any copyright.

Also, OA does not affect the attribution and moral rights of the authors who will continue to be recognized as creators of the work and will be remunerated for their research activity. In this respect, academic creators can find more satisfaction for their scholarly works by receiving ex ante revenues and career advancements by disseminating publications. On the other hand, to guarantee the pluralism of information sources, the emergence of OA does not necessarily imply that other models of knowledge circulation will disappear. Open and proprietary worlds are not mutually exclusive.

How to foster the development of OA while respecting the balance between the various interests at stake is the challenge that legislatures and research institutions are currently facing. In the Italian, German, and US legal systems, academic authors are the holders of rights in their creative works, thus preserving academic freedom, i.e., the researcher's independence from both the state and the research institution. Starting from the assumption that imposts end up limiting academic freedom, any provision that leads to a mandatory OA publication or re-publication following both the gold and green road may raise doubts of legitimacy.[163] Meanwhile, the plurality of sources of information and methods of sharing, and freedom of choice, help create a balance among constitutional values. It is therefore necessary to unleash science from the exclusivity of the traditional publishing system favoring the variety of communication channels without imposing any obligations on authors. Indeed, in the current transitional scenario, also considering the predominant research evaluation system in place and the small number of high-impact OA journals, the green road may allow authors to embrace the traditional publishing channels while also making their works available in OA. This represents a first step towards granting general access to

(continued)

[163] Meanwhile, the topic is analyzed with regard to the US legal framework by *Copyright and the Harvard Open Access Mandate*, cit.

scientific content, improving the preservation of works and the development of content databases, as well as promoting new research evaluation systems and value-added services. In addition, technologies based on data mining and the semantic web might support the creation of an infrastructure that could encourage authors to spontaneously enrich repositories, thus triggering a virtuous circle in the OA paradigm success. In other words, the results that OA will produce in terms of research evaluation improvements and value added for authors and users will be crucial in determining its success.

One of the obstacles to the development of green OA, as seen above, is copyright management. The discipline of copyright, as was already mentioned, has a number of limitations that are also due to the specific nature of scientific research production. Since academic authors hardly ever have financial incentives and, in any case, the right to share and access of knowledge, as expressions of academic freedom and engines of scientific and cultural progress, seems to override the right of commercial exploitation, there is no undeniable need to protect the author market. Furthermore, with the advent of digital technologies, copyright has become a tool in the hands of publishers that acquire the rights to financial exploitation and exert total control over information. *De iure condendo*, we might welcome a review of the current legislation on copyright in keeping with constitutional principles, taking into account the peculiarities of the scientific field.[164]

A copyright law reform at the European level might deal with different aspects, such as broadening copyright exceptions in favor of access to knowledge, granting a re-publication right to the author, providing the publisher with a nonexclusive license while keeping copyright in the hands of the author, or providing the author with a compulsory license granting the right to republish in OA. Finally, given the nature of academic written work, we might imagine, provocatively, a paradigm shift in the protection of these works. As previously mentioned, research—at least publicly funded research—is remunerated *ex ante*. That means it may no longer be necessary to hold exclusive economic rights to the written academic works. In defining the concept of original or creative work, academic written works might be considered a special category. In this field, while moral rights are a cornerstone, the creation of a market may not be desirable since it *de facto* benefits a few private publishers. Hence, a regulation that grants the academic author only moral rights in publications might be acceptable and not in conflict with

(continued)

[164] For an overview, see Van Eechoud et al. (2004). See also IVIR, *Study on the Implementation and Effect in Member States' Laws of Directive 2001/29, Final Report* (February 2007), available at http://www.ivir.nl/publications/guibault/Infosoc_report_2007.pdf.

the constitutional principles considered in this work. This perspective looks at the work in its ontological dimension, which is protectable as long as its market needs to be preserved. The concept of copyright-protected work could be defined by the reasons for such protection in the context of reference. Particularly in the case of the products of scientific research to be published in journals or research books, the work is not destined for a market favoring authors and their indipendence which needs to be protected from the various interests at stake, including those of the research institutions to which they belong.

Acknowledgment I am grateful to the Max Planck Institute for Innovation and Competition where I had the opportunity to conduct my work taking advantage of the lively research environment and the privilege to discuss my ideas with experts working on tangential research projects.

References

Adams (2007) Copyright and research: an archivangelist's perspective. SCRIPTed 4(3):285. doi:10.2966/scrip.040307.285

Albert KM (2006) Open access: implications for scholarly publishing and medical libraries. J Med Libr Assoc 94(3): 253–262

Armbruster C (2005) Open access in social and cultural science: innovative moves to enhance access, inclusion and impact in scholarly communication. Social Science Research Network. Retrieved September 28, 2006: http://papers.ssrn.com/sol3/cf_dev/AbsByAuth.cfm?per_id=434782

Berners-Lee T (1999) Weaving the web. The original design and ultimate destiny of the world wide web by its inventor. HarperCollins, San Francisco

Bethge H (2009) In: Sachs (ed) Grundgesetz Kommentar. C.H. Beck, Munich, p 220

Björk BC (2004) Open access to scientific publications – an analysis of the barriers to change. Inf Res 9(2):170. http://InformationR.net/ir/9-2/paper170.html

Björk BC (2012) The hybrid model for open access publication of scholarly articles – a failed experiment? J Am Soc Inf Sci Technol 63(8):1496–1504

Björk BC, Solomon D (2014) Developing an effective market for open access article processing charges, March 2014. Final Report to a consortium of research funders comprising Jisc, Research ibraries UK, Research Councils UK, the Wellcome Trust, the Austrian Science Fund, the Luxembourg National Research Fund and the Max Planck Institute for Gravitational Physics. http://www.wellcome.ac.uk/stellent/groups/corporatesite/@policy_communications/documents/web_document/wtp055910.pdf

Braegelmann T (2009–2010) Copyright law in and under the constitution – the constitutional scope and limits to copyright law in the United States in comparison with the scope and limits imposed by constitutional and European Law on copyright law in Germany. Cardozo Arts Entertain Law J 27:99–144

Breyer S (1970) The uneasy case for copyright: a study of copyright in books, photocopies, and computer programs. Harv Law Rev 84 (2):281–355

Brown AEL (2012) Intellectual property, human rights and competition. Edward Elgar, Cheltenham
Byrne JP (1989) Academic freedom: a “Special Concern of the First Amendment”. Yale Law J 99: 251, 259–260
Byrne JP (2006) Constitutional academic freedom after Grutter. Getting real about the four freedoms of a university. Univ Colorado Law Rev 77:929–953
Carroll MW (2008) Complying with the NIH public access policy – copyright considerations and options. SPARC/Science Commons/ARL
Caso R (2013) Scientific knowledge unchained: Verso una Policy dell’Università Italiana sull’ Open Access. The Trento Law and Technology Research Group Research Papers Series No. 16, http://ssrn.com/abstract=2264920 or http://dx.doi.org/10.2139/ssrn.2264920
Centivany A (2011) Paper tigers: copyright and scholarly publishing. Mich Telecommun Technol Law Rev 17:385–416. http://papers.ssrn.com/sol3/papers.cfm?abstract_id=1893590
Commager HS (1963) The university and freedom. J Higher Educ 34(7):361–370
Connolly J (2000) The Sovietization of higher education in the Czech Lands, East Germany, and Poland during the Stalinist period (1948–54). In: Péteri G, David-Fo M (eds) Academia in Upheaval. Greenwood Publishing Group, London, p 71
Daniel PTK, Pauken PD (1999) The impact of the electronic media on instructor creativity and institutional ownership within copyright law. Educ Law Rep 132:1–43
Daughtrey WH (1991) The legal nature of academic freedom in United States colleges and universities. Richmond Law Rev 25:213–271
Denicola R (2006) Copyright and open access: reconsidering university ownership of faculty research. Nebraska Law Rev 85(2). http://ssrn.com/abstract=2448356
Dershowitz A (2005) Rights from wrongs. A secular Theory of the Origin of Rights. Basic Books, New York
Dreier T (2013) How much property is there in intellectual property? The German civil law perspective. In: Howe H, Griffiths J (eds) Concepts of property in intellectual property law. Cambridge University Press, Cambridge, p 94
Dreier H, Schulze G (2013) UrhG IV ed., 2013, § 43 Urheber in Arbeits- oder Dienstverhaelt-nissen. C.H. Beck, Munich, pp 1 ff
Drexl J, von Lewinski S (2007) The digitizing of literary and artistic works. Electronic J Comp Law 11:3. http://www.ejcl.org
Dupré J (2001) Human nature and the limits of science. Oxford University Press, Oxford
Dusollier S (2002) Fair use by design in the European Copyright Directive of 2001: an empty promise. University of Namur. Communication of the ACM 46: 51. http://www.cfp2002.org/fairuse/dusollier.pdf
Dusollier S (2008) The role of the lawmaker and of the judge in the conflict between copyright exceptions, freedom of expression and technological measures. Copyright and Freedom of Expression. In: ALAI 2006 Barcelona, Huygens Editorial, p 569–578
Eger T, Scheufen M, Meierrieks D (2013) The determinants of open access publishing: survey evidence from Germany (March 13, 2013). Available at SSRN: http://ssrn.com/abstract=2232675
Epping V, Hillgruber C (2009) Kommentar, C.H. Beck, Munich, p 179
Eve MP (2013) Before the law: open access, quality control and the future of peer review. In: Vincent N, Wickham C (eds) Debating open access. The British Academy. Carlton House Terrace, London, p 68. http://issuu.com/thebritishacademy/docs/debating_open_access-ed_vincent_and
Farell J, Shapiro C (2004) Intellectual property, competition and information technology. Working paper no. 45, University of California. http://papers.ssrn.com/sol3/papers.cfm?abstract_id=527782
Fechner F (1999) Geistiges Eigentum und Verfassung, Mohr Siebeck, Tübingen
Fehling M (2010) In: Bonner Grundgesetz Kommentar, C.F. Müller Verlag, Heidelberg p 74

Fitzpatrick K, Santo A (2012) Open review: a study of contexts and practices. The Andrew W. Mellon Foundation White Paper, Media Commons Press. http://mcpress.media-commons.org/open-review/files/2012/06/MediaCommons_Open_Review_White_Paper_final.pdf
Frosio GF (2014) Open access publishing: a literature review. CREATe working paper 2014/1. http://www.create.ac.uk/publications/000011
Galimberti P (2012) Qualità e Quantità: Stato dell'Arte della Valutazione della Ricerca nelle Scienze Umane in Italia. JLIS 3(1). doi:10.4403/jlis.it-5617
Gasaway L (2010) Archiving and preservation in US Copyright Law. In: Derclay E (ed) Copyright and cultural heritage. Edward Elgar, Cheltenham
Geiger C (2006) Copyright and free access to information for a fair balance of interests in a globalised world. Eur Intellect Prop Rev 28(7):366–373
Geiger C (2013) The social function of intellectual property rights, or how ethics can influence the shape and use of IP law. In: G.B. Dinwoodie (ed.), Intellectual Property Law: Methods and Perspectives, Edward Elgar, Cheltenham, p. 153
Geller PG (2010) A German approach to fair use. Test cases for TRIPS criteria for copyright limitations. J Copyright Soc U S A 57:553–571
Guarda P (2013) Creation of software within the academic context: knowledge transfer, intellectual property rights and licenses. Int Rev Intellect Prop Competition Law 44(5):494–523
Guarda P (2014) Consortium agreement and intellectual property rights within the European Union Research and Innovation Programs. EIPR (forthcoming)
Guedòn JC (2001) In Oldenburg's long shadow: librarians, research scientists, publishers and control of scientific publishing. Association of research library, Washington. http://www.arl.org/storage/documents/publications/in-oldenburgs-long-shadow.pdf
Guibault L (2002) Copyright limitations and contracts: an analysis of the contractual overridability of limitations on copyright. Wolters Kluwer, The Hague
Guibault L (2011) Owning the right to open up access to scientific publications. In: Guibault L, Angelopolous C (eds) Open content licensing from theory to practice. Amsterdam University Press, Amsterdam
Guibault L (2013) Licensing research data under open access condition. In: Beldiman D (ed) Information and knowledge, 21st century challenges in intellectual property and knowledge governance. Edward Elgar, Cheltenham
Haberstumpf H (2001) Wem gehören Forschungsergebnisse? ZUM 819–828
Harnad S, Brody T, Vallieres F, Carr L, Hitchcock S, Gingras Y, Oppenheim C, Stamerjoanns H, Hilf ER (2004) The Access/Impact Problem and the green and the gold roads to open access. Serials Review 30(4). doi:10.1016/j.serrev.2004.09.013
Heerman P (1999) Gewerblicher Rechtsschutz und Urheberrecht. GRUR, 468–476
Helfer LR (2011) Human rights and intellectual property. Mapping the global interface. Cambridge University Press, Cambridge
Herb U (February 2010) Sociological implications of scientific publishing: open access, science, society, democracy and the digital divide. First Monday 15(2)
Herrera Diaz JR (2010) Ownership of copyright in works created in employment relationships: comparative study of the Law of Colombia, Germany and the United States of America. Revista la propriedad Immaterial 14:95–113
Hilty R (2006) Five lessons about copyright in the information society. J Copyright Soc U S A 53: 103–118
Hilty R, Köklü K (2013) Access and use: open vs. proprietary worlds. Max Planck Institute for Innovation & Competition Research Paper, No. 14-07, 29 April 2013. http://ssrn.com/abstract=2425637 or http://dx.doi.org/10.2139/ssrn.2425637
Hilty R, Peukert A (eds) (2004) Balance of interests in copyright law, Nomos, Baden Baden
Hilty R, Kruijatz S, Bajon B, Frueh A, Kur A, Drexl K, Geiger C (2009) European Commission – Green Paper: copyright in the knowledge Economy – Comments by the Max Planck Institute for Intellectual Property, Competition and Tax Law. IIC 40:309–327

Hilty RM, Köklü K, Hafenbrädl F (2013) Software agreements: stocktaking and outlook – lessons from the UsedSoft v. Oracle Case from a comparative law perspective. IIC 44(3):263–293
Horowitz P (2007) Evaluate me!': conflicted thoughts on gatekeeping in legal scholarship's new age. Conn L Rev 39(1):38–52
Jarass H, Pieroth B (2014) Grundgesetz Kommentar. C.H. Beck, Munich, p 121
Jordan KA (2003) Financial conflicts of interest in human subjects research: proposals for a more effective regulatory scheme. Wash Lee Law Rev 60:17–108
Karran T (2007) Academic freedom in Europe: a preliminary comparative analysis. Higher Educ Policy 20:289–313
Kaufman R (2008) Publishing forms and contracts. Oxford University Press: New York
Kaufman JM (2012) The Creative Rights Act of 2020, a new deal for promoting the progress of creativity, 17 April 2012. http://ssrn.com/abstract=2135862
Kommers PD (1997) The Constitutional Jurisprudence of the Federal Republic of Germany. Duke University Press, Durham-London
Krasser R, Schricker G (1998) Patent und Urheberrecht an Hochschulen. Nomos, Baden-Baden
Kuhlen R (2013) Stellungsname del Aktionbündnisses zum Entwurf eines Dritter Gesetzes zur Änderung Hochschulrechtlicher Vorschriften des Ministeriums für Wissenschaft, Forschung und Kunst (MWK), Baden-Wurttemberg. Stand 15.11.2013. http://www.urheberrechtsbuendnis.de/docs/stellungnahme-AB-auf-MWK-Ba-Wue.pdf
Krujatz S (2012) Open Access: Der Offene Zugang Zu Wissenschaftlichen Informationen Und Die Okonomische Bedeutung Urheberrechtlicher Ausschlussmacht. Mohr Siebeck, Goettingen
Lametti D (2010) How virtue ethics might help erase C-32's conceptual incoherence. In: Geist M (a cura di) From "Radical Extremism" to "Balanced Copyright": Canadian Copyright and the Digital Agenda. Irwin Law, Toronto, p 309
Landes WM, Posner R (2003) The economic structure of intellectual property law, Belknap Press, US
Lape L (1992) Ownership of copyrightable works of university professors: the interplay between the copyright act and university copyright policies. Vill Law Rev 37:223–265
Laughlin K (2000) Who owns the copyright to faculty-created web sites?: The work for hire doctrine's applicability to internet resources created for distance learning and traditional classroom uses. B C Law Rev 41:549–567
Leinemann F (1998) Die Sozialbindung des Geistigen Eigentums, Nomos, Baden Baden
Leistner M (2004) Farewell to the "Professor's Privilege". Ownership of patents for academic inventions in Germany under the reformed employees' Inventions Act 2002. IIC 35:859–871
Lorenzato F (2009) Titolarità e contratti sulle pubblicazioni scientifiche. In: Caso (ed) Pubblicazioni scientifiche, diritto d'autore e Open Access. Atti del Convegno tenuto presso la Facoltà di Giurisprudenza di Trento il 20 giugno 2008, Universitá degli Studi, Facoltá di Giurispridenza, Trento p 47
Ludington H (2011) The dogs that did not bark: the silence of the legal academy during World War II. J Legal Educ 60 (3):397–432
Lutz A (2012) Zugang zu Wissenschaftlichen Informationen in der digitalen Welt. Göttingen
Mangolt H, Klein F, Starck C (2010) Das Bonner Grundgesetz. Kommentar, Verlag Vahlen, Munich p 57
Marzetti M (2013) Argentina passes open access act for publicly funded research, 16 December 2013. http://www.ip-watch.org/2013/12/16/argentina-passes-open-access-act-making-publicly-funded-research-available/
Mazziotti G (2013) Copyright in the EU digital single market. Centre for European Policy Studies, Brussels
Merloni F (1990) Autonomie e libertà nel Sistema della ricerca scientifica. Giuffré, Milano
Merton RK (1942) The normative structure of science. In: Merton RK (ed) The sociology of science: theoretical and empirical investigations. University Chicago Press, Chicago

Metzger W (1988) Profession and constitution: two definitions of academic freedom. Tex Law Rev 66:1265–1275
Migheli M, Ramello GB (2013) Open access, social norms and publication choice. Eur J Law Econ 35(2):149–167
Migheli M, Ramello GB (2014) Open access journals & academics' behaviour. Working paper no. 3/2014. http://www.icer.it/docs/wp2014/ICERwp03-14.pdf
Millington P (2011) SHERPA/RoMEO, 60 % of journals allow immediate archiving of peer-reviewed articles – but it gets much much better..., 24 November 2011. http://romeo.jiscinvolve.org/wp/2011/11/24/60-of-journals-allow-immediate-archiving-of-peer-reviewed-articles-but-it-gets-much-much-better/
Monotti A, Ricketson S (2003) Universities and intellectual property: ownership and exploitation. Oxford University Press, New York
Morelli S (1996) L'applicazione diretta della Costituzione nei rapporti interindividuali. Giust. civ. II:537
Moscarini A (2006) Proprietà private e tradizioni costituzionali comuni. Giuffré, Milano
Moscon V (2013) Misure tecnologiche di protezione (Technological proctection measures). In Digesto civ., Agg., Utet, Torino, p 386
Mueller-Langer F, Scheufer M (2013) Academic publishing and open access. In: Handke, C. / Towse R. (eds.): Handbook of the Digital Creative Economy. Edward Elgar, Cheltenham, p. 365
Netanel NW (2008) Copyright paradox. Oxford University Press, New York
Niioka H (2001) Klinische Versuche im Patentrecht. Heymanns, Munich
Nordemann W, Nordemann A, Nordemann JB (eds) (2008) Urheberrecht, Kommentar zum Urheberrechtsgesetz, Verlagsgesetz, Urheberrechtswahrnehmungsgesetz, § 43 Urheber in Arbeits- oder Dienstverhaeltnissen. C.H. Beck, Munich
Oldaker L (1992) Threats to academic freedom in higher education. In: ERIC (conference paper)
Orsi Battaglini A (2007) Libertà scientifica, Libertà accademica e valori costituzionali, in Scritti giuridici, Giuffré, Milano
Packard A (2002) Copyright or copy wrong: an analysis of university claims to faculty work. Comm Law Policy 7:275–316
Pascuzzi G, Caso R (2011) Valutazione dei prodotti scientifici nell'area giuridica e ruolo delle tecnologie digitali. Riv.dir. civ., 685
Perlingeri P (1980) Norme costituzionali e rapporti di diritto civile. Rass. dir. civ. 1:95
Pernice I (2004) Kunst und Wissenschaft, Forschung und Leher sind frei. Die Freiheit der Lehre entbindet nicht von der Treue zur Verfassung. In: Dreier H (ed) Grundgesetz Kommentar, Mohr Siebeck , Tuebingen p 715
Pflueger T, Ertmann D (2004) E-Publishing und Open Access Konsequenzen für das Urheberrecht im Hochschulbereichin. ZUM 436–441
Pila J (2010) Who owns the intellectual property rights in academic work? Eur Intellect Prop Rev 609
Pinxten H (2012) The humanities under fire? In: Vanderbeeken R, Le Roy F, Stalpaert C, Aerts D (eds) Drunk on capitalism. An interdisciplinary reflection on market, economy, art and science. Springer, Berlin p 25
Pramann O (2007) Publikationsklauseln in Forschungsverträgen und Forschungsprotokollen. Springer, Berlin
Press E, Washburn J (2000) The Kept University. Atlantic Monthly, 285(3):39–54
Priest E (2012) Copyright and the Harvard open access mandate. Northwestern J Technol Intellect Prop 10:377. http://ssrn.com/abstract=1890467
Reichman JH, Okediji R (2012) When copyright law and science collide: empowering digitally integrated research methods on a global scale. Minn Law Rev 96(4):1362–1480
Rice A (1990) Licensing the use of computer program copies and the copyright act first sale doctrine. Jurimetrics J 30:157–172

Robertson JA (1977–1978) The scientist's right to research: a constitutional analysis. Calif Law Rev 1203–1279

Roosendaal HE, Geurts PA (1997) Forces and functions in scientific communication: an analysis of their interplay. In: Proceeding of Cooperative Research Information System in Physics (CRISP 97), Oldenburg, 91.08.1997–4.9.1997

Ruffert M, Steinecke S (2011) The global administrative law of science. Springer, Heidelberg

Russel RD (2008) The business of academic publishing: a strategic analysis of the academic journal publishing industry and its impact on the future of scholarly publishing. The Electronic Journal of Academic and Special Librarianship. http://southernlibrarianship.icaap.org/content/v09n03/mcguigan_g01.html

Sanberger G (2006) Behindert das Urheberrecht den Zugang zu wissenschaftlichen Publikationen? ZUM 818–831

Santosuosso A, Sellaroli V, Fabio E (2007) What constitutional protection for freedom of scientific research? J Med Ethics 33(6):342–344

Scaccia G (2005) Il bilanciamento degli interessi in materia di proprietà intellettuale. AIDA 198

Schack H (2010) Urheber- und Urhebervertragsrecht. Mohr Siebeck, Tübbing

Schricker G (1998) Wer ist der Verfasser? Die Autorenangabe bei wissenschaftlichen Veröffentlichungen. Forschung & Lehre 5(11):584–587

Schricker G (2004) German and comparative intellectual property law. Efforts for a better law on copyright contracts in Germany. A never-ending story? IIC, 35:850–858

Schricker G, Krasser R (2004) Urheber- und Erfinderrecht des wissenschaftlichen Personals, in Hochschulrecht. Ein Handbuch für die Praxis, M. Hartmer/H. Detmer, Bonn

Shavell S (2010) Should copyright of academic works be abolished? J Legal Anal 2(1):301–358

Shirky C (2008) Here comes everybody: the power of organizing without organizations. Penguin Press, New York

Snyder S (2009) Free-for-all: public access and publisher rights collide in the fair copy-right in Research Works Act of 2009. DePaul J Art Technol Intellect Prop Law 20:127–135

Sprang C (2014) JustiziarStellungnahme zum Entwurf eines Dritten Gesetzes zur Änderung hochschulrechtlicher Vorschriften des Landes Baden-Württemberg, Frankfurt am Main, 9 February 2014. http://www.boersenverein.de/sixcms/media.php/976/stellungnahme_3.hrag_bawu_20131128.pdf

Steinhauer EW (2010) Das Recht auf Sichtbarkeit, Überlegungen zu Open Access und Wissenschaftsfreiheit. Münster, Hagen

Sterckx S (2012) Enclosing the academic commons – increasing knowledge transfer or eroding academic values? In: Vanderbeeken R, Le Roy F, Stalpaert C, Aerts D (eds) Drunk on capitalism. An interdisciplinary reflection on market, economy, art and science. Springer, Berlin, p 49

Stevenson A (2010) The economic case for open access in academic publishing. Ars Technica, 29 November 2010. http://arstechnica.com/science/news/2010/11/the-economic-case-for-open-access-in-academicpublishing.ars

Strauss NS (2011) Anything but academic: how copyright's work-for-hire doctrine affects professors, graduate students, and K-12 teachers in the information age. Richmond J Law Technol: 1–47

Suber P (2012) Open access. MIT Press, Harvard

Suber P (2013) Second shoe drop: new White House directive mandates OA, 22 February 2013. https://plus.google.com/109377556796183035206/posts/8hzviMJeVHJ

Suber P (2014) New open-access mandates in the US, 17 January, 2014. https://plus.google.com/+PeterSuber/posts/BxaAbKqv5HS

Tartari V, Breschi S (2012) Set them free: scientist's evaluations of the benefits and costs of university – industry research collaboration. Ind Corp Change 21(5):1117–1147

Torremans PLC (2008) Copyright (and other intellectual property rights) as a human right. In: Torremans PLC (ed) Intellectual property and human rights. Kluwer Law International, The Hague, p 197

Torremans P (2010) Archiving exceptions: where are we and where do we need to go? In: Derclay E (ed) Copyright and cultural heritage. Preservation and access to works in a digital world. Edward Elgar, Cheltenham
Townsend E (2003) Legal and policy responses to the disappearing "teacher Exception", or copyright ownership in the 21st century university. Minn Intellect Prop Rev 4:209
Towse R (2001) Creativity, incentive and reward: an economic analysis of copyright and culture in the information age. Edward Elgar, Cheltenham
Turner GRG (1988) The price of freedom. In: Tight M (ed) Academic freedom and responsibility. Stony Stratford, England, Open University Press
Ubertazzi LC (2003a) Introduzione al diritto europeo della proprietà intellettuale. Contratto e impresa Europa, 1054–1108
Ubertazzi LC (2003b) Le invenzioni dei ricercatori. Contratto e impresa Europa, 1109–1122
Ulrici B (2008) Vermögensrechtliche Grundfragen des Arbeitnehmerurheberrechts. Mohr Siebeck, Tubingen
Van Bouwel J (2012) What is there beyond Mertonian and dollar green science? exploring the contours of epistemic democracy In: Vanderbeeken R, Le Roy F, Stalpaert C, Aerts D (eds) Drunk on capitalism. An interdisciplinary reflection on market, economy, art and science. Springer, Berlin, p 35
Van Eechoud M, Hugenholtz PB, Guibault L, Van Gompel S, Helberger N (2004) Harmonizing European copyright law. The challenges of better lawmaking. Alphen aan den Rijn Kluwer Law International, The Hague
VerSteeg R (1990) Copyright and the educational process: the right of teacher inception. Iowa Law Rev 75:397–407
von Falck, Schmaltz C (2005) University inventions: classification and remuneration in Germany, the Netherlands, France, the UK, the U.S. and Japan. IIC, 36:912–927
von Lewinski S, Thum D (2011) Spezifisce Fragen zum Auslandsbezug des geplanten Zweitveroeffentlichunggsrechts nach § 38 Abs. 1 S. 3 and 4 UrhG neu. IUWIS. http://www.iuwis.de/publikation/spezifische-fragen-zum-auslandsbezug-des-geplanten-zweitver%C3%B6ffentlichungsrechts-nach-%C2%A7-3
Wandtke A, Bullinger W (2014) Praxiskommentar zum Urheberrecht, IV edn. § 43 Urheber in Arbeits- oder Dienstverhaeltnissen. C.H. Beck, Munich, p 30
Yu PK (2009) The objectives and principles of the TRIPS agreement. Houston Law Rev 46:979–1046

The manufacturer's authorised representative in the EU is Springer Nature Customer Service Centre GmbH, Europaplatz 3, 69115 Heidelberg, Germany. If you have any concerns regarding our products, please contact ProductSafety@springernature.com

Printed and bound by CPI Group (UK) Ltd, Croydon, CR0 4YY
22/09/2026
02220945-0020